THE ELEMENTS OF ETHICS

THE ELEMENTS OF ETHICS

G. E. MOORE

Edited and with
an Introduction by
TOM REGAN

TEMPLE UNIVERSITY PRESS
Philadelphia

Temple University Press, Philadelphia 19122
Copyright © 1991 by Temple University. All rights reserved
Published 1991
Printed in the United States of America

Library of Congress Cataloging-in-Publication Data
Moore, G. E. (George Edward), 1873–1958.
The elements of ethics / G. E. Moore : edited and with an
introduction by Tom Regan.
p.   cm.
Includes bibliographical references and index.
ISBN 0-87722-770-5 (alk. paper)
1. Ethics.   2. Moore, G. E. (George Edward), 1873–1958—Ethics.
I. Regan, Tom.   II. Title.
B1647.M73E43   1991
170—dc20   90-46948

To Timothy and Diana

Contents

Preface

The original typescript of G. E. Moore's *The Elements of Ethics* is in the collection of Moore Papers at the main Library of the University of Cambridge, England. I am pleased to acknowledge the permission of the Syndics of Cambridge University Library to publish Moore's book for the first time.

The original typescript consists of ten lectures Moore delivered in the Autumn of 1898. Each lecture was written originally in long-hand (the handwritten version of the tenth lecture has been preserved), but Moore made arrangements to have the lectures typed when, in March 1902, he submitted them for publication to Cambridge University Press. In the typescript itself, only two of the lectures are titled. But in a syllabus for the course, Moore not only gave a title to each of the ten lectures, he also offered a brief summary of each. Moore's titles have been placed at the beginning of each lecture, and the full syllabus, which also includes recommended readings and a list of questions, appears after my Introduction.

In the body of the typescript Moore sometimes made minor changes; these have been incorporated into the present edition. During some of his lectures, moreover, he made reference to, and evidently read to his listeners from, the works of others. The authors and the works cited, along with page numbers, were given by Moore in the margins. Although these quotations were not present in the original typescript, they have been added here, because without them, Moore's discussion of the material he quoted would be all but unintelligible. Because Moore's discussions in *The Elements* often parallel his later discussions in *Principia Ethica*, I have relied on the latter work to help decide where to begin and end a given quotation in the former one.

Moore was not always consistent in the manner in which he footnoted the various sources he cited. Rather than follow his lead, I have tried to use the same bibliographical devices throughout this edition of the lectures. When, as he sometimes does, Moore makes reference to lesser known philosophers, I have added brief biographical sketches.

The text presented more serious problems. First, the manuscript pages sometimes are mistakenly numbered (for example, there are two different pages numbered 324, and there is no page 304). I have treated these matters as uncorrected errors on the part of the typist. Second, Moore's bibliographical references sometimes seem erroneous, and the text itself sometimes contains minor gaps (such as a missing word or expression). These problems have been duly noted, and I have explained my reasons for resolving them in the ways I have. In these cases, as in others, I have been aided by the advice and counsel of William Adler, David Falk, Andrews Reath, J. B. Schneewind, and James VanderKam. It is a pleasure to acknowledge their assistance.

Except for the changes indicated and some minor alterations, such as corrections of spelling and punctuation, the lectures as they appear here are those Moore submitted for publication in 1902.

In my Introduction I have sought to place Moore's lectures in a larger context than the obvious one—namely, the role they played in the development of his moral philosophy. I do address this question, especially in my discussion of how both *The Elements* and Moore's later book, *Principia Ethica* (1903), face some of the same problems while offering quite different solutions. But I address more than this important question. To know *where* Moore presented his lectures, and *why* he was asked to present them, provides a window through which we can glimpse the broad outlines of the social and philosophical aspirations of his time and place. And we can see more than this: persons of real standing and influence in that day, persons who today are all but forgotten— J. Passmore Edwards and Mary Ward, for example—form part of the larger context of which Moore's lectures were but a small part.

The attempt to do justice to this larger context is, of course, a quite different enterprise than the attempt to confirm or refute Moore's philosophical views, or to give a detailed comparison of *The Elements* and *Principia*. These challenges remain. My hope is that, with the publication of *The Elements*, other philosophers will more easily endeavor to meet them. In my Introduction I have chosen to explore a different direction.

That Moore's lectures are being published at all is a result of the generous permission given by his son, the composer-musician Timothy Moore. My personal gratitude to him is great. But when I thank him in public here, I believe I am thanking him for the many scholars who, in the years to come, will benefit from having his father's lectures readily available. The lectures themselves, some of the circumstances surrounding their origin and subsequent history, and the role they played in the composition of *Principia* will now be topics researchers can meaningfully discuss. For this, all students of the history of philosophy in general, and of the philosophy of G. E. Moore in particular, will be grateful.

I wish to acknowledge the wise and friendly guidance of Jane Cullen, senior editor of Temple University Press, the expert assistance of Linda Gregonis, who prepared the manuscript for publication, and Jennifer French, who oversaw its production. Gratefully acknowledged, too, was the always friendly assistance of the staff of the division of Rare Books and Manuscripts, University of Cambridge Library, most especially Godfrey Waller.

As always I owe a special debt to my wife Nancy. Not only did she spend many hours discussing this project with me and reading the various drafts of my Introduction, she also made many valuable suggestions. And she did all this with unflagging patience and understanding. Few people are so blessed, with so much, from many. How very fortunate I am, therefore—and how very thankful—to receive so much from one.

Raleigh, N.C.   Tom Regan
July 20, 1990

Editor's Introduction
Tom Regan

THE ANNOUNCEMENT

"I was much interested in noticing an announcement of your course of lectures for the 'Ethical Society' in the *Daily News*, one day last week." So writes Henrietta Moore to her son George on October 11, 1898.[1] The ten lectures Moore was scheduled to give at the London School of Ethics and Social Philosophy were advertised as "The Elements of Ethics, with a view to an appreciation of Kant's Moral Philosophy."[2] The plan proved to be too ambitious. As Moore states in his introductory remarks, "I shall not enter into the details of Kant's system at all" (*The Elements*, Moore's Introduction).[3] Instead, he announces that he intends to reserve Kant's moral philosophy "for a second course next term, if the committee of this School should desire me to deliver one" (ibid.). They did. And Moore did. But the written lectures (it was Moore's custom to write the full text of his lectures, in long-hand, and to read them) seem to have been lost; only notes taken by his brother

1. Quotations from letters are taken from correspondence between Moore and the person identified. The date of each letter is given in the text. The letters are part of the collection of unpublished material comprising The Moore Papers, Cambridge University Library.

2. Moore's syllabus is reprinted after my Introduction. The syllabus originally was printed by Kenny & Co., Trade Union Printers, 25 Camden Road N.W., London. This is historically significant, because it means that the outline of the lectures—and, thus, the main outline of *Principia Ethica*—did not emerge on a week-to-week basis during the time (the autumn of 1898) Moore wrote the lectures, but must have been settled upon by Moore *before* he began to give the lectures. For further discussion of this matter, see footnote 28.

3. Quotations from *The Elements of Ethics* refer to Moore's lectures as here reproduced. Quotations from the lectures hereafter are given in the body of the Introduction by citing *The Elements*, followed by the appropriate lecture.

Thomas (the poet Sturge Moore) and Sturge Moore's answers to examination questions survive. Because Kant's moral philosophy is barely touched upon in the lectures published here, they have been given the same title they came to have among Moore's contemporaries: *The Elements of Ethics*. The typescript on which they are based is the one submitted to and accepted for publication by Cambridge University Press in March 1902. Although for reasons explained in what follows Moore abandoned his plans to publish *The Elements*, these lectures are important to students of his life and work, if for no other reason than that they represent Moore's first effort as a systematic teacher.

That Moore should have been given the opportunity to offer lectures is itself a tribute to his youthful promise. At twenty-six and only recently named a Fellow of Trinity College, Cambridge, he had a modest record of publication (two reviews, a contribution to a symposium on the unreality of time, and a more substantial paper entitled "Freedom").[4] By contrast, the remaining lecturers at the London School of Ethics and Social Philosophy were mostly scholars of established reputation: T. H. Green, Leslie Stephens, Bernard Bosanquet, J. H. Muirhead, Samuel Alexander, G. F. Stout, and J. Ellis McTaggart, for example. Little wonder, then, that on October 10, 1898, Sturge Moore would write to his younger brother, perhaps in response to the same advertisement in the *Daily News* that had caught their mother's attention, "I congratulate you heartily on your success which I hope will lead to many others. We are all intending to help swell the audience to your lectures and look forward to gaining sound rudimentary notions." With his "Lectures on Ethics," Moore's reputation as one of his generation's leading philosophers was launched.

4. Moore's published work at this time included the following: (1) A contribution to an Aristotelian Society Symposium on the topic "In What Sense, If Any, Do Past and Future Time Exist?" *Mind*, n.s., v. 6, April 1897, pp. 235–40; (2) a review of Leon Brunschvicg, *La modalité du jugement* (Paris, 1897), *Mind*, n.s., v. 6, Oct. 1897, pp. 554–59; (3) his essay "Freedom," *Mind*, n.s., v. 7, April 1898, pp. 179–204; and (4) a review of J. G. Fichte, *The Science of Ethics, as Based on the Science of Knowledge* (translated by A. E. Kroeger, edited by the Hon. Dr. W. T. Harris, London, 1897), *International Journal of Ethics*, v. 9, October 1898, pp. 92–97.

THE SCHOOL

The London School of Ethics and Social Philosophy was a noble if short-lived experiment in alternative education. It was more a school in name than in fact. The Oxford philosopher Bernard Bosanquet served as its president, and among its three vice-presidents was Moore's former teacher at Cambridge, Henry Sidgwick. Beginning in the autumn of 1897, lectures were organized and presented at various places in London: Essex Hall and Morley College, for example, but mainly at the Passmore Edwards Settlement. According to its statement of "Aims and Methods," the school aimed at "supplying students of Philosophy in London with some of the teaching which the philosophy faculty of a teaching university might be expected to provide."[5] The school's founders believed they were responding to a real need. Both the University of London and existing auxiliary educational services, in their view, failed to supply adequate opportunities in London for the growing demand to study philosophy systematically. "That such additional opportunity for philosophic study is necessary is well known," Bosanquet writes in his First Report, "to all those familiar with the means already provided by existing institutions; that there exists a growing body of students willing to take advantage of such teaching seems to have been shown by the large measure of success which has attended the philosophical courses given from time to time by the London School for the Extension of University Teaching."[6]

Something better had to be tried. Bosanquet, Sidgwick, and the other members of the school's committee decided to break new ground, standing apart from both the University of London and the Extension Society. "The object of ceasing to work under the University Extension Society," Bosanquet writes, "was to give the Committee an absolutely free hand both in the arrangement of

5. The School's "Aims and Methods" are set forth by its president, Bernard Bosanquet, in both his "First Annual Report, The London School of Ethics and Social Philosophy, 1897–1898," and in his "Second Annual Report, The London School of Ethics and Social Philosophy, 1898 to 1899." The Moore Papers, Cambridge University Library.

6. The quotation is from Bernard Bosanquet's "First Report," p. 3.

courses of lectures with a view to systematic teaching, and in securing the services of teachers of high standing on terms which would make it worth their while to give fresh courses of lectures, specially adapted to their place among the other courses."[7]

Such independence had its price. That price was money, mainly the lack thereof. Finances for operating the school came largely from contributions made by subscribers, less so from the nominal fees charged for some of the lectures themselves. It was not enough. To make matters worse, the school's major benefactor gave notice of withdrawing his support on the grounds that the school should be self-supporting. In his letter of October 27, 1900, in which he announces the committee's decision to dissolve the school only three years after its founding, Bosanquet sadly notes that "it was necessary, therefore, for purely financial reasons, to close the School. And we must insist," Bosanquet continues—inaccurately, as will be explained below—"that these reasons were purely financial."[8] The one possible remedy, namely, to have the school's lecturers recognized as teachers in the University of London, came to naught when the university commissioners "felt unable to accede to the application" because the commissioners judged that the school failed to qualify as a Public Educational Institution, according to the University of London Act of 1898.

Bosanquet's bitter disappointment is apparent when he writes that "we cannot think that the absence, in the greatest city in the world, of adequate means for the systematic study of the central theory of life, will be permitted to continue. . . . [S]ooner or later, we must believe, the governing body of the University will grabble seriously with the problem of philosophical teaching," adding (ominously), "our students, we feel sure, will use . . . any influence they may possess."[9] Whatever practical "influence" these students may have had is unclear. What is clear, is that the not inconsider-

7. Bernard Bosanquet, "Memorandum on the Work of the London School of Ethics and Social Philosophy," June 1899, p. 1. The Moore Papers, Cambridge University Library.

8. Quoted from Bernard Bosanquet's letter to subscribers of The London School of Ethics and Social Philosophy, October 27, 1900, p. 2. The Moore Papers, Cambridge University Library.

9. Ibid.

able demands placed on the school's youngest teacher, George Edward Moore, the newly appointed Fellow, Trinity College, Cambridge, played a decisive role in the development of his own, and in the history of this century's, moral philosophy.

BRICKS AND MORTAR

The school's central meeting place, where Moore delivered his lectures, was Passmore Edwards Settlement, 9 Tavistock Place, in the Bloomsbury section of London. The settlement's social mission was the same as its major benefactor's, J. Passmore Edwards. A true son of poverty, Passmore Edwards amassed an enormous fortune in the newspaper and periodical business. Once empowered by his riches, he set himself the task of making the world at least a little less inequitable, vowing to insure that future generations of the multitudinous poor might be spared the hardships he had faced alone. The luxury of "the helots of Park Lane" never tempted him. Literally scores of public buildings—libraries, galleries, hospitals, orphanages, convalescent homes, technical schools, and settlements (but no churches)—were built throughout England as a result of his largesse. His was the spirit of the optimistic philanthropist, his the perspective of the political visionary. His fierce utilitarian motto was, "Do the best for the most." In his conception of "the best," it was the quality of pleasure, not its mere quantity, that mattered. "When I read an interesting book," he writes, "I long to place it within reachable distance of anyone, however poor and lonely, who would like to read it; or when I hear fine music I say to myself, 'Oh that the people, the multitudinous people, had the requisite tastes and opportunities to enjoy similar satisfaction'; and as with literature and music so with the other privileges of life."[10] Passmore Edwards's object was to use his wealth to elevate the tastes of the poor until they became those of the rich.

Few others could have more fully shared these same values than the founder of Passmore Edwards Settlement, the indomitable

---

10. J. Passmore Edwards, *A Few Footprints* (London: Clement's House, 1905), p. 34n.

Mary Ward, better known as Mrs. Humphry Ward, the author of *Robert Elsmere*. This remarkably successful novel, which sold more than a million copies soon after its publication in 1888, is the story of a young clergyman who loses his faith, leaves parish life, and together with his wife moves to one of London's least desirable areas, Bedford Square, Bloomsbury. There Elsmere creates a mission whose primary purpose is to serve the needy. The novel ends with Elsmere's death, but the author's message is one of hope: people *can* make a difference.

The parallel between the fictional Robert Elsmere and the flesh-and-blood Mary Ward, whom Dean Inge eulogized at her funeral as "perhaps the greatest English woman of our time,"[11] is unmistakable. Like her fictional counterpart, Mary Ward was a tireless crusader for social reform, a woman so passionately committed to every noble cause that she ran the risk, and sometimes encountered the fact, of public ridicule at the hands of the British aristocracy. But Mary Ward rarely bent and never broke. "The pleasures and opportunities which civilization brought and developed came mainly to the rich," she states in her remarks on the occasion of the informal opening of Passmore Edwards Settlement, "and yet if the state was to grow healthily, they must in time be brought down to the market-place and distributed far and wide. Hitherto they had been sadly lacking to the great mass of our people. It was for the equalisation and distribution of these advantages that Settlements were specifically meant."[12] And none more so, in Mary Ward's vision, than Passmore Edwards Settlement. As her biographer Enid Huws Jones observes, Passmore Edwards Settlement was Mary Ward's way of realizing "the dreams of Robert Elsmere in bricks and mortar."[13] It was Mary Ward's good fortune to find in Passmore Edwards a man who, in addition to sharing her vision, was able to pay for most of the building materials. It was not in her, nor was it in his, character to build with

---

11. Quoted in Enid Huws Jones, *Mrs. Humphry Ward* (London: Heinemann, 1973), p. 166.

12. Mary Ward, "Social Ideals," *The Manchester Guardian*, October 11, 1897.

13. Enid Huws Jones, *Mrs. Humphrey Ward* (London: Heinemann, 1973), p. 3.

anything less than total commitment to improving the minds of the workingmen for whom the settlement was mainly intended.

THE SETTLEMENT

The impressive structure housing the settlement was designed by two young architects, Dunbar Smith and C. Brewer, on land leased by the Duke of Bedford for 999 years. An 1899 volume of *The Studio* heralds the building as "a triumph of the Arts and Crafts movement."[14] Rooms were provided for the warden and eighteen resident scholars. In addition, space was provided for classrooms, club rooms, entertaining rooms, a gymnasium, a large hall with a seating capacity of five hundred, and a library with the initials "THG" on the fireplace, to honor the philosopher T. H. Green, after whom the library was named. The architects overcame the depressing mood that characterizes this genre of building. The settlement "is the most charming and least vulgar advertisement imaginable," Mary Ward writes.[15] She must have been pleased, and J. Passmore Edwards not a little relieved.

The "advertisement" of which Mary Ward spoke was the fresh, positive image she wished to bring to the educational and social reform movements of which she was so vital a part. Hers was the gospel of good works, not good intentions, of devotion to this-worldly duty, not other-worldly dreams. Like Robert Elsmere she had lost her faith in God, and yet like him she never ceased to see her mission in missionary terms. "The ideal settlement," she writes, "presents itself almost wholly in religious guise."[16] As was true of her fictional hero, Mary Ward's faith was her works.

The creation of Passmore Edwards Settlement was one work among many. The settlement's primary purpose was to serve the needs of workingmen in a decaying neighborhood. Though then dotted with islands of affluence, the Bloomsbury area before and after the turn of the century was predominately poor. The set-

14. Quoted in ibid., p. 118.
15. Quoted in ibid., p. 116.
16. Quoted in ibid., p. 137.

tlement's mission was to give the working poor food for their thought, not just their stomachs. "It seemed impossible," Enid Huws Jones writes, "that this life of regular and sociable meals, of civil exchange of ideas, of enjoyment . . . of the arts, of contact with the mighty past and dreams of a mightier future—a life that was so rich and sweet to Mary Ward and her circle—should not elevate those to whom the door of the Settlement was now open."[17] As George R. Sims, writing in *Living London*, observes: "Here are potential hooligans sitting clean and in their right mind, at tea with the refined and refining colonists."[18] If only enough "potential hooligans" could be exposed to great ideas, great art, ennobling discussion, their own life would be ennobled. This was the raison d'être of the Passmore Edwards Settlement. Soon after its opening Mary Ward's critics charged that she had lost sight of why the settlement had been created.

A CHORUS OF CRITICS

Grounds for criticism came from diverse sources. One concerned the substantial commitment Mary Ward made to serving young children instead of the workingmen for whom the settlement was mainly intended; another concerned the status of the resident scholars, who (the critics charged) were treated as a class apart, there to pursue "their studies"; a third concerned—paradoxical though it may at first appear—the growing success of The London School of Ethics and Social Philosophy. Whereas the original hope had been to make the civilizing influence of high culture available to the underprivileged many, critics wondered aloud whether those who were benefiting were not a privileged few. As Enid Huws Jones observes, the students who paid their fees to hear Moore and the other lecturers were not "the shop-lads from Tottenham Court, as the founders had hoped."[19] They were people like Moore's friends from Cambridge, Desmond MacCarthy and

17. Ibid., p. 121.
18. Ibid., pp. 120–21.
19. Ibid., p. 90.

Crompton Llewelyn Davies, and Moore's brother, Sturge Moore, and others who, in the latter's revelatory words, were "intending to help swell the audience" at Moore's lectures.

For his part Moore must have anticipated the make-up of his audience more than he lets on. Although he remarks at the first meeting that he was "told that I must not assume in my class any large acquaintance with philosophic ethics" (*The Elements*, Moore's Introduction), he was only too happy to recommend Sidgwick's *The Methods of Ethics*, Mill's *Utilitarianism*, Plato's *Gorgias*, and, more respectfully, though less confidently, Kant's *Grundlegung*. This was hardly bedtime reading for weary, hungry workingmen. When, amid the torrents of the debate about whether the school had lost its rudder, Enid Huws Jones invites us to imagine the warden looking incredulously down the class rolls, it is not difficult to understand his worry that things perhaps were not going as the subscribers had intended.

Bosanquet and the other founders of the school must have been aware of the growing chorus of criticism, even as early as Bosanquet's "First Report" at the end of the 1897–1898 term. It was true, he allows, that because of the reputations of some lecturers, they drew "their own audiences from different parts of London" (not to mention Cambridge!); still, "there is . . . a certain nucleus of people who attend regularly, drawn chiefly from the neighborhood."[20] Somehow (or other) the tastes of the poor were being elevated until they were those of the rich.

The myth could not long endure. The success of the London School of Ethics and Social Philosophy, apart from its financial failure, doomed it. It may have been in the right place, and it may have been at the right time, but it was the wrong idea, or at least wrongly implemented. The reasons for its short-lived and all but forgotten demise were not "purely financial," Bosanquet's protestations to the contrary notwithstanding. They were sociological and political. Whereas another friend of Moore's from Cambridge, the soon-to-be eminent historian G. M. Trevelyan, who lectured at

20. Bernard Bosanquet, "First Report," p. 6. The Moore Papers, Cambridge University Library.

the Working Men's College in London, was able to say that "the name of the College helped to keep the snobs away,"[21] Moore and the other lecturers at the London School of Ethics and Social Philosophy lacked a similar protection. "Shop-lads" was not part of the school's name. At this place, and in that time, many of the snobs from Cambridge and London were in, and the hooligans from Tottenham Court, out. Small wonder that the warden—and others—persisted in feeling that the settlement was not being used by the people for whom it had been built. Small wonder that this bold experiment, fathered by Bosanquet and the others, entered the world all but stillborn.

REVISING THE REVISIONS

Moore presented his ten lectures on Thursday evenings during the autumn term. They were well attended. Thirty-six people paid fees ranging from one to five shillings for the full course; the average attendance was twenty-nine. The plan was for Moore to read a prepared lecture for an hour, then to lead a half hour's open discussion, an arrangement that allowed Moore to take the last train back to Cambridge. But things did not always work out as planned. The lectures average thirty-six double-spaced typed pages (hard to read aloud in an hour's time), and in some cases the discussions lasted longer than a half-hour. This regimen was not easy for Moore. He sometimes lost his patience during the discussion period, "in the heat of the moment," as he describes it, adding that the demands placed upon him are "so trying (to the nerves, I suppose I must say), that it is difficult to keep quite cool" (*The Elements*, Lecture III). Certainly the discussions must have been out of the ordinary, a development that led Bosanquet to draw particular attention to them because of their "unusual value and interest."[22] The young Moore, it would seem, had found a true admirer

21. G. M. Trevelyan, *An Autobiography and Other Essays* (London: Longman, Green and Company, 1949), p. 24.

22. Bernard Bosanquet, "Second Report," p. 6. The Moore Papers, Cambridge University Library.

in the energetic president of the London School of Ethics and Social Philosophy.[23]

Moore submitted *The Elements of Ethics* to Cambridge University Press on March 6, 1902. Within a fortnight word came that the book had been accepted. The Cambridge philosopher W. R. Sorley evidently championed Moore's cause, observing in a letter to Moore, dated March 16, 1902, that he "was responsible for the Syndice's decision." Sorley's good news was a mixed blessing. All was not well with *The Elements*. Because he had played a key role in having the book accepted, Sorley writes that he feels "almost bound to put the other side before you (I mean of course the 'other side' of the case as it presents itself to my own mind—not what other people said)."

At least part of what "other people said" is to be found in a neatly hand-written page of criticisms, not in Sorley's hand, that

---

23. Appearances may be deceiving. Bosanquet and Moore had a history of personal enmity, and although its causes remain obscure, its deleterious effects on Moore's early career are clear. During the years 1896 and 1897, Moore wrote two dissertations on Kant's moral philosophy, both of which are in the holdings of the Trinity College Library, University of Cambridge. Moore submitted both for a coveted Prize Fellowship. The first was unsuccessful; the second earned Moore a six-year fellowship (1898–1904) at Trinity, with rooms and meals provided, and an annual stipend of £200. Moore's former teacher, James Ward, presented Moore's case before the Board of Electors. He more than had his work cut out for him.

Bosanquet served as the outside reader of the second dissertation, and to say that he found it less than satisfactory is to understate his severe judgment. In his "Report" (also in the Trinity College Library) he declares that he finds "a difficulty in regarding (Moore's philosophical position) as serious." Moore's views, he states, "appear to me to lie beyond the limit of paradox permissible in philosophy." If he had been asked to review Moore's work for *Mind*, Bosanquet explains, "I should have treated it as a brilliant essay by a very able writer, but should have endeavoured to point out that its positive stand-point and consequently its treatment of the subject were hopelessly inadequate." "Hopelessly inadequate." It is a tribute to James Ward's rhetorical skills (or to his political connections) that, in the face of Bosanquet's acid assessment, the Board of Electors was convinced to award Moore a Prize Fellowship.

Moore was aware of Bosanquet's unflattering report, and Bosanquet was aware that Moore was aware of it. Writing to Moore on October 30, 1898, Bosanquet proposes that they have lunch, after which they might have "an hour's talk. . . . It would be pleasant for me to improve your acquaintance . . . even apart from the question of the Dissertation." Because Moore was then offering a course of lectures at a school Bosanquet headed, the tone of the latter's letter is predictably conciliatory: "I should be uncomfortable if I did not say that I hope we meet as fellow students of philosophy. I formed a clear opinion about the Dissertation and will tell you what it is as well as I can. But I do not feel any mission to

accompanied his letter. The overall finding is simple: The manuscript stands in need of extensive revision if Moore is to make a successful transition from a course of lectures to a book. For example, "the repetitions are far more frequent than is desirable in a book with a consecutive argument, and they seem sometimes to be introduced at places which do not suit a reader though they would suit a lecture audience." Of course, even in his most polished philosophy, the mature Moore has a marked tendency to repeat himself; it is part of his unique philosophical style. As a young lecturer, however, as we find him in *The Elements*, this tendency sometimes is near obsessional. Sorley knew that recasting the lectures would not be easy, but he encouraged Moore to persevere: "I hope that you will not hesitate to put a good deal of time into it," he writes. Because Moore *already* had put "a good deal of time" into revising the lectures, the prospect of having to do more could not have been pleasant.

---

speak as an authority or to 'give advice' in any sense of that kind. We will talk over our views, and we ought to be able to understand each other. I thought the Dissertation full of interest, though as you have heard I took a strong view against its main contentions" (The Moore Papers, Cambridge University Library).

Possibly Moore and Bosanquet joined for lunch. Possibly they had a hour's talk about their philosophical differences. The available evidence is moot. Talk or no, Bosanquet's less than enthusiastic opinion of Moore's philosophical views remained unchanged in the years ahead and twice worked against Moore's chances for continued support from Cambridge—first, in 1900, when Moore applied for the position of Knightsbridge Professor of Philosophy that became available when Sidgwick fell mortally ill, and second, in 1904, when Moore applied for a research fellowship. It could not have come as good news to Moore to read, in an undated letter written to him by the university vice-chancellor, that, in addition to the references Moore had supplied for his candidacy as Knightsbridge professor, the vice-chancellor was "writing to ask Dr. Ward and Dr. Bosanquet to send me such a letter with regard to your qualifications as I can read to the electors" (The Moore Papers, Cambridge University Library). Whatever the real merits of the youthful Moore's candidacy may have been—and even a partisan on Moore's side would have to concede that they were less than spectacular—they were not as bad as Bosanquet likely said they were, neither in this case nor, four years later, when Moore applied for a research fellowship. As Moore was to learn ten years later (the information is contained in an entry in his diary for April 27, 1914, The Moore Papers, Cambridge University Library), "why the older members of Council voted against my Research Fellowship was because of unfavourable reports from English philosopher Bosanquet." It is a fine irony that a man who hurt Moore's early chances for a more permanent position at Cambridge would, by having him offer a series of lectures at the school over which he presided, help sustain the young Moore in the composition of *Principia Ethica*. An immortal work is the best answer to one's harshest critics.

The earliest evidence we have that Moore continued to work on his lectures after 1898 is a letter to his mother, dated February 27, 1900, where he writes that he is working on his "old volume of Ethical lectures." Soon thereafter, on March 18, he writes again to tell her that he has "begun revising" them. Even as he worked on revising them, rumor had it that they *already* had been published. "Moore!" writes Henry Sidgwick in a letter from 1900, "I did not know he had published any *Elements of Ethics!*"[24] Impatient with the pace at which the project moved, Moore labored on, lamenting to his mother, in a letter dated September 12, 1901, more than a year and a half after he had begun revising them, "But lately I have made very little progress with what I intended to do—rewriting parts of my Ethics."

More regrettable still, in Moore's view, was the absence of the published lectures when he applied for Sidgwick's vacant professorship. "I fear the hope [of his receiving the appointment] is quite absurd," he writes to Desmond MacCarthy on June 2, 1900, adding: "I feel perhaps I ought to regret now that I did not make more effort to get my Lectures published. Now it is too late." Too late to strengthen his candidacy, that is. But it was not too late to revise his lectures with a view for eventual publication, which is what Moore continued to do until March 10, 1902, when, as noted earlier, he submitted them to Cambridge University Press.

When thus submitted, only four of the ten lectures had been revised, and in the page of criticisms accompanying Sorley's letter he was informed that "the criticisms apply to the four chapters revised for press as well as to the remainder of the book." Even the revisions needed to be revised. It was more than Moore could bear. When he writes to his mother on March 18, 1902, to share the good news that his lectures have been accepted for publication, Moore notes ruefully that "I shall have to alter them a good deal, which may take some time and will not, I'm afraid, make a very good job, after all." Clearly, Moore's enthusiasm already was wan-

---

24. From a letter of Sidgwick's to Henry Graham Dakyns, dated February 3, 1900. Quoted in J. B. Schneewind, *Sidgwick's Ethics and Victorian Moral Philosophy* (Oxford: Clarendon Press, 1977), p. 17.

ing. After this period there is no evidence that he continued to work on *The Elements*. Another project would soon command most of his time and energy. That project was *Principia Ethica*.

THE MAIN OUTLINE

Though his memory is not always reliable, we have it on Moore's own authority that *The Elements of Ethics* was the parent, *Principia* the child. "It was in writing the course on Ethics," Moore recalls, "that I developed the main outline of *Principia Ethica*."[25] This may be true in spirit but perhaps not in letter. Although Moore wrote his lectures each week throughout the autumn term of 1898, the professionally printed course syllabus was prepared and distributed no later than and possibly before the first meeting. To read the syllabus and the summaries of the several lectures is to recognize the "main outline" of *Principia* in embryonic form. Since the syllabus was prepared *before* Moore had written a single lecture, the "main outline" of *Principia* actually can be placed somewhat further back in time than Moore remembers.

In his "Autobiography," after noting the connection between the lectures and *Principia*, Moore observes that "*Principia* was almost an entirely new, and was a much longer, work, and the latter part of those six years [that is, 1898–1904] was mainly occupied in writing it."[26] Again, Moore's memory is faulty. *Principia* was essentially finished by March 1903, while his fellowship did not elapse until the end of September 1904. And it proves even more unreliable when he writes that his "first course [of lectures for the London School of Ethics and Social Philosophy] was on Kant's Ethics, and the second on Ethics simply."[27] Just the opposite is true. Faulty memory and the precise date of the beginning of *Principia*[28] to one side, "the main outline" of this later book is apparent in the structure of the earlier lectures.

25. G. E. Moore, "An Autobiography," *The Philosophy of G. E. Moore* (New York: Tudor, 1952), p. 24.
26. Ibid.
27. Ibid., p. 23.
28. Fixing the "precise" date of *Principia*'s beginning probably is impossible. There are

The ten lectures, as they were listed in the syllabus, have the following titles:

Lecture I. The Subject-Matter of Ethics
Lecture II. Naturalistic Ethics, Especially the Ethics of Evolution
Lecture III. Hedonism
Lecture IV. Hedonism Continued
Lecture V. Some Main Forms of Metaphysical Ethics
Lecture VI. Ethics in Relation to Conduct
Lecture VII. Free Will
Lecture VIII. The Ethics of the Inner Life
Lecture IX. Practical Applications
Lecture X. General Conclusions

Principia, by contrast, has only six chapters:

Chapter I. The Subject-Matter of Ethics
Chapter II. Naturalistic Ethics

---

some clues, however. Starting in 1900, and continuing for a few years thereafter, Moore kept records of his philosophical work (preserved in The Moore Papers, Cambridge University Library), records that not only mention what projects he worked on but also how long he worked on them. Citing an entry for May 23, 1902, which reads "Begin writing at my book," Paul Levy concludes that this is the fateful day on which Moore began to write *Principia* (Paul Levy, *Moore: G. E. Moore and the Cambridge Apostles* [Oxford: Oxford University Press, 1981], p. 233). The initial plausibility of Levy's finding is strengthened by the unhappy prospects Moore faced if he was to continue to revise his lectures to meet the criticisms lodged against them. It is easy to imagine Moore deciding to abandon the latter project altogether and instead to strike out in a new direction. This may be true. But there is other evidence that challenges this finding.

Certainly the *idea* of writing a book that stood apart from *The Elements* was one Moore had entertained before May 23, 1902. As early as September 12, 1901, in a letter to his mother, cited earlier in my Introduction, Moore writes that he "has made very little progress with what I intended to do—rewriting parts of my Ethics and *beginning my new book*" (emphasis added). Moreover, Moore refers to *The Elements* as "Ethics," "my Ethics lectures," "my Ethics," or simply "my lectures." When he refers to his "book," he evidently has *Principia* in mind. If true, then Levy is mistaken when he fixes the date of *Principia's* beginnings as May 23, 1902. As early as the Long Term of 1901, that is, between July 30 and August 27, Moore writes that he "work(s) at book." Thus, if we assume that when Moore uses the word 'book' he is referring, not to *The Elements* but instead to *Principia*, then the date of Moore's commencing to write *Principia* actually is some nine months earlier than the date Levy chooses.

Against this suggestion it can be argued that Moore does say, quite clearly, that he "begins writing at my book" in his entry for May 23, 1902. If he "begins writing at my book" on this day, then this is the day he begins to write it. What could be clearer? But things are not as clear as they seem. In his written records of his work Moore often writes of "beginning this" or "beginning that" in ways that do not imply that he has begun

Chapter III. Hedonism

Chapter IV. Metaphysical Ethics

Chapter V. Ethics in Relation to Conduct

Chapter VI. The Ideal

Despite the numerical difference between the ten lectures and the six chapters, the overlap between the two is evident, especially between the first six lectures and the first five chapters. Moore's lectures, one might say, gave him the structure for his book. His challenge was to fill in the details, mindful that this time he was obliged to write for readers, not listeners.

On this latter point Moore himself proved to be a good listener. When Sorley wrote to him to explain the "other side" regarding *The Elements*, he passed along the suggestion that "the main divisions of your argument should be made the divisions of the chapters, and if possible the chapters divided into paragraphs

---

something new. For example, during the period April 19 to June 17, 1902, Moore writes that he "begin(s) writing" a review of McTaggart's *Ethics* for the *International Journal of Ethics*; on July 15, however, almost three months later, he again notes that he "begin(s) working" on this same review. How are we to make sense of his confusing diction? The most obvious answer is that the former entry refers to Moore's work on McTaggart's book during the May Term of 1902, while the latter refers to his work on this *same* review during the Long Term. What it means, then, for Moore to say that he "begins" to do something, is not necessarily that he has begun a new project; it could just as well mean that within a particular period of time (say, the Long Term) there is a particular date when he *renews* his work on an old one. That Moore should write, "Begin writing at my book May 23," therefore, does not entail that this was the date on which, for the first time, he began to work on *Principia*.

In light of the above, it is entirely possible that Moore was at work on *Principia* from (roughly) August 1901 onward, that he continued to work on it sporadically even as he worked on revising his lectures, but that he decided to cease working on the latter project and instead to work exclusively on *Principia* owing to the great difficulties he would have faced had he continued to revise *The Elements*. The available evidence is consistent with this finding, a finding that is strengthened when we recall that Moore was hardly a speedy writer. "I write very slowly and with great difficulty," he observes in his "Autobiography," recalling his work on *Principia* in particular, "and I constantly found that I had to rewrite what I had written, because there was something wrong with it" ("An Autobiography," *The Philosophy of G. E. Moore* [New York: Tudor, 1952], p. 24). If Levy is right, and Moore wrote all of *Principia* between May 23, 1902, and the Lent Term of 1903, which is when he sent the final chapter of *Principia* to Cambridge University Press, Moore would have had to have written a book of 225 printed pages in less than ten months! Though possible, this hardly seems to be consistent with the pace at which Moore, who wrote *Principia* "very slowly and with great difficulty," could write.

This finding, if true, makes a difference to how *The Elements* should be understood.

corresponding with the steps of the argument." Moore's brother Bertie also offered some friendly advice, sending along detailed comments on the lectures and suggesting, in a letter dated merely "'00," that they "would perhaps gain in clearness if you gave a concise summary at the end of each lecture . . . as Darwin does." None of these suggestions found its way into *The Elements*, but all were incorporated into *Principia*. In addition to being a good teacher, Moore was a good student.

A DIFFERENT LIGHT

The differences between *The Elements* and *Principia* concern more than matters of style and are not attributable merely to the fact that the lectures were read by Moore, the book by his readers. *Principia* is, quite simply, a vastly better work of philosophy. Whereas in *The Elements* Moore flounders, loses the thread of his argument, and makes leaps of faith when reason prohibits him from reaching the conclusions he desires (see, for example, his appeal to "Common Sense" in the final pages of Lecture X), *Principia* is a work of great rigor, a philosophical treatise (in the best sense) in which the author endeavors relentlessly—and, no less important, passionately—to extract every ounce of truth. To read it afresh is to encounter a young thinker (Moore was still in his twenties when *Principia* was finished) who is totally in control of where the argument is headed and why. Not so in *The Elements*. Here we find Moore confused about where he is going, and how to get there. Why, then, if *The Elements* are inferior philosophically, publish these lec-

---

Readers familiar with *Principia* will find some striking similarities between this work and *The Elements*—for example, both contain essentially the same account of natural and nonnatural properties, the same discussion of whether a beautiful world would be good even if no one was aware of it, and much of the same criticisms of hedonism in general and Mill in particular. Heretofore the reigning view has been that Moore took various parts of *The Elements* and inserted them into *Principia*. This is a natural interpretation, given *The Elements'* earlier date of composition. It is possible, however, that the reverse is true: Parts of *Principia* may have been inserted into *The Elements* as Moore struggled to revise the latter at the same time as he "slowly" crafted the former. It may prove to be impossible to know which way the borrowing went. It is even possible that it went in both directions. But since uncertainty hardly justifies dogmatism, the reigning view is at best one possibility among others.

tures today, more than ninety years after they were originally presented and almost ninety years after Moore abandoned them?

To begin with, publication of *The Elements* enables contemporary scholars to gain access to an important source of Moore's influence. Heretofore Moore has been known mainly through his published work, yet during his early years at Trinity, first as a student, then as a fellow, his unpublished papers and lectures helped make him a major figure in late Victorian and early Edwardian intellectual life in general and in philosophy in particular. In no small measure this was due to Moore's membership in the Apostles.[29] The unpublished papers he prepared and read before this semi-secret society, often on philosophical questions at the very heart of his developing philosophy, helped shape beliefs and attitudes well beyond his own and the small circle of the sons of privilege to whom he read them. A committed student today can find and read these papers, but, as they will not be published, what we might call the "unpublished Moore" would be all but inaccessible if it were not for the publication of *The Elements*. To read these lectures now is to open a door previously closed, and to remove some of the mystery about what lies behind it.

More significantly, having access to *The Elements* permits a new generation of scholars to recognize the problems Moore was grappling with in his lectures and to use this insight when reading *Principia*. For more than the main outline of this latter book is to be found in the lectures. Many of the same questions are asked and answered in both, and although some of the answers differ in many important ways there is reason to believe that Moore's answers in *Principia* can be better understood if they are considered alongside the ones he offers in *The Elements*. Moreover, much of the basic metaphysical and epistemological framework that undergirds Moore's ethical teachings in *Principia* already is in place in *The*

---

29. The fullest account of Moore's membership in the Apostles is Paul Levy, *Moore: G. E. Moore and the Cambridge Apostles* (Oxford: Oxford University Press, 1981). Moore's unpublished Apostles' papers play an important role in my account of the development of his moral philosophy. See my *Bloomsbury's Prophet: G. E. Moore and the Development of His Moral Philosophy* (Philadelphia: Temple University Press, 1986).

Elements. And this is important: past generations of Moorean scholars, lacking access to the lectures, and having interpreted *Principia*
in the vocabulary of the philosophical fashions peculiar to their
place and time, have failed to recognize and to do justice to
Moore, the metaphysical and epistemological realist. The hope,
then, is that by publishing *The Elements*, another generation of
scholars might read *Principia* in a different light and thereby understand Moore's actual position better than their predecessors. Just
two examples of how this hope might be realized will be offered
here.

MOORE'S PLATONISM

The first concerns Moore's understanding of Good. In *Principia*, as
is well known, he argues that the word 'good', when it is used to
mean "that which is good in itself", names a nonnatural property
that is unique, simple, unanalyzable, and indefinable. These claims
have occasioned an enormous outpouring of critical commentary,
much of which misses Moore's meaning. Access to *The Elements*
should help remedy this. In this work Moore's Platonism (with a
capital P) is in some ways more obvious than it is in *Principia*, where
it is no less real.

The broad outlines of Moore's metaphysic at this time are in
part as follows. There exists a world of individual things (tables
and chairs, minds and their contents, for example). These things
all are in time, and some are in space as well. They are constituted
by those natural properties that together make them what they
are. There is no substantial "something I know not what" in which
these properties subsist; the natural properties are *themselves* substantial.

In addition to the world of particular things in space or time,
Moore recognizes a second, radically different order of being. The
denizens of this world are not individual things but *concepts* or
universal meanings (for example, yellowness, not this or that yellow
thing). These concepts are not in space or time, do not come into
being and pass away, and are not subject to qualitative change.

Moreover, "of *all* concepts," Moore writes in *The Elements* (Lecture V), "it is true that they *are* whether they exist or no." Since this is true of all concepts, it is true of the concept Good.

The similarities between Moore's views and those of Plato are unmistakable, something Moore himself explicitly notes in *The Elements*. "The chief significance of Plato's doctrine of Ideas," he states, is that it recognizes "this peculiar kind of being which belongs to concepts as such"; what Plato calls Ideas or Forms, Moore adds, is "what I have called concepts" (ibid.).

No reader will find as clear a debt expressed to Plato in *Principia*. But the debt is there, between the lines, and Moore's Platonism makes an enormous difference to how he should be understood. For what Moore means when he claims that "Good is indefinable" is barely distinguishable (if distinguishable at all) from what Plato would mean if he said "the Form (or Idea) of Good is indefinable." One looks in vain throughout most commentaries on Moore's moral philosophy to find an appreciation of the metaphysical backdrop against which Moore's famous discussion of the naturalistic fallacy takes place.[30] Indeed, Moore is more often credited with, and praised for, being *anti*-metaphysical![31] If nothing else, ready access to *The Elements*, where Moore explicitly acknowledges the Platonic roots of the metaphysic that grounds his ethical theory, should help future scholars read *Principia*'s repeated critique of naturalism with a fresh view. It is only if or as we understand *what it is* that Moore there claims is unique, simple, indefinable, and

---

30. A notable exception is Robert Peter Sylvester, *The Moral Philosophy of G. E. Moore*, edited and with an introduction by Ray Perkins, Jr., and R. W. Sleeper (Philadelphia: Temple University Press, 1990). Sylvester's book is the more remarkable because it was written without his having had access to Moore's unpublished work.

31. Thus G. J. Warnock writes that Moore "did not borrow a modish metaphysical idiom to make up for, or to conceal, his own lack of relish for any such thing." *English Philosophy Since 1900* (London: Oxford University Press, 1959), p. 12. Nothing could be further from the truth concerning the *early* Moore, the Moore we find up to, and in, *Principia Ethica*. Moore's genuine "relish" for metaphysics during this period is confirmed by his other writings of this time, both published and unpublished. For some of his relevant published work see Tom Regan, ed., *G. E. Moore: The Early Essays* (Philadelphia: Temple University Press, 1986).

nonnatural, that we can presume to decide whether he is right, and his naturalistic opponents, wrong.

PRACTICAL ETHICS

A second example of the light *The Elements* can cast on *Principia's* pages concerns Moore's practical ethic—his ethic in relation to conduct. Throughout both *The Elements* and *Principia* Moore emphasizes that Ethics, as he understands this science, is concerned with more than right conduct. Its object, he writes, is "the general enquiry into what is good" (*The Elements*, Lecture I). The ethics of conduct—practical ethics—is only one part of this more general inquiry. It is a part that caused great difficulties to Moore and one that has occasioned all but unanimous misinterpretation among those commentators who have written about *Principia's* fifth chapter, where Moore confronts these difficulties in that work.

In *The Elements* Moore is as much a consequentialist as he is in *Principia*. The criterion of right action is good results, intrinsically good results. Generally speaking, right acts are good as means to intrinsically good ends. To know what is right, therefore, requires that we know what is good. To know the latter, in the *strict* sense of 'know', however, requires that we know the best possible, the *Summon Bonum*. Because in *The Elements* Moore's view is that this Ideal consists of an infinite number of instances of an infinite number of different positive goods (see Lecture X), and because in his view *we cannot know* what the Ideal is, his practical ethic stands in real danger of ending in moral skepticism. If we cannot know the end, how can we know the means?

Moore offers the following answer:

I think we can still say what is best *in general*. . . . Most questions of practical conduct are for the most part questions of means and not of ends. The possible effects of our choice are, in any case, very small: the amount of good attainable is whether by choice or not also very small in comparison of the ideal: we need therefore, in general ask no more than what is possible, and that we shall commonly arrive at the best answer that can be given to this question, evolution guarantees us. It is only those who on the whole were best at foreseeing what will be the effect of what who could have come to survive as we have survived. [*The Elements*, Lecture X]

Moore's position here is more than a little unMoorean. To be able to foresee "what will be the effect of what" no doubt is necessary if a species such as the human species is to survive, and possibly "evolution guarantees" that we are able to know the effects of what we do, at least to some degree. But what evolution does not guarantee is that our ability to see into the future gives us the ability to know what is intrinsically good.

Remarkably, Moore thinks otherwise. "In the case of ends," he writes, "we have a similar guarantee. We shall not in general, be able to think that anything is good besides what other people think so. For what we think has also been determined by evolution" (ibid.). Not only is this "similar guarantee" similarly unMoorean, it flies directly in the face of claims made by Moore a week earlier, in Lecture IX. There he writes the following:

In the matter of opinion as to what is good as an end, evolution indeed may shew that people on the whole are likely to agree. It may shew that common sense is strong. But it can never shew that common sense is right. For that purpose it must first shew that the course of evolution has on the whole tended to good.

But "common sense," even buttressed by "evolution," cannot show this. When it comes to common sense and evolution establishing what is best, Moore writes that "I can see no ground for admitting any probability at all" (Lecture IX). And there's the rub. For if knowledge of what is best is beyond our reach, and if Moore dispenses with his all but scandalous (judged by Moorean standards) appeals to "evolution" as a basis for deciding what is right, then the unwelcome specter of moral skepticism remains. How, rationally, can one avoid this? That is one question the Moore of *The Elements* not only fails to answer; he fails grandly.

This same problem—how to avoid moral skepticism—haunts the pages of *Principia*, as well it should. Because what is right depends on the value of consequences, Moore is faced with two daunting challenges: first, to find some things, short of the *Summum*

Bonum, in whose goodness we can *rationally* believe, and, second, to find some way to make *rational* judgments about what is right even in the face of our ignorance about the long term future consequences of our actions. Readers familiar with *Principia* will recognize in that work's famous "method of isolation" Moore's attempt to meet the first challenge. This is well known. What many readers have failed to recognize is how Moore endeavors to meet the second challenge in this work. The crucial passage occurs in chapter five, where Moore insists upon "the general truth" of certain principles, "which ordinary moral rules are apt to neglect." Two of these "general truths" are the following:

(1) That a lesser good, for which any individual has a strong preference (if only it be a good, and not an evil), is more likely to be a proper object for him to aim at, than a greater one, which he is unable to appreciate. For natural inclination renders it immensely more easy to attain that for which such an inclination is felt. (2) Since almost every one has a much stronger preference for things which closely concern himself, it will in general be right for a man to aim rather at goods affecting himself and those in whom he has a strong personal interest, than to attempt a more extended beneficence. Egoism is undoubtedly superior to Altruism as a doctrine of means: in the immense majority of cases the best thing we can do is to aim at securing some good in which we are concerned, since for that very reason we are more likely to secure it.[32]

There is here no mention of the "guarantee" afforded by "evolution," no appeal to "what other people think," no convenient fatalistic inference to the conclusion that "what we think also has been determined by the course of evolution." A very different practical ethic, one that encourages individuals to decide and choose for themselves, on the basis of their own judgment (so long as they are for "a good, and not an evil"), emerges in *Principia*.[33] But even though Moore's practical ethic in *Principia* takes a much different form than the one he sets forth in *The Elements*, *Principia's*

---

32. G. E. Moore, *Principia Ethica* (Cambridge: Cambridge University Press, 1960), pp. 166–67.

33. I attempt to explain the neglected but vital importance of individual choice and judgment in Moore's practical ethic in my *Bloomsbury's Prophet*.

practical ethic still is offered as a solution to the same fundamental problem Moore failed (grandly) to solve in his lectures, namely the problem of how to avoid moral skepticism.

Whether Moore's *Principia* account of right conduct succeeds in avoiding the moral skepticism to which his account in *The Elements* seems doomed, save for his expedient appeal to what evolution "guarantees," is too large a question to be pursued here. It is, besides, the wrong question to ask in the present context. What is of importance here is the recognition that, as is true in the case of Moore's views in *Principia* regarding the indefinability of Good, so also in the case of his views regarding practical ethics: a close study of *The Elements* can help make a new study of *Principia* both more perspicuous and more rewarding.

ECHOES

The compact five-story building at 9 Tavistock Place where Moore gave his lectures still stands. But the name was changed to Mary Ward House after Passmore Edwards died in 1910—still the fierce utilitarian philanthropist, still endowing all manner of public buildings, hoping to do "the best for the most" to the end. The initials "P E" that are inscribed on the brass door furniture of the main rooms, Enid Huws Jones observes, "puzzle an age which does not remember [Passmore Edwards] very well."[34] She might just as well have said the same of the initials "THG" above the library's fireplace, and of the name "Mary Ward" itself.

This indomitable woman survived the criticisms that greeted her early years at the Passmore Edwards Settlement and used the facility to launch the evening play center movement for children. From a weekly average of 2,000 students attending her program at the Settlement in 1900, the movement grew rapidly; by 1914 eight schools served this purpose in the greater London area, with more than a million and a half children participating. Her visionary commitment to social ideals led her to create a Foundling Hospital

34. Enid Huws Jones, *Mrs. Humphrey Ward* (London: Heinemann, 1973), p. 116.

and, with the assistance of a familiar benefactor, the Passmore Edwards School for Invalid Children.

Even as she labored for social causes, Mary Ward continued to write, averaging almost a book a year until her death on March 24, 1920. Not one of her books currently is in print. Unlike the settlement's near neighbor, Virginia Woolf, who moved to Bloomsbury's Gordon Square in 1905—there to form the nucleus of what in time was to become known as the Bloomsbury Group, a group of artists, writers, and intellectuals who, in a twist of fate Mary Ward must have witnessed in stunned incredulity, claimed the philosopher who delivered the lectures that comprise *The Elements of Ethics* as their prophet and his later book, *Principia Ethica,* as their bible—unlike Virginia Woolf, Mary Ward has all but faded from the contemporary world of literature. "She did not write by ear," Enid Huws Jones notes, "unlike the generation of Virginia Woolf, who rejected her."[35] And yet in 1953 Violet Markham, a sister warrior of Mary Ward's during the British suffragette movement, which, not uncharacteristically, Mary Ward led, is quoted as saying, "I am rash enough to prophesy that within another fifty years Mrs Humphrey Ward will know a comeback."[36] The stark fact is, time is running out.

The same is not true of the young philosopher who made his teaching debut in the building Mary Ward conceived. For a time in the not so distant past the moral theories of G. E. Moore, like the novels of Mary Ward and the teachings of Bernard Bosanquet, were in danger of vanishing from the philosophical scene. David Garnett senses this when he writes, in a letter to Moore in June of 1949, that "the thing which I don't like . . . is the assumption that nobody reads you any more." Garnett's worry was a serious one for a time, but no longer. Each year sees new work by another generation of scholars that challenges slumbering dogmas about Moore's thought and helps restore both Moore and his ideas to their rightful place in the history of moral philosophy.[37] This process of

35. Ibid., p. 169.
36. Quoted in ibid., p. 169.
37. For helpful surveys of both recent and historically relevant literature, see the

restoration can only be assisted as more is learned about this remarkable man and the development of his thought. To walk past Mary Ward House today, even amid the noise of London traffic gone mad, is to hear the echoes of lectures past, lectures which, with their publication here, permit them to be heard again— afresh and anew. It is possible that Moore himself would say of some of them what he actually said of his 1898 article "Freedom": "though I have not looked at that article for a long time, I have no doubt that it was absolutely worthless."[38] Still, one must hope that even Moore's severest critic—Moore himself—would approve of permitting his new generation of students to judge for themselves.

---

discussions by Ray Perkins, Jr., and R. W. Sleeper in Robert Peter Sylvester, *The Moral Philosophy of G. E. Moore*, edited and with an introduction by Perkins and Sleeper (Philadelphia: Temple University Press, 1990). Also noteworthy are the ongoing activities of The Moore Society, founded in 1986. For information contact Professor Dennis Rohatyn, University of San Diego, Department of Philosophy, Alcala Park, San Diego, California, 92110.

38. G. E. Moore, "An Autobiography," *The Philosophy of G. E. Moore* (New York: Tudor, 1952), p. 21.

LONDON SCHOOL OF ETHICS AND
SOCIAL PHILOSOPHY.

PASSMORE EDWARDS SETTLEMENT,

TAVISTOCK PLACE, W.C.

AUTUMN TERM, 1898.

SYLLABUS

OF A

COURSE OF TEN LECTURES

ON

"The Elements of Ethics,

with a view to an appreciation of Kant's
Moral Philosophy,"

BY

MR. G. E. MOORE,

Trinity College, Cambridge.

LONDON:
KENNY & CO., TRADE UNION PRINTERS, 25 CAMDEN ROAD N.W.

1898.

The Elements of Ethics, with a view to an appreciation of Kant's Moral Philosophy.

Lecture I.

The Subject-matter of Ethics.—The ethical problem is involved in the question of conduct: What ought I to do or be? What is right? This presupposes a more fundamental question, not confined to conduct: What ought to be? What is good? The meaning of this question. It cannot be answered by psychology, by sociology, or by any of the natural sciences; hence it distinguishes Ethics from all these. The failure to observe this distinction is responsible for some main forms of ethical doctrine. Hedonistic Ethics, Evolutionistic Ethics and the Metaphysical Ethics of Will are largely due to the fallacy of Naturalism.

Lecture II.

Naturalistic Ethics, especially the Ethics of Evolution.—Naturalism rests on supposed impossibility that 'good' should mean anything except something 'natural': hence it cannot be an ethical doctrine at all. But it may be illogically used in support of such, *e.g.*, by Bentham in support of his Hedonism. So, too, in the common doctrine 'This is good, because it is natural.' Apart from this fallacy, it is soon obvious that everything that is natural is not good. Special form of fallacy connected with Evolution. As ethical doctrine, this involves the bare postulate of optimism, and does not follow even from that.

Lecture III.

Hedonism.—Naturalistic Hedonism rests on a false theory of the relation between pleasure and desire. Intuitionistic Hedonism may, however, be held, when this is disposed of, either as Egoism or as Utilitarianism. What is common to both, if their meaning be logically developed, seems very like an absurdity. To distinguish them, they must be treated as not purely hedonistic: they then become less paradoxical but indefinite. Utilitarianism must, however, be preferred to Egoism. The preference of the latter seems due either to the naturalistic fallacy or to confusion with Egoism as a doctrine of means.

Lecture IV.

Hedonism continued.—The doctrine of Utilitarianism. It cannot be a pure Hedonism. The objections applying to it, as generally understood, are those which apply to the theory that pleasure is a criterion of good, though not itself the sole good. This theory is either a baseless postulate, or else must minimise the value of pleasure even as a criterion. In the latter case, it seems to rest largely on false psychological analysis. Besides the defects which it shares with Egoism, and which seem enough to justify the rejection of any so-called Hedonism, Utilitarianism has practical difficulties of its own.

Lecture V.

Some main forms of Metaphysical Ethics.—Metaphysical Ethics are mainly of the Naturalistic type, if for Nature be substituted the metaphysical conception of Reality. Stoicism, Spinozism, and Kant are all liable to this objection. If it be contended that Reality is good and that we must therefore conform to it, proof seems lacking to the premise, and the deduction will hardly furnish practical guidance, being a reason for nothing, and apt to be a cause of fatalism. If, on the other hand, we depend with Kant on a Pure, and with Hegel on a Universal Will, there is no proof of such entities nor of their connection with the good. 'Self-realisation' either contains no practical guidance or implies an inconsistency.

Lecture VI.

Ethics in relation to conduct.—So far we have been mainly concerned with proposed Ends. The necessity for consistency in conduct follows immediately from this conception, together with a self-evident practical axiom. With the problem of the proper means to attain an End, 'scientific' knowledge is seen to be necessary to practical Ethics. Rational action thus implies a consideration of the possible as well as of the good. Difficulties thus introduced.

Lecture VII.

Free Will.—This problem is properly connected only with practice, not with the determination of the ideal. Kant's contrary view seems due to confusion. The vagueness of common ideas with regard to freedom: only a limited freedom maintained. In fact, freedom must either involve an un-caused event, or lose its opposition to Determinism. This dilemma is obscured (1) by asking the question with regard to free action, instead of free choice, (2) by lack of analysis of the conception of agent or self. Determinism is necessary and in no way contrary to morality. Meaning of Responsibility.

Lecture VIII.

The Ethics of the Inner Life.—Connected with the doctrine of Free Will and with Christian morals. Internal rightness presupposes the possibility of external rightness, since Kant's purely formal determination is a chimæra. Hence 'moral goodness' can only be considered as a part of goodness in general. Its value is obviously enhanced by external rightness, and depends, quite as much as that of the latter, on its utility. Hence this doctrine cannot claim to be a self-subsistent system.

Lecture IX.

Practical Applications.—The correspondence of internal and external goodness to faith and works is not insignificant; the nature of belief helps largely to determine the former. Tests of a rational belief. Application of these to moral judgments and to religious belief. Difficulty of deducing external duties from any one single principle. Negative rule may be of service, if properly applied, but is at least as apt to be applied improperly. Illustrations. Egoism as against Altruism: superiority of former largely due to practical superiority of feeling over principle.

Lecture X.

General Conclusions.—Above results mainly negative. Reason for this in complexity of ideal, and impossibility of fully conceiving it. Some main constituents may be named, but the degree of each and their proportion must be left indeterminate. The subordination of the æsthetic to the moral ideal. The practical problem being still further complicated by the question of possibility, we must trust in most cases to the particular judgments of conscience or common sense. Ethical doctrine can be at most a negative safeguard; but for this it is valuable, if it be definite. Summary of ethical elements: points of agreement and disagreement with Kant.

BOOKS

H. Sidgwick, 'The Methods of Ethics' (5th ed., MacMillan, 14s.).

J. S. Mackenzie, 'A Manual of Ethics' (University Correspondence College, 6s. 6d.).

For Reference:—

On Evolution:—H. Spencer, 'The Data of Ethics.'

On Hedonism:—J. S. Mill, 'Utilitarianism'; H. Sidgwick, 'Methods of Ethics.'

On Metaphysical Ethics:—Kant, 'Grundlegung zur Metaphysik der Sitten,' 'Kritik der praktischen Vernunft'; translated by T. K. Abbott (Longmans); F. H. Bradley, 'Ethical Studies' (very rare); T. H. Green, 'Prolegomena to Ethics.'

For general reference:—Plato, 'Gorgias,' 'Philebus,' translated by Jowett; Aristotle, 'Ethics,' translated by F. H. Peters (Kegan Paul): H. Sidgwick, 'History of Ethics' (MacMillan).

Lecturer's Address: Trinity College, Cambridge.

QUESTIONS

1. How is the province of Ethics to be defined?
2. What is the meaning of ethical obligation?
3. What is Naturalism?
4. Expose the fallacy involved in naturalistic Ethics.
5. Explain briefly the doctrine of evolution, and how it is thought to bear upon Ethics.
6. What is Psychological Hedonism?
7. Discuss the relations of pleasure and desire.
8. What is the meaning of 'end' and 'means'?
9. State as clearly as possible the fundamental postulate of Ethical Hedonism.
10. What is Utilitarianism?
11. Distinguish the different meanings of Egoism, and discuss its merits as an ethical doctrine.
12. Enumerate the reasons for and against the contention that pleasure is a criterion of the good.
13. State briefly the difference between the metaphysical conception of Reality and the common conception of Nature.
14. How is it proposed to found an Ethics on the conception of a Pure Will?
15. Give an account of volition.
16. How are practical precepts related to Ethics?
17. When may conduct be said to be inconsistent?
18. Define rational action.
19. Discuss the common notion of Free Will.
20. Why should it be thought that Free Will has any bearing upon Ethics?
21. Analyse voluntary action.
22. Are we responsible agents? Give reasons for your answer.

23. Distinguish fatalism from determinism.
24. What bearing has the notion of the 'self' upon the problem of Free Will?
25. Why is a good character to be valued?
26. Distinguish 'internally' from 'externally' right conduct.
27. How is 'moral goodness' related to goodness in general?
28. What is a rational belief?
29. Discuss the ethical considerations for or against the common estimate of any so-called virtue or vice.
30. Discuss the value of Altruism.
31. How must the ethical ideal be conceived?
32. What is the relation of the beautiful to the good?
33. What is conscience?

THE ELEMENTS OF ETHICS

Moore's Introduction

Before I begin the special subject of to-day's lecture, as announced in the Syllabus, I wish to say something about the general nature of my whole course.

The title announces that it is given 'with a view to an appreciation of Kant's Moral Philosophy'. Now it is only fair to warn you that in the ten lectures, of which the outline is before you, I shall not enter into the details of Kant's system at all. If any of you have come here with the sole object of learning what Kant's views on Ethics were, I am sorry to say you will be disappointed. Kant's Moral writings form a subject large enough for a complete course to themselves; it is impossible, too, to give a just idea of them, without some preliminary explanation of his general philosophy: This subject will, therefore, be reserved for a second course next term, if the committee of this School should desire me to deliver one.

In my course this term I have been kindly allowed to lead up to Kant as I thought best; and I have chosen to do so, by what, after all, I believe to be the shortest road. It is an *appreciation* of his moral teaching that I have in view: that is to say, I wish to make it plain how far his views were true, and how far false.

Now in any philosophical study, such as ethics, it is impossible to speak with authority. I cannot, as a scientific lecturer could, ask you to take what I shall tell you upon trust. In science there is an immense body of facts, not generally known, which have been proved by unquestionable methods, and which can therefore be taught authoritatively and illustrated by experiments, without any need that the evidence on which they rest should be set forth in detail. In philosophy this is not so. In philosophy there is hardly a single point, upon which there is now, or has ever been, agreement among experts. When, therefore, I tell you, as in an 'appreciation' I must do, that this which Kant has said is true, and that, which Kant has said, is false, you may be sure that many people, who have more right than myself to speak, would give me the lie direct. If this, therefore, were all I did for you, I should be giving you no information about ethics, but merely about my own opinions; and you might be justly indignant at my presumption. My object therefore must be to *convince* you that what I say is true, by giving you the reasons on which my opinions are based—by giving you reasons, which are, as far as possible, evident to yourselves. I am well aware that there is very little hope that I shall so convince you of much that I shall say. But in some things I may succeed; and, whether I succeed or no, this is certainly the only way in which ethical or other philosophical instruction can be profitably given. In philosophy, progress is only possible by a free and sceptical discussion of every question, which human ingenuity can possibly devise: there is not, as in science, any ready-made supply of certificated knowledge, which can be safely purveyed as the genuine article. If any of you expected something different—if you came here expecting to be easily informed of what nobody would dispute, I am sorry to say again that you must go away disappointed. I can appeal to nothing but your own reason for the truth of what I say; and, if you are not prepared blindly to take my word for gospel, you will have no reason to think that you have learnt anything of value from my lectures, except, indeed, such reasons as you yourselves shall have tested and approved.

In this respect my desire will be to imitate the method of Socrates as he is made to state it in one of those Platonic dialogues, to which I have referred you—the dialogue named *Gorgias*.[1] In that dialogue Polus has been urging that certain successful criminals must be happy: anybody, says he, would change places with them. 'My dear Sir' says Socrates,

1. The reference is to Plato's *Gorgias*, 471C–472B. There is every reason to believe that the translation is Moore's.

you are certainly a very good orator. You are just like the speakers in a court of law, who think that they have proved their point, when they bring forward many reputable witnesses to the truth of what they say, while the counsel on the other side perhaps brings none. But this sort of proof is worth nothing to get at the truth; since it is possible a man may be falsely convicted on the testimony of many respectable people. So now, almost all the men of Athens will bear you witness, if you care to call them. Yet I, who am but one among so many, cannot agree with you: for you do not force me so to do, but try by means of your false witnesses to rob me of my property which is the truth. On my side, unless I get you, and you alone to bear me witness and agree to what I say, I shall think I have done nothing to my purpose.

This, I say, is the method, which I *desire* to imitate; but, in fact, I daresay you may often produce in me that state of dumbness, which Socrates produced in others. If that should happen, I would like to say that I am not totally without authority: some good writers do agree with me on most of the points which I shall argue, and besides I claim to have common sense on my side in almost all these matters upon which it can be said to have an opinion.

But this process of giving reasons must obviously be a long one; and that is why I am proposing to give you a whole course of lectures upon general Ethics, before attempting to 'appreciate' Kant's special system. In this course I shall try to tell you quite plainly and definitely what I myself believe to be the true principles of Ethics; and, as far as may be, to convince you that they are so. Perhaps even more I shall try to convince you that principles held by other ethical teachers, and which you yourselves, it may be, now think true, are false. On almost all the points, which I shall thus discuss, you will afterwards find that Kant has much to say; and it is only when you have thoroughly examined them yourselves that you can hope fairly to estimate the value of his teaching. Moreover, Kant was a German philosopher, and even those late writings of his, with which we shall have to deal, were written more than a century ago. Those of you who have read the philosophy of any of the great Germans, will know how hard it is for Englishmen, familiar chiefly with the ideas of modern science, even to understand the meaning of much that they have written, and how, when you think you understand it, their meaning often seems a mere absurdity. It is only within the last fifty years that any large number of English philosophical writers have been at all influenced by German thought: the prevailing tone of English philosophy, as represented by such men as Locke, Berkeley, Hume, Reid, and more recently by Mill and Herbert Spencer, has always been of an entirely different cast from that of the Germans. They have been chiefly occupied with questions which we have never asked, and our method of discussing those which we have asked has been freer and less encumbered with that apparatus of technical formalities, which in them is apt to seem grotesque. Coleridge, one of the first Englishmen to excite our interest in German thought, has remarked that, in spirit, the Germans have tended to be enthusiastic and visionary. Coleridge also says that 'there is a nimiety' a 'too-muchness' about all Germans: and this characteristic certainly appears in their philosophical method. This character of their method is partly due, no doubt, to what he calls their 'totality' of intellect—their encyclopaedic learning, their desire to exhaust a subject, their 'passion for completion and love of the complete'; but partly it is due to the fact that philosophy has so long been taught in the German universities, in such a systematic and orderly fashion, that in England the teaching of Latin grammar alone can bear comparison with it.

This being so, it seems best to introduce to you maybe in an English dress those thoughts, which seem so foreign and outlandish when they are first met in Kant. In treating him it will be convenient to refer, on each point, to the more intelligible names and forms, under which I shall hope to have made you familiar with his problems in the present course of lectures. In these, therefore, I shall endeavour to refer mainly to English and more modern writers, and shall mention only in passing where I have been dealing with a notion, which will play a large part in the discussion of Kant.

Finally, I must beg your indulgence, if I appear to treat at too great length matters, with which some of you are quite familiar. I was told that I must not assume in my class any large acquaintance with philosophic ethics; and my chief fear will therefore be lest I fail to make myself intelligible, owing to the use of technical language.

For that, *discussion*
books.

LECTURE I

The Subject-Matter of Ethics

Most of you, probably, have some idea what Ethics is supposed to be about. You know that when you say 'So and so is a good man' or 'That fellow is a villain'; when you ask 'What ought I to do?' or 'Is it wrong for me to do like this?'[,] when you hazard such remarks as 'Temperance is a virtue and drunkenness a vice'—you know that it is the business of Ethics to discuss such questions and such statements; to argue what is the true answer, when you ask what is your duty, and to give reasons for thinking your statements about the character of persons or the morality of actions to be true or false. It is in such forms as these that ethical judgments are most familiar to us, though we do not commonly call them by that name. We all make such judgments daily: nobody will deny that they are of some importance; and nobody again, can have failed to observe that there is much difference of opinion about them.

Well, it is the business of Ethics to consider such matters, to try to diminish that difference of opinion. And the province of Ethics is to be defined as the treatment of the notion or notions which are common to all such statements. But what is it that is common to all these subjects of enquiry? If we take the examples I have given, we shall not be far wrong in saying that they are all concerned with the question of conduct—with the question what, in the conduct of us human beings, is good, and what is bad, what is right and what is wrong. For when we say that a man is good, we commonly mean that he acts rightly; when we say that drunkenness is a vice, we commonly mean that to get drunk is a wrong or wicked action. And this in fact is what the name 'Ethics' implies. You may know that that name was first given to a book of Aristotle's, in which he discusses what men ought to aim at, and what are their virtues and their vices; and that the name is derived from the Greek word ἦθος, which denotes what we call 'moral character'. The common word 'morals', too, comes directly from the Latin word, which exactly corresponds, both in its meaning and its history, with the Greek original of Ethics: 'mores' is equivalent to 'ἦθος' and 'moralis' to 'ἠθικός'. Who, therefore, talks of Ethics, is talking of 'morality'. The former name is to be preferred, only because it has been more generally employed for the attempt to give a 'scientific' account of the subject—an account systematically arranged and one in which all the points are, as far as may be, strictly proved. 'Morality', too, has tended to acquire a meaning even more limited to a mere part of the subject, than that of Ethics; and for this reason also the latter term is to be preferred.

And yet the meaning of Ethics even has been limited. Many people would accept as an adequate definition of the science, the statement made above that it deals with the question what is good or bad in human conduct. They hold that its enquiries are properly confined to 'conduct' or to 'practice'; they hold that the name 'practical philosophy' covers all the matter with which it has to do. Now, without discussing the proper meaning of the word (for verbal questions are properly left to the writers of dictionaries and other persons interested in literature; philosophy as we shall see, has no concern with them), I may say that I intend to use 'Ethics' to cover more than this—a usage, for which there is, I think, quite sufficient authority. I am using it to cover an enquiry for which, at all events, there is no other word: the general enquiry into what is good. Ethics is undoubtedly concerned with the question what good conduct is; But, if it is concerned with this, it does not start at the beginning, unless it is prepared to tell us what is good as well as what is conduct. For 'good conduct' is a complex notion: all conduct is not good; for some is certainly bad and some may be indifferent. And on the other hand, other things, beside conduct, may be good; and if they are so, then, 'good' denotes something, that is common to them as well as conduct, and if you examine good conduct alone of all good things, then you will be in danger of mistaking, for what is good in it something which is not common to those other things: and thus you will have made a mistake about Ethics even in your own sense; for you will not know what good conduct really is. This is a mistake which many writers, as we shall see, have actually made, by limiting their enquiry to good conduct. And hence I shall try to avoid it by considering first what is good in general, hoping, that if we can arrive at any certainty about this, it will be much easier to settle the question of good conduct: for we all know pretty well what 'conduct' is. This, then, is my question: What is good? and What is bad? and to the discussion of this question (or these questions) I give the name of Ethics, which must, at all events, include it.

But this is a question, which may have many meanings. If, for example, I were to ask you 'What is good?' and you were to answer me 'This particular lecture which you are now delivering is good', that would certainly be some sort of answer to my question, although perhaps a false one. But I am not asking the question in this sense. I am not intending to enquire what it is right for me to do, or for you to do, under the actual circumstances in which we stand; I am not going to discuss whether Professor Sidgwick's *Methods of Ethics* is a good book or a bad one; whether London is a good city, Lord Salisbury a good Prime Minister, or whether the dinner I have just had was a good dinner. All these, no doubt, are in some ways interesting questions; but the answering them does not belong to Ethics in the sense in which it is generally understood. If you were to ask a friend what school you ought to send your son to, his answer would certainly be an ethical judgment. Such ethical judgments, too, are delivered from the pulpit, rarely now as they once were, about the personal matters of the congregation, but often still about politics or public characters. But I am not going to usurp this part of a moral teacher's functions; nor do such ethical judgments form a part of Ethics, for the simple reason that there are far too many persons, things and events, in the world, past, present, or to come, for a discussion of their individual merits to be embraced in any science. Ethics, therefore, does not deal at all with facts of this nature, facts that are unique, individual, absolutely particular; facts with which such studies as history, geography, astronomy, are compelled, in part at least, to deal. And, for this reason, it is not the business of the ethical philosopher to give personal advice or exhortation.

But there is another meaning which may be given to the question, 'What is good'? 'Lectures are good' would be an answer to it, though an answer obviously false; for some lectures are very bad indeed. And ethical judgments of this kind do indeed belong to Ethics; though I shall not deal with many of them. Such is the judgment 'Pleasure is good'—a judgment, of which Ethics must discuss the truth, although it is not nearly as important as that other judgment, upon which I have promised you two lectures 'Pleasure alone is good.' It is judgments of this sort, which are made in any book on Ethics, which contains a list of 'virtues'—in Aristotle's 'Ethics' for example. But it is judgments of precisely the same kind, which form the substance of what is commonly supposed to be a study different than Ethics, and one much less respectable— the study of casuistry. You will be told that casuistry differs from ethics, in that it is much more detailed and particular, ethics much more general. But it is most important you should notice that casuistry does not deal with anything that is absolutely particular—particular in the only sense in which a perfectly precise line can be drawn between it and what is general. It is not particular in the sense just noticed, the sense in which this lecture is a particular lecture, and your friend's advice particular advice. Casuistry may indeed be *more* particular and Ethics *more* general; but that means that they differ only in degree and not in kind. And this is universally true of 'particular' and 'general', when used in this common, but inaccurate, sense. So far as Ethics allows itself to give lists of virtues or even to name constituents of the ideal, it is indistinguishable from casuistry. Both alike deal with what is general, in the sense in which physics and chemistry deal with what is general. Just as chemistry aims at discovering what are the properties of oxygen, *wherever it occurs*, and not only of this or that particular specimen of oxygen; so casuistry aims at discovering what actions are good, *whenever they occur.* In this respect ethics and casuistry alike are to be classed with such sciences as physics, chemistry and physiology in their absolute distinction from those of which history and geography are instances. And it is to be noted that the detailed nature of casuistical investigations actually brings them nearer to physics and to chemistry than are the investigations usually assigned to ethics. For just as physics cannot rest content with the discovery that light is propagated by waves of ether, but must go on to discover the particular nature of the ether-waves corresponding to each several colour; so casuistry, not content with the general law that charity is a virtue, must attempt to discover the relative merits of every different form of charity. Casuistry forms, therefore, part of the ideal of ethical science: ethics cannot be complete without it. The defects of casuistry are not defects of principle; no objection can be taken to its aim and object. It has failed only because it is far too difficult a subject to be treated adequately in our present state of knowledge. The casuist has been unable to distinguish, in the cases which he treats, those elements upon which their value depends. Hence he often thinks two cases to be alike in respect of value, when in reality they are alike only in some other respect. It is to mistakes of this kind that the pernicious influence of casuistry has been due. For casuistry is the goal of ethical investigation. It cannot be safely attempted at the beginning of our studies, but only at the end.

But our question 'What is good?' may have still another meaning. We may, in the third place, mean to ask, not what thing or things are good, but how 'good' is to be defined. This is an enquiry which belongs only to ethics, not to casuistry; and this is the enquiry which will occupy us now. I want you to attend most specially to what I have to say on this point. It is the most fundamental point in all Ethics. Until you have made up your minds about *it*, you cannot hope to understand the subject. If I cannot make you understand me now, if I cannot persuade you that the answer I shall give you is the true one, the rest of this course will be as good as useless from the point of view of scientific knowledge. For, though you may still be able to make true ethical judgments of the two kinds last mentioned; though you may live as good lives without an answer to this present question, as with it: you cannot possibly, without such answer, *know what is the evidence* for your ethical beliefs; you will never be able to give a satisfactory reason for them to any one who presses you to the end. The object of Ethics is just this that you should *know* the reasons for thinking that this or that is good; and if you are to know those reasons, you must know the answer to this question. My object in these lectures is only to teach you what is true about the good, not to make you do the good. If I wished to make you good, I might very possibly succeed just as well without discussing this subject of definition: many preachers do so succeed every Sunday. But my office is not that of the preacher; my only direct object is to help you to know the truth, and, though I certainly hope some other good effects may follow, especially in leading you to reject false principles of action, yet I should have done my duty even if the reverse were to be the case.

What, then, is good? How is good to be defined?—Now, you may think this is a verbal question. A definition does indeed often mean the expressing of one word's meaning in other words. But this is not the sort of definition I am asking for. Such a definition can never be of ultimate importance in any study except lexicography—the writing of dictionaries. If I wanted that kind of definition I should have to consider in the first place how people generally used the word 'good'. But my business is not with its proper usage, as established by custom. I should, indeed, be foolish, if I tried to use it for something which it did not usually denote: if for instance I were to announce that whenever I used the word 'good' you must understand me to be thinking of that object which is usually denoted by the word 'table'. I shall, therefore, use the word in the sense in which I think it is ordinarily used; but at the same time I am not anxious to discuss whether I am right in thinking that it is so used. My business is solely with that object or idea, which I hold, rightly or wrongly, that the word is generally used to stand for. What I want to discover is the nature of that object or idea, and about this I am extremely anxious that you should agree with me.

Well, if we understand the question in this sense, my answer to it may seem a very disappointing one. If you ask me 'What is good?' my answer is that good is good, and that is the end of the matter. Or if you ask me 'How is good to be defined?' my answer is that it cannot be defined, and that is all I have to say about it. But disappointing as these answers may appear, they are of the very last importance. To any of you who are familiar with philosophic terminology, I can express this importance by saying that they amount to this: that propositions about the good are all of them synthetic and never analytic, and you will know that that is no trivial matter. And the same thing may be expressed more popularly, by saying that, if I am right, then nobody can foist upon us such an axiom as that 'Pleasure is the only good' or that 'The good is the desired' on the pretence that this is 'the very meaning of the word'.

Well then, let us consider this position. My point is that 'good' is a simple notion, just as 'yellow' is a simple notion; that, just as you cannot by any manner of means explain to any one who does not already know it, what yellow is, so you cannot explain what good is. Definitions of the kind that I was asking for, definitions which describe the real nature of the object or notion denoted by a word, and which do not merely tell us what the word is used to mean, are only possible when the object or notion in question is something complex. You can give a definition of a horse, because a horse has many different properties and qualities, all of which you can enumerate. But when you have enumerated them all, when you have reduced a horse to his simplest terms, then you can no longer define those terms. They are simply something which you think of or perceive, and to any one who cannot think of or perceive them, you can never, by any definition, make their nature known. You may perhaps object to this that you are able to describe to others, objects which they have never seen or thought of. You can, for instance, make a man understand what a chimaera is, although he has never heard of one or seen one. You can tell him that it is an animal with a lioness's head and body, with a goat's head growing from the middle of its back, and with a snake in place of a tail. But note that here the object which you are describing is a complex object; it is entirely composed of parts, with which we are all perfectly familiar—a snake, a goat, a lioness; and we know too the manner in which those parts are to be put together, because we know what is meant by the middle of a lioness's back, and where her tail is wont to grow. And so you will find it is with all objects, not previously known, which you are able to define: they are all complex; all composed of parts, which may themselves in the first instance, be capable of similar definition, but which must in the end be reducible to simplest parts, which can no longer be defined. But yellow and good, we say, are not complex: they are notions of that simple kind, out of which definitions are composed and with which the power of further defining ceases.

Consider yellow, for example. You may try to define it for me, by telling me of its physical equivalent; you may tell me what kind of light-vibrations must stimulate the normal eye, in order that we may perceive it. But, if you think a moment, you must be aware that those light-vibrations are not themselves what we mean by yellow. *They* are not what we perceive. Indeed we should never have been able to discover their existence, unless we had first been struck by the patent difference of quality between the different colours. The most we can be entitled to say of those vibrations is that they are what corresponds in space to the sensation of yellow in our minds.

Yet a mistake of this simple kind has commonly been made about good. It may be true that all things which are good are *also* something else, just as it is true that all things which are yellow produce a certain kind of vibration in the light. And it is the fact that Ethics aims at discovering what are those other properties belonging to all things which are good. But far too many philosophers have thought that when they named those other properties they were actually defining good; that these properties, in fact, were simply not 'other', but absolutely and entirely the same. This

14

is the view which I have called the 'naturalistic fallacy' and of which I shall now endeavour to dispose.

Let us consider what it is they say. And first it is to be noticed that they do not agree among themselves. They not only say that they are right as to what good is, but they endeavour to prove that other people who say that it is something else, are wrong. One, for instance, will affirm that Good is pleasure, another, perhaps, that Good is that which is desired; and each of these will argue eagerly to prove that the other is wrong. But how is that possible? One of them says that good is nothing but the object of desire, and yet he tries to prove that it is not pleasure. Now, if he is serious in his first assertion that good just means the object of desire; then one of two things follows. Either he must be trying to prove that the object of desire is not pleasure; and, in that, I hold he will be right. But, then, where is his Ethics? The position he is maintaining is merely a psychological one. Desire is something which occurs in our minds, and pleasure is something else which so occurs; and our would-be ethical philosopher is merely holding that the latter is not the object of the former. But what has that to do with the question? His opponent held that pleasure was the good, and although he should prove a million times over that pleasure is not the object of desire, he is no nearer proving his opponent to be wrong. The position is like this. One man says a triangle is a circle: another replies a triangle is a straight line, and I will prove to you that I am right: for (this is the only argument) a straight line is not a circle. That is quite true, the other may reply; but nevertheless a triangle is a circle, and you have said nothing whatever to prove the contrary. What is proved is that one of us is wrong, for we agree that a triangle cannot be both a straight line and a circle: but which is wrong, there can be no earthly means of proving, since you define triangle as straight line and I define it as circle.—Well, that is one alternative which any naturalistic ethics has to face: If good is *defined* as something else, it is then impossible either to prove that any other definition is wrong or even to deny such definition.

The other alternative will scarcely be more welcome. It is that the discussion is after all a verbal one. When *A* says Good means pleasant and *B* says good means desired, they may merely wish to assert that most people have used the word for what is pleasant and for what is desired respectively. And this is quite an interesting subject for discussion: only it is not a whit more an ethical discussion than the last was. Nor do I think that any exponent of naturalistic ethics would be willing to allow that this was all he meant. They are all so anxious to persuade you that what they call the good is what you ought to do. "Do, pray, act so, because the word 'good' is generally used to denote such actions"; such is the substance of their teaching. And in so far as they tell you how you ought to act, their teaching is truly ethical, as they mean it to be. But how perfectly absurd is the reason they would give for it! "You are to do this, because most people use a certain word to denote conduct such as this." "You are to say the thing which is not, because most people call it lying." That is an argument just as good! My dear sirs, what we want to know from you as an ethical teacher, is not how people use a word; it is not even, what kind of actions they approve, which the use of this word 'good' may certainly imply: what we want to know is simply what good is. We may indeed agree[1] that what most people do think good, is actually so; we shall at all events be glad to know their opinions: but when we say their opinions about what is good, we do mean what we say; we do not care whether they call that thing which they mean horse or table or chair, 'gut' or 'bon' or 'ἀγαθός' we want to know what it is that they so call good. When they say 'Pleasure is good', we cannot believe that they merely mean 'Pleasure is pleasure' and nothing more than that.

Well then, Naturalism is not Ethics. It may be psychology, anthropology, sociology, or any other science whatever; it may be

1. An alternative to the passage beginning with the words, "We may indeed agree," written in longhand by Moore, appears on the back of Moore's typescript. It reads as follows: We may indeed agree that the actions and things people call good are actually good; we shall at all events be glad to know their opinions; but what we must know is the meaning of such assertions [written just above the last five words is 'their meaning in calling things good'], whether the term used be 'bon' or 'ἀγαθός', or its application true or untrue."

lexicography: but it is not Ethics. If there is to be any Ethics at all, good must mean good and must not mean something else; good must be undefinable. I confess I feel no fear whatever of any one who tries to attack this position. He must, as we have seen, either admit that he means to use the word good arbitrarily to mean some definite thing; and then he is not attacking my position: or else he must be laying down the law about the general use of words, and then, again, he is not attacking my position. The only position which can be logically held against me, and which I cannot directly meet, is the position that there is no such subject as Ethics at all, that good means absolutely nothing, which cannot be put into other words. Against any one who takes up this position the only method open by the nature of the case, is to try and shew him out of his own mouth that he himself and other people are constantly using another notion—the indefinable notion which I mean by good. And that method may be a very long one. On the other hand, he is equally powerless to attack me directly, who believe myself conscious of this other notion, irreducible to any other which he can suggest. The position is like that of one who should try to prove to a man born blind, that there is such a thing as colour: only in this case I do not believe that anyone is born blind—morally blind.

Assuming, then, that good is good, and undefinable, I think you will be surprised to find what important consequences follow from a position apparently so barren. In my next lecture I shall try to shew in detail how it robs Naturalistic Ethics of a great part of their speciousness. At present, I only wish to point out how it immediately solves the riddle of those puzzling words 'Obligation' and 'Sanction'. People are fond of asking Why should I do my duty? Under what obligation am I? and they are almost as fond of finding the answer in a Sanction: Because you will be rewarded if you do, and punished if you don't. But in reality the question is meaningless, and the answer is illogical. For to ask 'Why should I do my duty?' means simply 'Why is it good for me to do it?' 'What is the good of doing it?' And since duty can only be defined as what it is good to do, this puzzling question of obligation is

17

reduced to one of these: 'Why is duty duty?' or 'Why is good good?' For it is perfectly obvious that ethical obligation does not mean that you are forced to do your duty, that, in short, you cannot help it. If it meant this, why then you would always do your duty, and no question could arise. And in fact it is obvious that everybody does not always do his duty.

And as for the Sanction of punishment or reward, why, that answer itself raises a new question which is much more serious than the question of obligation which it tries to answer. For it is really pertinent to ask: Why should I care about rewards and punishments? That question is by no means absurd. And the only possible answer is because it is good to have rewards, and bad to suffer punishment. And that answer is by no means always true. So that whenever the question of obligation is answered by the assertion of sanction, you may know that the answer is merely trying to persuade you (and that often falsely) that the winning of rewards and the avoiding of punishments are in themselves that very thing, namely duties which *ex hypothesi* the action by which you are to win the one and to avoid the other is already known to be. No further reason can possibly be given for doing what is duty, than simply that it is a duty so to do. Thus our apparently barren statement that good is good, at once removes from the sphere of Ethics, two discussions over which a great deal of trouble has been wasted—the discussion of obligation and of sanction.

LECTURE II

Naturalistic Ethics, Especially the Ethics of Evolution

I announced to you last Thursday, that in the present course of lectures I should not directly deal with Kant; and I explained to you my reasons for lecturing first on Ethics generally. My reasons were partly that Kant, being a German and not a very modern writer, presents peculiar difficulties to English students who are not already familiar with ethical and philosophical problems; but my chief reason was that the correctness of almost every proposed ethical principle is now, and has always been, a matter of hot dispute among writers whose claims to pronounce on the matter appear to be of equal weight. This being so, I wished to warn you that I could not claim authority for my own exposition of the Elements of Ethics; the only method open to me was the lengthy one of trying to convince you, by giving you the *reasons* for my opinions, by instituting a perfectly frank and sceptical discussion of every moral dogma, which might offer, however indisputable such dogma might at first appear, and however respectable might be the names of its supporters. You may perhaps recognise as a truism, that the wisest men have been mistaken before now: well, please, remember to apply that truism to those of whom I shall speak; and remember, too, that when I attack a view of Herbert Spencer, I may probably have Kant upon my side, or when I attack a view of Kant, Plato, perhaps, or some other great name will be with me. Once more let me remind you of the words of Socrates: I do not fear your witnesses: nor will I rest my case on mine: so far as the counting of *their* voices goes, I am content your verdict should be, what in justice I think it must be, 'non liquet'— not proven: my only hope lies in the strength of my arguments, whereby I may compel you to agree with me and be my witnesses yourselves. This is a quixotic hope, no doubt, but it is all I have. And I am most anxious that you should imitate my method. Take nothing upon trust, examine every statement to the very best of your ability: only then, will you have learnt anything of value from these lectures, but something you will have learnt then even should you still be unconvinced.

Well, I proceeded to point out that the commonest matters of ethical or moral judgment were the characters of persons or actions, with which you are concerned: that you make an ethical judgment, whenever you answer the question 'Is so and so a good man?' or 'What ought I to do?' The Science of Ethics, however, cannot include such judgments as those, except by way of illustration: the actual persons or actions, which offer matter for these judgments, are too many and too various for any science to discuss them all. Ethics proper can only give the *reasons*, on which these absolutely particular judgments are based. It must attempt to make general rules of the form, 'This kind of thing is good' 'That kind of thing is bad', so that you may know, if your actual case is of that kind, that then it is good or bad. I pointed out that Ethics thus included casuistry, which also always lays down *general* rules and never deals with what is absolutely particular, though it may be *more* particular than Ethics.

But Ethics, I said, must also include another enquiry. Other things beside conduct may be good, and, if they are, then what is good must be something sufficiently general to embrace them as well as conduct. Ethics, therefore, besides its judgments on the kind of character or conduct, which is good whenever it occurs,— besides these judgments, which alone are usually called 'moral'— must make judgments of the same nature, general judgments, about every kind of thing or event which may be good or bad: the so-called 'moral' judgments form only a part of its sphere.

Finally, I said, Ethics must decide on what is meant by good. If we really want to *know*, here is obviously something to be known; and that alone would be a sufficient justification for seeking an answer to this question. Moreover it is by its dealing with the notion 'good' that Ethics is distinguished; and it is the duty of every science, so far as possible, not to use any term of which it does not know the meaning—far more, then, should it know the meaning of its fundamental term. But I had still another reason to justify my insistence on this question of what good means. It was this: That the failure to be clear upon this point seems to have led to grave error with regard to these general ethical principles, which are all important as a basis both for conduct and for judgment. I attributed to this mistake, which I called the naturalistic fallacy, several widely accepted ethical doctrines; and this charge I am to justify in the present lecture.

You will remember my own answer to this question what good means. My answer was that good just means good; that it is undefinable. This statement seems to have been a stumbling-block to some of you; and I am very glad indeed that you discussed it, both because the discussion shewed me that I must try to make myself clearer to you and because it has led me to make my position clearer to myself. I said that good was undefinable and your questions shewed that you were not clear as to what I meant by definition. Well, I do not wish to assert that I used the words 'definition' or 'definable' in the proper sense. And if any of you were ready with an exact definition of the word 'definition', and prepared to maintain that your definition of it was the right one, the one in accordance with ordinary usage, I certainly owe you apologies. But I hardly suppose that you were so prepared; and I think, in fact, that my use of the word was as near to ordinary usage, as is possible in the case of a notion, like this of definition, of which the true nature is still a moot point in philosophy. In any case, I am willing to admit that my use of the word was arbitrary; I was only anxious that you should understand what I meant by it: it would have served my purpose just as well, if I had used the word 'photograph' instead of definition, and had said that good was unable to be photographed. For I tried to *explain* what I meant in terms, about which there could be no doubt, and I think I can explain it still more clearly now.

Well, there are two other kinds of things, that might be called definitions, from which I wished to distinguish the kind of thing, I meant by definition, when I said that good was undefinable. When you say as Webster says, 'The definition of horse is 'A hoofed quadruped of the genus Equus',' you may mean three things. (1) You may mean merely: 'When I say 'horse', you are to understand that I am talking about a hoofed quadruped of the genus Equus'. Well, that might be called the arbitrary verbal definition: and I do not mean that good is undefinable in that sense. (2) You may mean, as Webster probably means: 'When most English people say horse, they mean a hoofed quadruped of the genus Equus'. This may be called the proper verbal definition, I would not say that good is undefinable in this sense either; for it is certainly possible to discover how people use a word: otherwise, we could never have known that good may be translated by *gut* in German and by *bon* in French. But now for (3). You may, when you define horse, mean something much more important. You may mean that a certain object, which we all of us know, is composed in a certain manner: that it has four legs, a head, a heart, a liver, etc., etc., all of them arranged in a definite relation to one another. It is in this sense that I deny good to be definable. I say that it is not composed of any parts, which you can substitute for it in your minds when you are thinking of it; just as you might think just as clearly and correctly about a horse, if you thought of all its parts and their arrangement instead of thinking of the whole: you could, I say, think how a horse differed from a donkey just as well, just as truly, in this way, as now you do, only not so easily; but there is nothing whatsoever which you could so substitute for good, and that is what I mean, when I say that good is undefinable.

But I am afraid I have still not removed your chief difficulty. I do not mean to say that *the* good, that which is good, is thus undefinable; if I did think so, I should not be lecturing on Ethics, for my main object is to help you towards discovering that definition. It is just because I think there will be less risk of error on our search for a definition of 'the good', that I am now insisting so that *good* is *undefinable*. I must try to explain the difference between these two. I suppose you will grant me that good is an adjective. Well 'the good', 'that which is good', must therefore be the substantive to which the adjective good will apply: it must be the whole of that to which the adjective will apply, and the adjective must *always* truly apply to it. But if it is that to which the adjective will apply, it must be something different from that adjective itself; and the whole of that something different, whatever it is, will be our definition of the good. Well, it may be that that something will have other adjectives, besides good that will apply to it. It may be full of pleasure, for example; it may be intelligent: and if these two adjectives are really part of its definition, then it will certainly be true, that pleasure and intelligence are good. And some of you appear to have thought that, if I said pleasure and intelligence are good, or if I said 'Only pleasure and intelligence are good' I shall be defining good. Well, I cannot deny that propositions of this nature may sometimes be called definitions; I do not know well enough how the word is generally used to decide upon this point. I only wish you to understand that that is not what I meant when I said there was no possible definition of good, and that I shall not mean this if I use the word again. I do most fully believe that some true proposition of the form 'Intelligence is good and intelligence alone is good' can be found; if none could be found, our definition of the good would be impossible. As it is, I believe *the* good to be definable, and yet I still say that good itself is undefinable.

One more point, by way of explanation. I believe it would at all events not be a strict use of the word definition, if it were applied to such a proposition as 'Pleasure is good'. My doubt is whether it can be properly applied even to such a proposition as 'Pleasure alone is good'. The point is important with regard to my expressed hope of finding a definition of *the* good. For I should not call it a definition proper unless the terms were convertible. For instance, if I said 'Intelligence is what is good' I should not call that a definition, unless it were equally true that 'What is good is intel-

23

ligence'. Thus, it would not be a definition of the good, if I said
'The good is intelligent, pleasant, etc., etc.,' because that would
not imply that everything which was intelligent, pleasant, etc.,
was also good. When, therefore, I offer any of the ethical propositions, by means of which I hope the end to define the good, such
as 'Pleasure is good', 'Intelligence is good', I must be understood to
mean that pleasure, intelligence, etc., are always good, but I must
not be understood to mean that they alone are good. And though,
if I said the latter, 'Pleasure alone is good', I should take that as
equivalent to a definition of 'the good'; yet 'Pleasure is good' would
not be a definition even of 'the good', far less then of good.

Well, I hope I may now return to our naturalistic fallacy without
further risk of misunderstandings. What I do fear is that, after
these explanations, you will think it cannot be important, that you
will be inclined to despise my vaunted statement that 'Good is
undefinable'. However, our first business is with its truth, and not
with its importance. You may remember how, in my last lecture, I
tried to establish that it was true. I pointed out that any writer, who
professed to define good, must either contradict himself, or else
must admit, what he cannot prove, that there is no such subject as
Ethics at all. Let us briefly reconsider the arguments for the former
position. In the first place, his definition may be a verbal definition:
he may merely assert 'This is how the word good is usually
employed'. But in that case, he cannot consistently maintain that
his system of Ethics is the true one. By recommending it, he must
imply 'This, which I tell you, is good: therefore do it'. But in fact he
has only proved 'This, which I tell you, is called good': and that is
no reason for telling you to do it. Or else, he may contend that his
definition is a real definition. A definition in the sense in which I
say that good is no definition. But, in this case, he is powerless to
contend that his definition is the right one. For if it is a real
definition at all, then you may substitute it for 'good' in all his
arguments: and, since his arguments against an opponent must
take the form 'What you define good as, is not good', then by
substitution we get the result 'What you define good as is not what

I define good as': a statement which both had admitted already, and which goes no way at all to prove what good really is.

Good, then, I maintain, is undefinable; and I mentioned in the discussion that Professor Sidgwick held the same view and argued for its truth in his 'Methods of Ethics'. I had forgotten to bring you the reference; I can give it you now: the subject is discussed from pp. 27–35 of the 5th edition (if you have not that edition it is from the 2nd edition onward in Book I. ch. iii. § 1–3). I have also stated in my Syllabus that Bentham supports his Hedonism by the naturalistic fallacy. You will find the evidence for that statement in a note on these same pages of Prof. Sidgwick's (p. 33, note 2).[1] Bentham explains, you will find, that his fundamental principle 'states the greatest happiness of all those whose interest is in question, as being the right and proper end of human action': and yet 'his language in other passages of the same chapter would seem to imply' that he *means* by the word right 'conducive to the general happiness'. Professor Sidgwick sees that, if you take these two statements together, you get the absurd result that 'greatest happiness is the end of human action, that is conducive to the general happiness'; and so absurd does it seem to him to call this result 'the fundamental principle of a moral system', that he suggests that

1. The passage from Sidgwick to which Moore refers, and the discussion that immediately follows, closely parallel Moore's discussion in *Principia*, pp. 18–19. In the typescript of *The Elements* Moore identifies the footnote from Sidgwick as note 3. In fact it is note 2. This correction has been made in the text. The footnote reads as follows:

> As, for instance, Bentham explains [*Principles of Morals and Legislation*, chap. I.i. note] that his fundamental principle "states the greatest happiness of all those whose interest is in question as being the right and proper end of human action," we cannot understand him really to mean by the word "right" "conducive to the general happiness," though his language in other passages of the same chapter [ix. and x.] would seem to imply this; for the proposition that it is conducive to general happiness to take general happiness as an end of action, though not exactly a tautology, can hardly serve as the fundamental principle of a moral system.

Moore's references to Sidgwick throughout the typescript of *The Elements* are to the fifth edition of *The Methods of Ethics* (London: Macmillan and Company, 1893). On some occasions Moore quotes material from Sidgwick's work and gives the page number in the typescript of *The Elements*. This bibliographical device has been retained throughout the present work.

Bentham cannot have meant it. Yet Prof. Sidgwick himself states elsewhere (p. 42) that Psychological Hedonism is 'not seldom counfounded with Egoistic Hedonism'; and that confusion, as we shall see next lecture, rests chiefly on that same fallacy, the naturalistic fallacy, which is implied in Bentham's statements. Prof. Sidgwick admits therefore that this fallacy is sometimes committed, absurd as it is; and I am inclined to think that Bentham may really have been one of those who committed it. Mill, as we shall see next lecture, certainly did commit it. In any case, whether Bentham committed it or not, his doctrine, as above quoted, will serve as a very good illustration of this fallacy, and of the importance of the contrary proposition that good is undefinable.

Let us consider this doctrine. Bentham seems to imply, so Professor Sidgwick says, that the word 'right' *means* 'conducive to general happiness'. Now this, by itself, need not necessarily involve the naturalistic fallacy. For the word right is very commonly appropriated to actions which lead to the attainment of what is good; which are regarded as means to the ideal and not as ends-in-themselves. This use of 'right', as denoting what is good as a means, whether or not it be also good as an end, is indeed the use to which I shall confine the word. Had Bentham been using 'right' in this sense, it might be perfectly consistent for him to *define* right as 'conducive to the general happiness', *provided only* (and notice this proviso) he had already proved, or laid down as an axiom, that general happiness was the good, or that general happiness alone was good. For in that case he would have already defined *the* good as general happiness, (a position perfectly consistent, as we have seen, with the contention that good is undefinable), and, since right was to be defined as 'conducive to *the* good', it would actually *mean* 'conducive to general happiness'. But this method of escape from the charge of having committed the naturalistic fallacy, has been closed by Bentham himself. For his fundamental principle is, we see, that the greatest happiness of all concerned is the *right* and proper *end* of human action. He applies the word right, therefore, to the end, as such, not only to the means which are conducive to it; and, that being so, right can no longer be defined as 'conducive

26

to the general happiness', without involving the fallacy in question. For now it is obvious that the definition of right as conducive to general happiness can be used by him in support of the fundamental principle that general happiness is the right end; instead of being itself derived from that principle. If right, by definition, means conducive to general happiness, then it is obvious that general happiness is the right end. It is not necessary now first to prove to assert that general happiness is the right end, before right is defined as conducive to general happiness—a perfectly logical procedure; but on the contrary the definition of right as conducive to general happiness proves general happiness to be the right end—a perfectly illogical procedure, since in this case the statement that 'general happiness is the right end of human action' is not an ethical principle at all, but either, as we have seen, a proposition about the meaning of words, or else a proposition about the *nature* of general happiness, not about its rightness or goodness.

Now, I do not wish you to misunderstand the place I assign to this fallacy. The discovery of it does not at all refute Bentham's contention that greatest happiness is the proper end of human action, if that be understood as an ethical proposition, as he undoubtedly intended it. That principle may be true all the same: we shall consider whether it is so, in the next two lectures. Bentham might have maintained it, as Professor Sidgwick does, even if the fallacy had been pointed out to him. What I am maintaining is that the *reasons* which he actually gives for his ethical proposition are fallacious ones, so far as they consist in a definition of right. What I suggest is that he did not perceive them to be fallacious; and that, if he had done so, he would have been led to seek for other reasons in support of his Utilitarianism, and that, had he sought for other reasons, he *might* have found none which he thought to be sufficient. In that case he would have changed his whole system—a most important consequence. It is undoubtedly also possible that he would have thought other reasons to be sufficient, and in that case his ethical system, in its main results would still have stood. But, even in this latter case, his use of the fallacy would be a serious objection to him as an ethical philosopher. For it is the business of Ethics, I must insist, not only to obtain true results, but also to find valid reasons for them. The direct object of Ethics is knowledge and not practice; and any one who uses the naturalistic fallacy has certainly not fulfilled this first object, however correct his practical principles may be.

My objections to Naturalism are then, in the first place, that it offers no reason at all, far less any valid reason, for any ethical principle whatever; and in this it already fails to satisfy the requirements of Ethics, as a scientific study. But in the second place I contend that, though it gives a reason for no ethical principle, it is a *cause* of the acceptance of false principles, it deludes the mind into accepting, ethical principles, which are false; and in this it is contrary to every aim of Ethics. You see that if we start with a definition of right conduct as conduct conducive to general happiness; then, knowing that right conduct is universally conduct conducive to the good, we very easily arrive at the result that the good is general happiness. If, on the other hand, we once recognise that we must start our Ethics without a definition, we shall be much more apt to look about us, before we adopt any ethical principle whatever; and the more we look about us, the less likely are we to adopt a false one. You may reply to this: Yes but we shall look about us just as much, before we settle on our definition, and are therefore just as likely to be right. But I will try to convince you that this is not the case. You see, if we start with the conviction that a definition of good can be found, we start with the conviction that good *can mean* nothing else than some one property or things; and our only business will then be to discover what that property is. But if we recognise that, so far as the meaning of good goes, anything whatever may be good, we start with a much more open mind. Moreover, apart from the fact, that when we think we have a definition, we cannot logically defend our ethical principles in any way whatever, we shall be much less apt to defend them well, even if illogically. For we shall start with the conviction that good must mean so and so, and shall therefore be inclined either to misunderstand our opponent's arguments or to cut them short with the reply 'This is not an open question: the very meaning of the word decides it; no one can think otherwise except through confusion'. This, I shall shew you, Herbert Spencer actually does.

Well, to these objections which I find against Naturalism, are two advantages which I find in my own contrary principle that good is undefinable. The first advantage which I claim, is simply— that it is true, and this, I am aware, may not seem to you a very great one. But I also claimed last Thursday that it was necessary, as a premise, to any ethical conclusion. Someone objected to this statement in the discussion, on the ground that it did not seem to fulfil the functions of a major premiss in Formal Logic. That is perfectly true; it does not fulfil them. But when I used the word 'premiss' I did not mean to confine myself to Formal Logic. It is a fact that very serious objections have long been urged against both the utility and the correctness of formal logic, and par-ticularly against the syllogistic doctrine of inference. These objec-tions begin at least as early as Hegel, and they have been well worked out by such writers as Lotze, Bradley and Bosanquet. It is not my business to discuss them here; but, speaking in terms of what I may perhaps be allowed to call this New Logic, I do contend that this proposition that good is undefinable must serve as a premiss to all ethical reasoning. I should give the name of premiss, to any proposition which is logically pre-supposed, in any conclusion; and, whether I am right in so naming it or no, what I wish to insist on is that this proposition is so pre-supposed, in any ethical conclusion. This is the second advantage which I claim for it. Take such a judgment as 'Pleasure is good'; well, if such a judgment is to have any ethical meaning at all, then it must be true that good is undefinable. And notice the consequences of this admission. It is at once plain that you cannot *deduce* the principle 'Pleasure is good', from any proposition whatever: if you mean to claim that it is true at all, you must base your claim on the ground that it is self-evident: and it is no slight gain to be clear upon this point, since the assertion of self-evidence is obviously risky. The naturalists, on the other hand, *can* deduce such a principle, if they have a definition of good,—and they will therefore feel far more

29

confidence in it—that confidence which leads to error. A principle, too, which is put forward as deduced, is so far better guarded
from attack than one which confessedly stands merely on its own
merits: and thus a pernicious fallacy can more easily creep into our
ethical reasoning, if it be not first acknowledged that good is
undefinable.

One more word about Naturalism. I have appropriated the
name to a particular method of approaching Ethics—a method
which strictly understood, is inconsistent with the possibility of
any Ethics whatsoever. This method consists in substituting for
'good', some one property of a natural object or of a collection of
natural objects; and in thus replacing Ethics by some one of the
natural sciences. In general, the science thus substituted is one of
the sciences specially concerned with man, owing to the general
mistake (for such I hold it to be) of regarding the matter of Ethics
as confined to human conduct. In general, Psychology has been
the science substituted, as by J. S. Mill; or Sociology, as by
Professor Clifford, and other modern writers. But any other science might equally well be substituted. It is the same fallacy which
is implied, when Professor Tyndall recommends us to 'conform to
the laws of matter:' and here the science which it is proposed to
substitute for Ethics is simply Physics. The name then is perfectly
general; and I have seen it used in the way in which I use it. But I
must warn you that I do not know this usage to be established;
naturalism may also mean something else: I only give you the
name, as the most convenient one I can find, for the doctrine
which I have been describing; and you must understand that if you
use it, particularly if you talk about the 'naturalistic fallacy', you
must expect not to be understood: it is the thing and not the name,
upon which you must rely, if you wish to argue the question; for
naturally, even those who call their Ethics a naturalistic one, do
not admit that it is therefore fallacious.

Well, now I hope to have convinced you that this is a fallacy,
whatever it be called; and I hope, too, that I have explained it
sufficiently for you to detect it, wherever it occurs. I must now
fulfil my promise for this lecture, and must point out some chief

cases in which this fallacy appears to have influenced ethical conclusions.

First, then, you have probably all heard something of 'living according to nature'. That was the principle of the Stoic ethics; but, since their ethics has some claim to be called metaphysical, I shall not attempt to deal with it more in detail till my fifth lecture. But the same phrase reappears in Rousseau; and it is not infrequently maintained even now that what we ought to do is to live naturally. Now let us examine this contention in its general form. It is obvious, in the first place, that we cannot say that everything natural is good, except perhaps in virtue of some metaphysical theory, such as I shall deal with later. If everything natural is good, then certainly ethics, as it is ordinarily understood, disappears: for nothing is more certain, from an ethical point of view than that some things are bad and others good; the object of ethics is, indeed, in chief part, to give you general rules whereby you may avoid the one and do the other. What, then, does natural mean, in this advice to live naturally, since it obviously cannot apply to everything that is natural?

Well, this phrase seems to me to point to a vague notion that there is some such thing as natural good; to a belief that nature may be said to fix and decide what shall be good, just as she fixes and decides what shall exist. For instance, it may be supposed that 'health' is susceptible of a natural definition, that nature has fixed what health shall be: and health, it may be said, is obviously good; hence in this case nature has decided the matter; we have only to go to her and ask her what health is, and we shall know what is good: we shall have based an ethics upon science. Well, but what is this natural definition of health? I can only conceive that health should be defined in natural terms as the *normal* state of an organism; for undoubtedly disease is also a natural product. To say that health is what is preserved by evolution, and what itself tends to preserve, in the struggle for existence, the organism which possesses it, comes to the same thing: for the point of evolution is that it pretends to give a causal explanation of why some forms of life are normal and others are abnormal; it explains the origin of

31

species. When therefore we are told that health is natural, we may presume that what is meant is that it is normal; and that when we are told to pursue health as a natural end, what is implied is that the normal must be good. But is it so obvious that the normal must be good? Is it really obvious that health, for instance, is good? Was the excellence of Socrates or of Shakespeare normal? Was it not rather abnormal, extraordinary? It is, I think, obvious in the first place, that not all that is good is normal; that, on the contrary, the abnormal is often better than the normal: peculiar excellence, as well as peculiar viciousness, must obviously be not normal but abnormal. Yet it may be said that nevertheless the normal is good; and I myself am not prepared to dispute that health is good. What I contend is that this must not be taken to be obvious; that it must be regarded as an open question. To declare it to be obvious is to suggest the naturalistic fallacy. Just as, in some recent books, a proof that genius is diseased, abnormal, has been used in order to suggest that genius ought not to be encouraged. Such reasoning is fallacious, and dangerously fallacious. The fact is that in the very words 'health' and 'disease' we do commonly include the notion that the one is good and the other bad. But, when a so-called scientific definition of them is attempted, a definition in natural terms, the only one possible is that by normal and abnormal. Now, it is easy to prove that some things commonly thought excellent are abnormal, and it follows that they are diseased. But it does not follow, except by virtue of the naturalistic fallacy, that those things commonly thought good, are therefore bad. All that has really been shewn is that in some cases there is a conflict between the common judgment that genius is good, and the common judgment that health is good. It is not sufficiently recognised that the latter judgment has not a whit more warrant for its truth than the former; that both are perfectly open questions. It may be true, indeed, that by 'healthy' we do commonly imply 'good'; but that only shews that when we so use the word, we do not mean the same thing, by it, as the thing which is meant in medical science. That health, when the word is used to denote something good, is good, goes no way at all to shew, that health, when the word is used to denote something normal, is also good. You might as well say that, because 'bull' denotes an Irish joke and also a certain animal, the joke and the animal must be the same thing. You must not, therefore, be frightened by the assertion that a thing is natural into the admission that it is good; good does not, by definition, mean anything that is natural; and it is therefore always an open question whether anything that is natural is good.

But there is another slightly different sense in which the word natural is used with an implication that it denotes something good. This is when we speak of natural affections, or unnatural crimes and vices. Here the meaning seems to be, not so much that the action or feeling in question is normal or abnormal, as that it is necessary. It is [in] this connection that we are advised to imitate savages and beasts. Curious advice certainly, but, of course, there may be something in it. I am not here concerned to enquire under what circumstances, some of us might with advantage take a lesson from the cow. I have really no doubt that such exist. What I am concerned with is a certain kind of reason, which I think is sometimes used to support this doctrine: a naturalistic reason. The notion sometimes lying at the bottom of the minds of preachers of this gospel, is that we cannot improve on nature. This notion is certainly true, in the sense that anything we can do, that may be better than the present state of things, will certainly be a natural product. But that is not what is meant by this phrase; again nature is used to mean only a part of nature, only this time the part meant is not so much the normal as an arbitrary minimum of what is necessary for life. And when this minimum is recommended as 'natural' as the way of life to which nature points her finger, then the naturalistic fallacy is used. Against this position I wish only to point out that though the performance of certain acts, not in themselves desirable, may be *excused* as necessary means to the preservation of life, that is no reason for praising them or advising us to limit ourselves to those simple actions, which are necessary, if it is possible for us to improve our condition, even at the expense of doing what is in this sense unnecessary. Nature does indeed set limits to what is possible; she does control the means we have at our disposal for obtaining what is good: and of this fact, practical ethics, as we shall see in our sixth lecture must certainly take account: but when she is supposed to have a preference for what is necessary, what is necessary means only what is necessary to obtain a certain end, pre-supposed as the highest good; and what the highest good is nature cannot determine. Why should we suppose that what is merely necessary to life is ipso facto better than what is necessary to the study of metaphysics, useless as that study may appear? It may be that life is only worth living, because it enables us to study metaphysics—is a necessary means thereto.—The fallacy of this argument from nature has been discovered as long ago as Lucian.[2] 'I was almost inclined to laugh' says Callicratidas in one of his dialogues

just now, when Charicles was praising irrational brutes and the savagery of the Scythians; in the heat of his argument he was almost repenting that he was born a Greek. What wonder if lions and bears and pigs do not act as I was proposing? That which reasoning would fairly lead a man to choose, can not be had by creatures that do not reason, simply because they are so stupid. If Prometheus or some other god had given each of them the intelligence of a man, then they would not have lived in deserts and mountains nor fed on one another. They would have built temples just as we do, each would have lived in the centre of his family, and they would have formed a nation bound by its mutual laws. Is it anything surprising that brutes, who have had the misfortune to be unable to obtain by forethought any of the goods, with which reasoning provides us, should have missed love too? Lions do not love; but neither do they philosophise; bears do not love; but the reason is they do not know the sweets of friendship. It is only men, who, by their wisdom and their knowledge, after many trials, have chosen what is best.

Well, now at last we come to Evolution: and I must frankly own that Herbert Spencer, whom I have chosen to discuss, does not

2. Moore here quotes from a dialogue which today, according to Professor William Adler, is attributed to an imitator of Lucian, not Lucian himself. Sometimes entitled *Affairs of the Heart (Amores)*, Professor Adler believes that a more accurate title would be *Two Types of Love*. As Moore was trained as a classicist, the translation likely is Moore's own. The dialogue concerns the merits of two kinds of love: conjugal and pederasty, with the latter emerging as superior. For Lucian's full dialogue, see *Affairs of the Heart (Amores)*, in *Lucian*, translated by M. D. MacLeod (Cambridge, Mass.: Harvard University Press, 1967), vol. VIII, pp. 147–236.

offer the best example of the naturalistic fallacy. I wished in this lecture to discuss a view which should maintain that the course of evolution, while it shewed us the direction in which we are developing, thereby and for the same reasons shewed us the direction in which we ought to develop. A much better example of this view I might have found in Guyan,[3] a writer who has lately had much vogue in France; but he is probably less well known to you. Guyan might almost be called a disciple of Spencer; he is frankly evolutionistic, and frankly naturalistic; and I may mention that he does not see that he differs from Spencer by reason of his naturalism. The point in which he has criticised Spencer concerns the question how far the ends of 'pleasure' and of 'increased life' coincide as motives and means to the attainment of the ideal: he does not seem to think that he differs from Spencer in the fundamental principle that the ideal is 'quantity of life, measured in breadth as well as in length' or as Guyan says 'Expansion and intensity of life': nor in the naturalistic reason which he gives for this principle. And I am not sure that he does differ from Spencer in these points. Spencer does, as I shall shew, use the naturalistic fallacy in details; but with regard to his fundamental principles, the following doubts occur: Is he fundamentally a Hedonist? And, if so, is he a naturalistic Hedonist? In that case he would better have been treated in my next lecture. Does he hold that a ten-

3. The reference is to the nineteenth-century French philosopher M. Guyan and, in particular, to his *A Sketch of Morality Independent of Obligation*, translated from the French by Gertrude Kapteyn, 2d ed. (London: Watts & Co., 1898). Even while he worked on his lectures for the London School of Ethics and Social Philosophy, Moore reviewed Guyan's book (*International Journal of Ethics*, v. 9, Jan. 1899, pp. 232–36). He was scandalized by the defects of the translation ("It may perhaps be useful to give a few of the grossest mistranslations I have noticed; but it must not be assumed that the list is exhaustive" [p. 233]). No friend of shoddiness, Moore saved his finer vehemence for Guyan (who "appears to have some reputation" [p. 236]) and his views. The book, Moore writes, does not "seem to fulfil the promise of the title. It might, I think, be more appropriately described as 'General remarks on psycho-physics, including hortative parentheses, and followed by an appendix on rewards and punishments'" (p. 233). Despite his low opinion of the book, Moore concludes his review by noting that Guyan's "justification of the need for 'metaphysical hypotheses' against 'the English utilitarians and evolutionists' seems even to show some vague notion of what is the proper object of ethics" (p. 236). The discussion of the relationship between Guyan's and Spencer's views, as presented in *The Elements*, is carried over verbatim to *Principia*. See *Principia Ethica*, pp. 46–47.

dency to increase quantity of life is merely a criterion of good conduct? Or does he hold that such increase of life is marked out by nature as an end at which we ought to aim?

I think his language in various places would give colour to all those hypotheses, though some of them are mutually inconsistent. I will try to discuss the main points.

You probably know that the modern vogue of 'Evolution' owed its origin to Darwin's investigations as to the origin of species. Darwin formed a strictly biological hypothesis as to the manner in which certain forms of animal life became established, while others died out and disappeared. His theory was (I speak under correction) that this might be accounted for, partly at least, in the following way. When certain varieties occurred (the cause of their occurence is still a matter of dispute), it might be that some of the points, in which they varied from their parent species or from other species then existing, made them better able to persist in the environment in which they found themselves, less liable to be killed off. They might, for instance, be better able to endure the cold or heat or changes of the climate; better able to find nourishment from what surrounded them; better able to escape from or resist other species which fed upon them; better fitted to attract the other sex. Being thus, less liable to die, their numbers relatively to other species would increase; and that very increase in their numbers might tend towards the extinction of those other species. Well this theory was called the theory of survival of the fittest. The natural process which it thus described was called evolution. It was very natural to suppose that evolution meant evolution from what was lower into what was higher; in fact it was observed that at least one species, commonly called higher—the species man—had so survived, and among men again it was supposed that the higher races, ourselves for example, had shewn a tendency to survive the lower, such as the North American Indians. We can kill them more easily than they can kill us. The doctrine of evolution was then represented as an explanation of how the higher species survives the lower. Spencer, for example, constantly uses more evolved as equivalent to higher. But, please, note that this forms no part of

Darwin's scientific theory. That theory will explain, equally well, how by an alteration in the environment, the gradual cooling of the earth, for example, quite a different species from man, a species which we think unfinitely lower, might survive us. The survival of the fittest does *not* mean, as one might suppose, the survival of what is fittest to fulfil a good purpose—best adapted to a good end: at the last, it means merely the survival of the fittest to survive, and the value of the scientific theory, and it is a theory of great value, just consists in shewing what are the causes which produce certain biological effects. Whether these effects are good or bad, it cannot pretend to judge.

Well, now let us hear Mr. Spencer:

I recur to the main proposition set forth in these two chapters, which has, I think, been fully justified. Guided by the truth that as the conduct with which Ethics deals is part of conduct at large, conduct at large must be generally understood before this part can be specifically understood; and guided by the further truth that to understand conduct at large we must understand the evolution of conduct; we have been led to see that Ethics has for its subject-matter, that form which universal conduct assumes during the last stages of evolution. We have also concluded that these last stages in the evolution of conduct are those displaying the *highest* type of being when he is forced, by increase of numbers, to live more and more in presence of his fellows. And there has followed *the corrolary that conduct gains ethical sanction* in proportion as the activities, becoming less and less militant and more and more industrial, are such as do not necessitate mutual injury or hindrance, but consist with, and are furthered by, co-operation and mutual aid.[4]

Now, you note, in Mr. Spencer's conclusion that the last stages in the evolution of conduct are displayed by the highest type of being. This he considers himself already to have proved. But you will look, in vain, for any proof that man is the highest type of being. Yet this point is essential if Mr. Spencer's conclusion is to have any ethical value, as he obviously thinks it has. He assumes it throughout the previous argument, and quite consistently too: I give him credit for that. Can this be because he has committed the

4. Herbert Spencer, *The Data of Ethics* (New York: P. F. Collier & Son, 1902), p. 21. I assume the material quoted from Spencer in Moore's lectures coincides with that quoted in *Principia Ethica*, p. 48. The italics were added by Moore in *Principia* and have been allowed to stand here.

naturalistic fallacy? In any case, I must contend that he has prejudiced our minds to accept his ethical conclusion, by the unproved assumption that the more evolved is ipso facto the higher.

Spencer goes on to shew that 'Always, [then], acts are called good or bad, according as they are well or ill adjusted to ends'.[5] In this I think I smell the naturalistic fallacy. Can Mr Spencer point out any act which is not adjusted to an end? The fact is there are two alternatives, with regard to end, if that word be used, as Mr. Spencer uses it, as applicable to other things besides a conscious purpose. Either 'end' is simply equivalent to 'effect'; and in that case no act can be better or worse adapted to an end than any other; since every act must produce its appropriate effect and can produce no other. If end mean this, then according to Mr. Spencer no act can be better or worse than another: and consequently his Ethics disappears. Or else end may mean what is good: then indeed some acts are better adjusted than others to ends; for the effect which each must produce, is now a good effect and now a bad one. But in this case we have something very like the naturalistic fallacy: Mr. Spencer had prejudiced our minds, by using end, where it can only mean what is good, to denote the effect of evolution.

But now we come to Mr. Spencer as a Hedonist. Mr. Spencer admits, nay enforces, the proposition: that all depends upon the question is life worth living.[6] Evolution fosters life; but evolution may, after all, have been a mistake. Pessimists hold that it has been; and how are we to decide between them and optimists, as to whether we are to aim at conduct more evolved and higher, or at conduct less evolved and lower? This is how: says Spencer: 'There

5. Ibid., p. 26. The word 'then' occurs in the sentence as written by Spencer but was omitted by Moore. It has been added here.

6. In *The Elements* Moore simply cites a page number of Spencer's *Data of Ethics*. In *Principia* he quotes Spencer as follows: "The question to be definitely raised and answered before entering any ethical discussion, is the question of late much agitated—Is life worth living? Shall we take the pessimist view? or shall we take the optimist view? . . . On the answer to this question depends every decision concerning the goodness or badness of conduct." Ibid., p. 28.

is one postulate'.[7] That statement is absolutely false. But it shews us at all events what Mr. Spencer assumes. Every one, he thinks, must hold that conduct is good or bad according as its total effects are pleasurable or painful. Why must? This is the 'must', which, as I have pointed out, suggests the naturalistic fallacy. We expect to hear Mr. Spencer answer: Because that is the very meaning of the words. He does not give this answer expressly, I confess. We find him arguing against the belief that virtue can be defined otherwise than in terms of happiness, and if Mr. Spencer holds to the doctrine that virtue cannot be otherwise defined; then we have caught him as a naturalist. This is the root of the argument against Carlyle to which he proceeds. Some of you may think, I hope, that Thomas Carlyle is as prima facie likely to be quite as good a moral teacher as Herbert Spencer; and, if so, you will be pleased to find that the latter's argument against the former rests on nothing stronger than this naturalistic fallacy.

Well, I am afraid I have time to say no more of Herbert Spencer. But I want you not to mis-understand the object of my criticism. I do not mean to imply that Spencer's writings on Ethics are not full of interesting and even instructive, observations; I shall hope to shew later in what way I believe his general theory may be of use to Ethics: all that I contend is that the reasons he gives for his main principle are very poor indeed, and that if the object of Ethics is to be methodical and scientific, instead of being merely based on science, the Data of Ethics is quite a good distance away from fulfilling the demands which may justly be addressed to an ethical writer.

7. In *The Elements* Moore quotes Spencer as above and inserts the page reference in the body of the typescript. In *Principia* he quotes Spencer at somewhat greater length. "Yes, there is one postulate in which pessimists and optimists agree. Both their arguments assume it to be self-evident that life is good or bad, according as it does, or does not, bring a surplus of agreeable feeling." Ibid., pp. 29–30.

LECTURE III

Hedonism

Ladies and gentlemen, before I begin to-day's lecture, I wish to say a few words with regard to the discussions, by which my lectures are followed. If I left these remarks to the end, I fear I might forget some of them, which I want very much to remember.

First of all, I believe I owe you a public apology for my behaviour during part of the discussion last Thursday. To one gentleman, in particular, I do owe such an apology. In the heat of the moment I certainly entertained, and implied by my words, the belief that one question which he addressed to me was not due to any serious difficulty felt by him, with regard to the matter in question. I had no right to that belief and still less right to express it. My feeling that the question was merely a vexatious one, was indeed only momentary; but that does not excuse it. My only excuse is that the delivery of an hour's lecture, followed by half-an-hour's discussion, is so trying (to the nerves, I suppose I must say), that it is difficult to keep quite cool. I am sure you will allow for this, even if you do not understand it: it is indeed very difficult to understand the state of mind produced by such an effort, until you have experienced it. Nevertheless, I hope that you all, and that gentleman in particular, will forgive me.

I was particularly anxious to make this apology, not only because I believe it is justly due, but also because I should be extremely sorry if anything I may have said or done in the last discussion, were to make you less ready to question me in future. I am still as anxious as ever to invite discussion. That is my *deliberate*

41

wish: but you must all be aware that it is very difficult always to *act* deliberately. However, I will do my best to prevent anything similar from happening again; I think I can prevent it, now that I have once been warned. But I wish to suggest one or two ways in which you can help me to make the discussions as useful as possible. In the first place, I doubt if they can be profitably prolonged beyond three-quarters of an hour: an hour and three-quarters' almost continuous talking is perhaps as much as I can manage with any credit on so difficult a subject; and this arrangement has the additional advantage that it allows me to catch the last train back to Cambridge. But I wish you to understand that, if it should turn out (as I trust it will) that I am still fit to answer, and you still ready to raise objections, beyond that time, I am perfectly ready to remain in town on any night and to prolong the discussion to any length. In the second place, I could wish that more of you found opportunity to formulate your objections in writing: I shall be always glad to consider such, whether you find it convenient to put them in the form of answers to my questions or not. This procedure, I venture to think, will enable you to put your own position in a clearer form, as it will undoubtedly enable me to appreciate your arguments more fully and to reply to them more adequately. Both you and I should have a better chance of convincing one another, if you would only write me papers; and it is the producing such conviction as to what we each sincerely believe to be the truth, that I wish to be the sole object of the discussion. Any amusement or interest, that it may excite, is only to be regarded as a means to this. But I am aware that you may not have time to write me anything, and in that case I will do my best to satisfy you by word of mouth. Again, I wish you to understand that I think it extremely desirable, that you should discuss among yourselves, if any of you differ in opinion, and not solely, as hitherto, with me. Such discussion would not only lighten the strain which is put upon me, but might also help to the production of better arguments, than I can offer. It is natural that I, who am supposed to be familiar with much philosophy, that may be new to some of you, should be less able to understand your difficulties with regard to it, than those who are more nearly your equals in this respect. Finally, if any of you are familiar with only one school of ethical thought (that represented by Herbert Spencer, for example), I cannot but think that you would approach the subject with a much more open mind, if you would read some one of the many writers, whose works are of an opposite tendency. Surely you ought in justice to hear both sides, before you settle your opinions. Read the *Gorgias* of Plato, read the first two books of Aristotle's *Ethics*, read Kant's *Foundation of the Metaphysic of Morals*: all of these books are short, all of them are interesting quite apart from their ethical value, and all of them are written by men of first rate reputation for philosophic genius. For this purpose I could even advise you to read Green: his work will at least shew you what different opinions can be entertained by writers of acknowledged ability and influence. And, finally, I can only repeat my advice that you should read Professor Sidgwick. You will find most of the questions of paramount importance for Ethics argued in his book with exemplary care and precision: and, if you are serious in wishing to arrive at true ethical opinions, I may safely say that you will not be entitled to claim that you have done so, until you are prepared to refute Professor Sidgwick's arguments on all points where you disagree with his results. But this, I must admit, is a counsel of perfection: thoroughly to digest the *Methods of Ethics* is a labour requiring both time and patience; and it is a book which is of little use unless it be digested. But that is not so with the others I have mentioned: an easy reading of them may be very profitable; and I think you all ought to read one or other of them, if your reading hitherto has been one-sided.

Well, in this lecture I have promised to discuss Hedonism. Hitherto I have chiefly dealt with a theory which I have called Naturalism. I do not defend the name, but I do wish you to understand what the theory is. We shall return to it again in Lecture V, and Mill's Hedonism, which I shall discuss to-day, offers one of the clearest possible examples of the theory. There is, then, still hope, if you do not understand me yet, that you may do so before the course is over. But, with all these opportunities still in prospect, I wish to make one short effort to put the matter clearly now before we proceed to the discussion of Hedonism. Naturalism may be briefly defined as a theory which holds that good is not good but simply something else. It is therefore obvious that the term is a very wide one, capable of including infinite different opinions: the same theory may appear in any number of different forms. For, no matter what the something is that good is held to mean, the theory is still naturalism. Whether good be defined as yellow or green or blue, as loud or soft, as round or square, as sweet or bitter, as productive of life or productive of pleasure, as willed or desired or felt: whichever of these or of any other object in the world, good may be held to *mean*, the theory, which holds it to *mean* them, will be a naturalistic theory. I have called such theories naturalistic because all of these terms denote properties, simple or complex, of some simple or complex natural object; some object which exists in time, or in time and space; some object, such as are dealt with by the natural sciences, or by the natural science of mind, which is called psychology. With this definition of nature we shall have more to do in our fifth lecture: it can, I think, be made into a perfectly precise definition. But, if you will please attend, for the present, to the thing and not to the name, I will try to shew you shortly what it is I mean by the naturalistic fallacy.

Suppose you say 'I am pleased'; and suppose that is not a lie or a mistake but the truth. Well, if it is true, what does that mean? It means that your mind, a certain definite mind, distinguished by certain definite marks from all others, has at this moment a certain definite feeling called pleasure. 'Pleased' *means* nothing but having pleasure, and though you may be more pleased or less pleased, and even, we may admit for the present have one or another kind of pleasure; yet in so far as it is pleasure you have, whether there be more or less of it, and whether it be of one kind or another, that pleasure is one definite thing, absolutely undefinable, some one thing that is the same in all the various degrees and in all the various kinds of it that there may be. You may be able to say how it is related to other things: that, for example, it is in the mind, that it causes desire, that you are conscious of it, etc., etc. You can, I say, describe its relations to other things, but define it you can *not*. And if any-body tried to define pleasure to you, as being any other natural object; if any-body were to say, for instance, that pleasure *means* the sensation of red, and were to proceed to deduce from that that pleasure is a colour, you would be entitled to laugh at him and to distrust his future statements about pleasure. Well, that would be the same fallacy which I have called the naturalistic fallacy. That 'pleased' does not mean 'having the sensation of red', or anything else whatever, does not prevent you from understanding what it does mean. It is enough for you to know that 'pleased' does mean 'having the sensation of pleasure', and though pleasure is absolutely undefinable, though pleasure is pleasure and nothing else whatever, yet you feel no difficulty in saying that you are pleased. The reason is, of course, that when you say 'I am pleased', you do *not* mean that '*you*' are the same thing as 'having pleasure'. And similarly I cannot see what difficulty you need find in my saying that 'pleasure is good' and yet not *meaning* that 'pleasure' is the same thing as 'good', that pleasure *means* good, and that good means pleasure. If you were to imagine that when you said 'I am pleased', you meant that you were exactly the same thing as 'pleased', I should not indeed call that a naturalistic fallacy, although it would be the same fallacy as I have called naturalistic with reference to Ethics. The reason of this is obvious enough. When you confuse two natural objects with one another, defining the one by the other, when for instance, you confuse yourself, who are one natural object, with 'pleased' or with 'pleasure' which are others, then there is no reason to call the fallacy naturalistic. But when you confuse 'good', which is not in the same sense a natural object, with any natural object whatever, then there is a reason for calling that a naturalistic fallacy: its being made with regard to 'good' marks it as something quite specific, and this specific mistake deserves a name because it is so common. If you want to know, why I do not think good is a natural object, I must ask you to wait till my Fifth lecture. But, for the present, please notice this. Even if it were a natural object, that would not alter the nature of the fallacy nor diminish its importance one whit. All that I have said about it would remain quite equally true: only the name which I have called it would not be so appropriate as I think it is. And I do not care about the name: what I do care about is the fallacy. Call it what you like; call it 'rose' or 'sweet-heart' or 'morning-dew', 'John' or 'Thomas' or 'Catherine': only do understand what it is, and try to recognise it when you meet with it.

Well, I might multiply illustrations of this fallacy without end; I might spend years incessantly explaining to you what I mean when I say that good is undefinable. But the fact is a very simple fact indeed; and I hope you now may recognise it. For instance, when you say an 'orange is yellow' do you think that binds you to hold that 'orange' means nothing else than 'yellow', and that nothing can be 'yellow' but an 'orange'? Supposing the orange is also sweet! Does that bind you to say that 'sweet' is exactly the same thing as 'yellow', that 'sweet' must be defined as 'yellow'? And supposing it be recognised that 'yellow' just means 'yellow' and nothing else whatever, does that make it any more difficult to hold that oranges are yellow? Most certainly it does not: on the contrary, it would be absolutely meaningless to say that oranges were yellow, unless yellow did in the end mean just 'yellow' and nothing else whatever, unless it was absolutely undefinable. You would not get any very clear notion about things, which are yellow, you would not get very far with your science, if you were bound to hold that everything which was yellow, *meant* exactly the same thing as yellow. You would find you had to hold that an orange was exactly the same thing as a stool, a piece of paper, a lemon, anything you like. You could prove any number of absurdities; but would you think you had the truth? Well, then, why should it be different with 'good'? Why, if good is good and undefinable, should I be held to deny that pleasure is good? Is there any difficulty in holding both to be true at once? On the contrary, there is no meaning in saying that pleasure is good, unless good is something different from pleasure. It is absolutely useless, so far as Ethics is concerned, to prove, as Mr. Spencer tries to do, that increase of pleasure coincides with increase of life, unless good *means* something different from either life or pleasure. He might just as well try to prove that an orange is yellow by shewing that it always is wrapped up in paper.

Well, all this is a somewhat elaborate answer to that question I was asked last time. I hope it will appear now that the question was rather absurd. But, as we have seen, Bentham and Spencer did not see clearly that it was absurd: Mill as we *shall* see, did not see it either; and I myself thought it worthwhile to devote a great part of both my last two lectures to explaining its absurdity. I suppose, therefore, that it needed an answer. Well, now you have one. But I must not stop yet. There is another form of the naturalistic fallacy, which yet may cause some trouble. I have had a very kind letter from one of my hearers, warning me that difficulty may be felt about this point too. The question is roughly this. May good be said to mean something different, when it is applied to utterly different objects, as when we say a hat is good, the weather is good; that man is good at work, this man has a good character! Or again does 'good' differ with the times? When I say that it was good for the savage to kill his enemy, in prehistoric times, do I mean the same thing as when I say that it is good for you to save *your* enemy? Well, my answer to these questions is that I do and must mean absolutely the same thing by 'good' in all these cases. Let me take an illustration. Supposing you are pleased and I am pleased and several other people are pleased. Well, we may be pleased in different degrees, and our pleasures may be of many different kinds, but, if it is true that nevertheless we all are pleased, then 'pleased' must mean absolutely one and the same thing in all of us. Moreover, I may presently become displeased or pained, or I may think that I was not pleased when I said I was. Nevertheless, if it was true that I was pleased, it still is true that I was pleased and always was and always will be true, and no change that possibly can happen, not even if pleasure should cease to exist can make the slightest difference to the truth of that statement or to the meaning of 'pleased'. The same is true of 'good', with this one proviso, that in some of those instances good meant good as means, while in others it meant good as end. The meaning of this distinction I shall have to explain later on in this lecture. But it is as well to state at once that when I spoke of 'good' as the fundamental notion of Ethics, when I said that it was undefinable, I meant good as end. Well I do not imagine that my answer to this question, stated as I have stated it, will seem paradoxical, but, if there are any other difficulties still involved in it, I believe that my future lectures will remove them.

Well, now I hope we may start clear upon our discussion of Hedonism. 'Hedonism', as you probably know, denotes any ethical theory which holds, for whatever reason, that 'pleasure' is the only thing at which we *ought* to aim, the only thing which is good in itself. Hedonists hold that all other things but pleasure, whether conduct or virtue or knowledge, whether life or nature or beauty, are only good as means to pleasure or for the sake of pleasure, never for their own sakes or as ends in themselves. The name 'Hedonism' is derived from the Greek word ἡδονή which means pleasure; and this ethical theory about pleasure has been very widely held. It was held by Aristippus, the disciple of Socrates, and by the Cyrenaic school which he founded; it was held by Epicurus and the Epicureans; and it has been held in modern times, chiefly by those philosophers who call themselves 'Utilitarians'—by Bentham, and by Mill, for instance. Herbert Spencer, as we have seen, also says he holds it; and Professor Sidgwick, as we shall see, holds it too.

Yet all these philosophers differ from one another more or less, both as to what they mean by Hedonism, and as to the reasons for which it is to be accepted as a true doctrine. The matter is therefore obviously not quite so simple as it might at first appear. My own object will be to shew quite clearly what the theory must mean, if it is made precise, if all confusions and inconsistencies are removed from the conception of it; and, when this is done, I think it will appear that all the various reasons given for holding it to be true, are really quite inadequate, that they are not reasons for holding Hedonism, but only for holding some other doctrine which is confused and inconsistent with itself. In order to attain this object I propose to take first Mill's doctrine, as set forth in his book called *Utilitarianism*; we shall find in Mill a conception of

Hedonism, and arguments in its favour, which fairly represent those of a large class of hedonistic writers. To these representative conceptions and arguments grave objections, objections which appear to me to be conclusive, have been urged by Professor Sidgwick. These I shall try to give you in my own words; and shall then proceed to consider and refute Professor Sidgwick's own much more precise conceptions and arguments. With this, I think, we shall have traversed the whole field of Hedonistic doctrine. But this discussion, I must warn you, is by no means easy to follow: towards the end, especially, it will become extremely subtle. I must therefore beg to have your closest attention throughout. There are two principles, particularly, which it will help you greatly to keep constantly in your minds: one is, that the naturalistic fallacy must not be committed; the second is that the distinction between means and end must be observed.

Well, then, we begin with Mill's *Utilitarianism*. That is a book, which I should advise you all to read. It is a very short book, only 96 pages of large print in this edition; and you will find in it an admirably clear and fair discussion of many ethical principles and methods. Mill exposes not a few simple mistakes which are very likely to be made by those who approach ethical problems without much previous reflection. But I shall assume for the purposes of this lecture that you are not going to make those mistakes. What I am concerned with is the mistakes which Mill himself appears to have made, and these only so far as they concern the hedonistic principle. Let me remind you once again what that principle is. It is, I said, that pleasure is the only thing at which we ought to aim, the only thing that is good as an end and for its own sake. And now let us turn to Mill and see whether he accepts this description of the question at issue. 'Pleasure', he says at the outset, 'and freedom from pain, are the only things desirable as ends' (p. 10);[1] and again at the end of his argument 'To think of an object as desirable (unless for the sake of its consequences) and to think of it as pleasant are one and the same thing' (p. 58). Well, I perfectly

1. Moore's references throughout his discussion of Mill are to the latter's *Utilitarianism*, 13th ed. (London: Longmans, Green & Company, 1897).

accept those statements as expressing the fundamental principle of Hedonism. It is with them I am concerned, and if I succeed in shewing that Mill's reasons for them do not prove them, you will at least admit that I have not been fighting with shadows or demolishing a man of straw. You will have observed, of course, that Mill adds 'absence of pain' to 'pleasure' in his first statement, though not in his second. Well, I shall talk of 'pleasure' alone, for the sake of conciseness; but all my arguments will apply quite equally to 'absence of pain': you can easily make the necessary substitutions for yourselves.

Mill holds, then, that 'happiness is desirable, and the only thing desirable, as an end; all other things being only desirable as means to that end' (p. 52). Happiness he has already defined as 'pleasure, and the absence of pain'; (p. 10) he does not pretend that this is more than a verbal definition; and I have not a word to say against it. His principle, then, is 'pleasure is the only thing desirable', if I may be allowed, when I say pleasure, to include in that word absence from pain. And now what are his reasons for holding that principle to be true? He has already told us (p. 6) that 'Questions of ultimate ends are not amenable to direct proof. Whatever can be proved to be good, must be so by being shewn to be a means to something *admitted to be good without proof.*' With this, I perfectly agree: indeed the chief object of my first two lectures was to convince you that this is so. Anything which is good as an end must be admitted to be good without proof. We are agreed so far. Mill even uses the same examples which I used. 'How' he says 'is it possible to prove that health is good?' 'What proof is it possible to give that pleasure is good?' Well, in Chapter IV, in which he deals with the proof of his Utilitarian principle Mill repeats the above statement in these words: 'It has already' he says, 'been remarked, that questions of ultimate ends do not admit of proof, in the ordinary acceptation of the term' (p. 52). 'Questions about ends' he goes on in this same passage, 'are, in other words, questions what things are desirable'. I am quoting these repetitions, because they make it plain what otherwise you might have doubted, that Mill is using the word 'desirable' or 'desirable as an end' as absolutely and precisely equivalent to the words 'good as an end'. We are, then, now to hear, what reasons he advances for this doctrine that pleasure alone is good as an end.[2]

The only proof capable of being given that something is visible, is that people actually see it. The only proof that a sound is audible, is that people hear it; and so of the other sources of our experience. In like manner, I apprehend, the sole evidence it is possible to produce that anything is desirable, is that people do actually desire it. If the end which the utilitarian doctrine proposes to itself were not, in theory and in practice, acknowledged to be an end, nothing could ever convince any person that it was so. No reason can be given why the general happiness is desirable, except that each person, so far as he believes it to be attainable, desires his own happiness. This, however, being the fact, we have not only all the proof which the case admits of, but all which it is possible to require, that happiness is a good: that each person's happiness is a good to that person, and the general happiness, therefore, a good to the aggregate of all persons. Happiness has made out its title as *one* of the ends of conduct, and consequently one of the criteria of morality. (pp. 52–53)

There, that is enough. That is my first point. Mill has made as naive and artless a use of the naturalistic fallacy, as anybody could desire. 'Good' he tells us, means 'desirable' and you can only find out what is desirable by seeking to find out what is actually desired. This is, of course, only one step towards the proof of Hedonism; for it may be, as Mill goes on to say, that other things beside pleasure are desired. Whether or not pleasure is the only thing desired is, as Mill himself admits (p. 58), a psychological question, to which we shall presently proceed. The important step for Ethics, is this one just taken, the step which pretends to prove that 'good' means 'desired'.

Well, the fallacy in this step is so obvious, that it is quite wonderful how Mill failed to see it. The fact is that desirable does not mean 'able to be desired' as visible means 'able to be seen'. The desirable means simply what ought to be desired or deserves to be

2. Moore's reference here is simply to pp. 52–53. However, since his discussion of Mill's views at this point in *The Elements* corresponds to the one he offers in *Principia* (pp. 64ff), it is reasonable to believe that the particular passage he had in mind in *The Elements* is the same one he actually quotes in *Principia*. The passage in question is the one reproduced in the text (above).

desired, just as the detestable means not what can be but what ought to be detested and the damnable what deserves to be damned. Mill has then smuggled in, under cover of the word desirable, the very notion about which he ought to be quite clear. Desirable does indeed mean 'what is good to desire'; but when that is understood, it is no longer plausible to say that our only test of *that*, is what is actually desired. Is it merely a tautology when the Prayer Book talks of good desires? Are not bad desires also possible? Nay, we find Mill himself talking of a 'better and nobler object of desire' (p. 10), as if, after all, what is desired, were not ipso facto good, and the only good. Moreover, if the desired is ipso facto the good; then the good is ipso facto the motive of our actions, and there can be no question of finding motives for doing it, as Mill is at such pains to do. If Mill's explanation of 'desirable' be *true*, then his statement (p. 26)[3] that the rule of action may be *confounded* with the motive of it is untrue: for the motive of action will then be according to him ipso facto its rule; there can be no distinction between the two and therefore no confusion and thus he has contradicted himself flatly. These are specimens of the contradictions, which, as I have tried to shew, must always follow from the use of the naturalistic fallacy; and I hope I need now say no more about the matter.[4]

3. In *The Elements* Moore places the reference to p. 26 of Mill's *Utilitarianism* in the margin. In *Principia*, he inserts the page number in the text itself. The latter device has been used here.

4. Moore here makes a marginal reference to "Sidgwick pp. 110–13. Bk. 1, ch. 9." It is unlikely that he interrupted his critique of Mill to read the full text of his reference to Sidgwick, which reads as follows:

> § 3. What then can we state as the general meaning of the term 'good'? Shall we say that it is the object of Desire or the end aimed at in Volition? We certainly cannot affirm this of actual desires and volitions with quantitative precision: *i.e.* we cannot say that what I regard as 'best' is always what I most desire or make voluntary efforts to realize: for we often desire intensely, and even seek to realize, a result that we know to be bad in preference to another that we judge to be good. But I may say that, what I regard as on the whole 'good' for me, I regard as 'desirable' if not 'desired': *i.e.* I think that I should desire it if my impulses were in harmony with my reason,— assuming my own existence alone to be considered. Putting aside the conceivable case of its being my duty to sacrifice my own good, to realise some greater good outside my own existence, we may say that my good on

Well, then, the first step by which Mill has attempted to establish his Hedonism is simply fallacious. He has attempted to establish the identity of the good with the desired, by confusing the proper sense of desirable, in which it denotes that which it is good to desire, with the sense which it would bear, if it were analogous to such words as visible. If desirable is to be identical with good, then it must bear one sense; and if it is to be identical with desired, then it must bear quite another sense. And yet to Mill's contention that the desired is necessarily good, it is quite essential that these two senses of desirable should be the same. If he holds they are the same, then he has contradicted himself elsewhere; if he holds they are not the same, then the first step in his proof of Hedonism is absolutely worthless. But now we must deal with the second step.

Having proved, as he thinks, that the good means the desired, Mill recognises that, if he is further to maintain that pleasure alone

---

the whole is what I 'ought' to desire: but—since irrational desires cannot always be dismissed at once by voluntary effort—we cannot say this in the strictly ethical sense of 'ought.' We can only say it in the wider sense, in which it merely connotes an ideal or standard, divergence from which it is our duty to avoid as far as possible, though, even when it is distinctly recognized, we may not always be able to avoid it at will.

The distinction, however, that has just been drawn between what is 'desirable' and what is actually 'desired' would not be universally accepted. Some who would admit 'desirable' as an interpretation or equivalent of 'good,' would maintain that by either term no more is signified than the object of actual desire, whatever that may be. They would admit that we all recognize some desires to be directed to what is not really good for us on the whole: but they would explain this by saying that such desires prompt to actions for the consequences of which, when they arrive, we feel, on the whole, aversion more intense than the former desire. On this view, then, my 'good on the whole' may be taken to mean what I should actually desire and seek if all the future aversions and desires, which would be roused in me by the consequences of seeking it, could be fully realized by me at the time of making my choice.

There is much in this view that seems to me true and important. I hold myself that the satisfaction of any desire is *pro tanto* good; and that an equal regard for all the moments of our conscious experience—so far, at least, as the mere difference of their position in time is concerned—is an essential characteristic of rational conduct. I cannot, however, admit the fact, that a man does not afterwards feel for the consequences of an action aversion strong enough to cause him to regret it, to be a complete proof that he has acted for his 'good on the whole.' Nor do I think that this is in accordance with common sense: for we commonly reckon it among the worst conse-

is good, he must prove that pleasure alone is really desired. This doctrine that 'pleasure alone is the object of all our desires' is what I have called in the Syllabus 'a false theory of the relation between pleasure and desire'. It is the doctrine which Prof. Sidgwick has called Psychological Hedonism: and it is a doctrine which most eminent psychologists are now agreed in rejecting. But it is a necessary step in the proof of any such Naturalistic Hedonism as Mill's; and it is so commonly held, by people not expert either in psychology or in philosophy, that I wish to treat it at some length. You will see that Mill does not hold it in this bare form. He admits that other things than pleasure are desired; and this admission is at once a contradiction of his Hedonism. Some of the shifts by which he seeks to evade this contradiction we shall afterwards consider. But some of you may think that no such shifts are needed: you may say of Mill, what Callicles says of Polus in the

---

quences of some kinds of conduct that they alter men's tendencies to desire, and make them desire their lesser good more than their greater: and we think it all the worse for a man—even in this world—if he is never roused out of such a condition and lives till death the life of a contented pig, when he might have been something better. To avoid this objection, it would have to be said that a man's "true good" is what he would desire on the whole if all the consequences of all the different lines of conduct open to him were actually exercising on him an impulsive force proportioned to the desires or aversions which they would excite if actually experienced. So far as I can conceive this hypothetical object of desire, I am not prepared to deny that it would be 'desirable' in the sense which I give to the term: but such a hypothetical composition of impulsive forces involves so elaborate and difficult a conception, that it is surely paradoxical to say that this is what we *mean* when we talk of a man's 'good on the whole.'

I conclude, then, that "*my* ultimate good" must be taken to mean in the sense that it is "what is ultimately desirable *for me*," or what I should desire if my desires were in harmony with reason,—assuming my own existence alone to be considered,—and is thus identical with the ultimate end or ends prescribed by reason as what ought to be sought or aimed at, so far as reason is not thought to inculcate sacrifice of my own ultimate good. Similarly, "ultimate good" without qualification must be taken to mean what rational beings as such would desire, assuming them to have an equal and impartial concern for *all* existence. When conduct is judged to be 'good' or 'desirable' in itself, independently of its consequences, it is, I conceive, this latter point of view that is taken. Such a judgment differs, as I have said, from the judgment that conduct is 'right,' in so far as it does not involve a definite precept to perform it; since it still leaves it an open question whether this particular kind of good is the greatest good that we can under

Gorgias[5] that he has made this fatal admission through a most unworthy fear of appearing paradoxical; that you, on the other hand, will have the courage of your convictions, and will not be ashamed to go to any lengths of paradox, in defence of what you hold to be the truth.

Well, then, we are supposing you to say that pleasure is the object of all desire, that it is the universal end of all human activity. Now I suppose you will not deny that people are commonly said to desire other things: for instance, we usually talk of desiring food and drink, of desiring money, approbation, fame. The question, then, must be of what you mean by desire, and by the object of desire. You obviously are asserting some sort of necessary or universal relation between something which you call desire, and another thing which is called pleasure. The question is of what sort this relation is; whether, in conjunction with the naturalistic fallacy above mentioned, it will justify Hedonism. Now I am not prepared to deny that there is some universal relation between pleasure and desire; but I hope to shew, that, if there is, it is of such sort as will rather make against than for your Hedonism. You say that pleasure is always the object of desire, and I am ready to admit that pleasure is always, in part at least, the cause of desire. Do you understand this distinction? Both views might be expressed in the same language; both might be said to hold that whenever we desire, we always desire *because of* some pleasure: if I asked you 'Why do you desire that?' you might answer, quite consistently with your contention, 'Because there is pleasure there,' and if you asked me the same question, I might answer, equally consistently

---

the circumstances obtain. It differs further, as we may now observe, in so far as good or excellent actions are not implied to be in our power in the same strict sense as 'right' actions—any more than any other good things: and in fact there are many excellences of behaviour which we cannot attain by any effort of will, at least directly and at the moment: hence we often feel that the recognition of goodness in the conduct of others does not carry with it a clear precept to do likewise, but rather "the vague desire / That stirs an imitative will." In so far as this is the case Goodness of Conduct becomes an ulterior end, the attainment of which lies outside and beyond the range of immediate volition.

5. Moore's marginal note cites *Gorgias*, 481C–487B.

with my contention, 'Because there is pleasure here.' Only our two answers would not mean the same thing; it is this use of the same language to denote quite different facts, which I believe to be the chief cause why Psychological Hedonism is held, just as it was also the cause of Mill's naturalistic fallacy.

Let us try to analyse the psychological state which is called desire. That name is usually confined to the state of mind in which the idea of some object not actually possessed, is present to the mind. Suppose, for instance, I am desiring a glass of port wine. I have the idea of a glass of port wine before my mind, although I have not got that glass. Well, how does pleasure enter in to this relation? My theory is that it enters in, in this way. The *idea* of the wine causes a feeling of pleasure in my mind, which in contrast with the pain of not having the wine produces that state of tension, and incipient activity, which is called desire. It is, there-fore, because of a pleasure, which I already have, the pleasure excited by a mere idea, that I desire the wine, which I have not. And I am ready to admit that a pleasure of this kind, an actual pleasure, is always among the causes of every desire, and not only of every desire, but of every mental activity, whether conscious or sub-conscious. I am ready to *admit* this I say: I cannot vouch that it is the true psychological doctrine; I believe it is still a debated point among psychologists; but, at all events, it is not primâ facie quite absurd. And now, what is the other doctrine, the doctrine which I suppose you to hold, and which is at all events essential to Mill's argument? It is this. That when I desire the wine, it is not the wine which I desire but the pleasure which I expect to get from it. In other words, the doctrine is that the idea of a pleasure not actual, is always necessary to cause desire; whereas my doc-trine was that the actual pleasure caused by the idea of something else was always necessary to cause desire. It is these two differ-ent theories which I suppose the Psychological Hedonists to con-fuse: the confusion, is as Mr. Bradley puts it, 'between a pleasant thought and the thought of a pleasure'. It is in fact only where the latter, the 'thought of a pleasure' is present, that pleasure can be said to be the object of desire, or the motive to action. On the other hand, when only a pleasant thought is present, as, I admit, *may* always be the case, then it is the object of the thought—that which we are thinking about, which is the object of desire and the motive to action; and the pleasure, which that thought excites, may, indeed, cause our desire or move us to action, but it is not our end or object, nor our motive.

Well, I hope you will try to understand this distinction, and to bear it in mind. Now, let us see how it bears upon ethical Hedonism. I assume it to be perfectly obvious that the idea which is the object of desire, is not always and only the idea of a pleasure. In the first place, plainly, we are not always conscious of expecting pleasure, when we desire a thing. We may be only conscious of the thing which we desire, and may be impelled to make for it at once, without any calculation as to whether it will bring us pleasure or pain. And, in the second place, even when we do expect pleasure, it can certainly be very rarely pleasure only which we desire. For instance, granted that when I desire my glass of port wine, I have also an idea of the pleasure I expect from it, plainly that pleasure cannot be the only object of my desire, the port wine must be included in my object, else I might be led by my desire to take worm-wood instead of wine! If the desire were directed solely on the pleasure, it could not lead me to take the wine; if it is to take a definite direction, it is absolutely necessary that the idea of the object, from which the pleasure is expected, should also be present and should control my activity. The theory then that what is desired is always and only pleasure, must break down: it is impossible to prove that pleasure alone is good, by that line of argument. But, if we substitute for this theory, that other, possibly true, theory, that pleasure is always the cause of desire, then all the plausibility of our ethical doctrine that pleasure alone is good, straightway disappears. For in this case, pleasure is not what I desire, it is not what I want: it is something, which I already have, before I can want anything. And do you feel any inclination to maintain, that that which I already have, while I am still desiring something else, is always and alone the good?[6]

But now let us return to consider some of Mill's arguments for his position that 'happiness is the sole end of human action'. Mill admits, as I have said, that pleasure is not the only thing we actually desire. 'The desire of virtue' he says 'is not as universal, but it is as authentic a fact, as the desire of happiness' (p. 53).[7] And again 'Money is, in many cases desired in and for itself' (p. 55). These admissions are, of course, in naked and glaring contradiction, with his argument that pleasure is the only thing desirable, because it is the only thing desired. How then does Mill even attempt to avoid this contradiction? His chief argument seems to be that 'virtue', 'money' and other such objects, when they are thus desired in and for themselves, are desired only as 'a part of happiness' (pp. 56–57). Now what does this mean? Happiness, as we saw, has been defined by Mill, as 'pleasure and the absence of pain'. Does Mill mean to say that 'money', these actual coins, which he admits to be desired in and for themselves, are a part either of pleasure or of the absence of pain? Will he maintain that those coins themselves are in my mind, and actually a part of my pleasant feelings? If this is to be said, all words are useless: nothing can possibly be distinguished from anything else; if these two things are not distinct, what on earth is? We shall hear next that this table is really and truly the same thing as this room; that a cab-horse is in fact indistinguishable from St. Paul's Cathedral; that this book of Mill's which I hold in my hand, because it was his pleasure to produce, is now and at this moment a part of the happiness which he felt many years ago

6. Moore again makes a marginal reference to Sidgwick, which this time reads "Sidgwick I.IV. pp. 41–56." The reference is to the whole of Chapter IV of Book I, "Pleasure and Desire." In this chapter of The Methods of Ethics Sidgwick argues for essentially the same conclusions Moore does in The Elements. Presumably, then, the reference he makes here is intended to reinforce the largely critical character of his consideration of Hedonism, both here and in Principia, Chapter III, pp. 59–109.

7. In The Elements Moore dispenses with page references in this particular discussion of Mill's views. In Principia he includes the page references, giving them at the bottom of the page (Principia, p. 71) rather than inserting them in the body of the text. The latter device has been used here.

and which has so long ceased to be. Pray, consider a moment what this contemptible nonsense really means. Money, says Mill, is only desirable as a means to happiness. Perhaps so, but what then? Why, says Mill, Money is undoubtedly desired for its own sake. 'Yes, go on' say we. 'Well', says Mill, 'if money is desired for its own sake, it must be desirable as an end-in-itself: I have said so myself'. 'Oh', say we, 'but you also said just now that it was only desirable as a means'. 'I own I did', says Mill, 'but I will try to patch up matters, by saying that what is only a means to an end, is the same thing as a part of that end. I daresay the public won't notice'. Well, that is what Mill has done. He has broken down the distinction between means and ends, upon the precise obser-vance of which his Hedonism rests. And he has been compelled to do this, because he has failed to distinguish end in the sense of what is desirable, from end in the sense of what is desired: a distinction which, nevertheless, both the present argument and his whole book presuppose. This is a consequence of the natu-ralistic fallacy.

Well, Mill has nothing better to say for himself than this. His two fundamental propositions are in his own words 'that to think of an object as desirable (unless for the sake of its consequences) and to think of it as pleasant, are one and the same thing; and that to desire anything except in proportion as the idea of it is pleasant, is a physical and metaphysical impossibility' (p. 58).[8] Both of these statements are, we have seen, merely supported by fallacies. The first seems to rest on the naturalistic fallacy; the second rests partly on this, partly on the fallacy of confusing ends and means, and partly on confusing a pleasant thought with the thought of plea-sure. The second, the doctrine of Psychological Hedonism, is in addition palpably untrue.

But the first, the doctrine that pleasure alone is desirable, may still be true, although Mill's fallacies can not prove it so. This is the question which we have now to face. This proposition 'pleasure alone is good or desirable', belongs undoubtedly to that class of

8. Moore, in this case, gives the page reference in the margin. Here it has been incorporated into the body of the text.

propositions, to which Mill at first rightly pretended it belonged, the class of first principles, which are not amenable to direct proof. But in this case, as he also rightly says, 'considerations may be presented capable of determining the intellect either to give or withhold its assent to the doctrine' (p. 7). It is such considerations which Professor Sidgwick presents, and such also that I shall try to present for the opposite view. This proposition that 'pleasure alone is good as an end', the fundamental proposition of Ethical Hedonism, will then appear, in Professor Sidgwick's language, as an object of intuition. I shall try to shew you why my intuition denies it, just as his intuition affirms it. It *may* always be true notwithstanding: neither intuition can *prove* whether it is true or not; I am bound to be satisfied, if I can present considerations capable of determining your intellects to reject it.

Well, then we now proceed to discuss Intuitionistic Hedonism. And the beginning of this discussion marks, I would have you observe, a turning-point in my ethical method. The point I have been labouring hitherto, the point that 'good is undefinable', and that to deny this involves a fallacy, is a point capable of strict proof: for to deny it involves contradictions. But now we are coming to the question, for the sake of answering which Ethics exists, the question what things or qualities are good. Of any answer to *this* question no direct proof is possible, and that, just because our former answer, as to the meaning of good, direct proof *was* possible. We are now confined to the hope of what Mill calls 'indirect proof', the hope of determining one another's intellect; and we are now so confined, just because, in the matter of the former question we were not so confined. Now, then, for determining your intellects on the subject of Hedonism. Here is one intuition to be submitted to your verdict—the intuition that 'only pleasure is good, as an end, good in and for itself'.

Well, in this connection, it seems first desirable to touch on another doctrine of Mill's—another doctrine which, as it seems to me, Professor Sidgwick has done very wisely to reject. This is the doctrine of 'differences of quality in pleasures'. 'If I am asked', says Mill, what I mean by differences of quality in pleasures, or what makes one pleasure more valuable than another, merely as a pleasure, except its being greater in amount, there is but one possible answer. Of two pleasures, if there be one to which all or almost all who have experience of both give a decided preference, irrespective of any feeling of moral obligation to prefer it, that is the more desirable pleasure. If one of the two is, by those who are competently acquainted with both, placed so far above the other that they prefer it, even though knowing it to be attended with a greater amount of discontent, and would not resign it for any quantity of the other pleasure which their nature is capable of, we are justified in ascribing to the preferred enjoyment a superiority in quality, so far outweighing quantity as to render it, in comparison, of small account. [p. 12][9]

Now probably, some of you know that Bentham rested his case on 'quantity of pleasure' alone. It was his maxim, that 'quantity of pleasure being equal, pushpin is as good as poetry'. And Mill apparently considers Bentham to have proved that nevertheless poetry is better than pushpin; that poetry does produce a greater quantity of pleasure. But yet, says Mill the utilitarians 'might have taken the other, and as it may be called, higher ground, with entire consistency' (p. 11).[10] Now you see from this that Mill acknowledges 'quality of pleasure' to be another or different ground for estimating pleasures, than Bentham's quantity; and moreover, by that question-begging 'higher', which he afterwards translates into 'superior', he seems to betray an uncomfortable feeling, that, after all, if you take quantity of pleasure for your only standard, something may be wrong and you may deserve to be called a pig. Well, I shall presently try to shew, that you very likely would deserve that name. But, meanwhile, I only wish to shew that Mill's admissions as to quality of pleasures, are either inconsistent with his Hedonism, or else afford no other ground for it than would be given by mere quantity of pleasure.

9. In *The Elements*, once again, Moore merely cites a page reference: "p. 12." However, his discussion in *Principia* closely parallels the one he offers in *The Elements*, and in the former work he actually quotes the passage from p. 12 of Mill's *Utilitarianism* to which he merely refers in the typescript of the latter work. The passage in question has been incorporated into the text (above).

10. The page reference, which Moore placed in the margin in *The Elements*, has been incorporated into the text.

You see Mill's test for one pleasure's superiority in quality over another is the preference of most people who have experienced both. A pleasure so preferred he holds, is more desirable. But then as we have seen, he holds that 'to think of an object as desirable and to think of it as pleasanter are one and the same thing' (p. 58). He holds, therefore, that the preference of experts merely proves that one pleasure is pleasanter than another. But if that is so, how can he distinguish this standard from the standard of quantity of pleasure? Can one pleasure be pleasanter than another, except in the sense that it gives *more* pleasure? 'Pleasant' must, if words are to have any meaning at all, denote some one simple quality common to all the things that are pleasant; and, if so, then one thing can only be more pleasant than another, according as it has more or less of this one quality. But, then, let us try the other alternative, and suppose that Mill does not seriously mean that this preference of experts merely proves one pleasure to be pleasanter than another. Well, in this case what does 'preferred' mean? It cannot mean more desired, since, as we know the degree of desire is always according to Mill in exact proportion to the degree of pleasantness. But, in that case, the basis of Mill's Hedonism, collapses, for he is admitting that one thing may be preferred over another, and thus proved more desirable, although it is not more desired. In this case Mill's judgment of preference is just a judgment of that intuitional kind which I have been contending to be necessary to establish the hedonistic or any other principle. It is a direct judgment that one thing is more desirable, or better than another: a judgment utterly independent of all considerations as to whether one thing is more desired or pleasanter than another. This is to admit that good is good and undefinable.

And note another point that is brought out by this discussion. Mill's judgment of preference so far from establishing the principle that pleasure alone is good, is obviously inconsistent with it. He admits that experts can judge whether one pleasure is more desirable than another, because pleasures differ in quality. But what does this mean? If one pleasure can differ from another in quality, that means, that *a* pleasure is something complex, something composed, in fact, of pleasure *in addition to* that which produces pleasure. For instance, Mill speaks of 'sensual indulgences' as 'lower pleasures'. But what is a sensual indulgence? It is surely a certain excitement of some sense *together with* the pleasure caused by such excitement. Mill, therefore, in admitting that a sensual indulgence can be directly judged to be lower than another pleasure, in which the degree of pleasure involved may be the same, is admitting that other things may be good, or bad, quite independently of the pleasure which accompanies them. *A* pleasure is, in fact, merely a misleading term which conceals the fact that what we are dealing with is not pleasure but something else, which may indeed necessarily produce pleasure, but is nevertheless quite distinct from it.

Mill, therefore, in thinking that to estimate quality of pleasure is quite consistent with his hedonistic principle, that pleasure and absence of pain alone are desirable as ends, has again committed the fallacy of confusing ends and means. For take even the most favourable supposition of his meaning; let us suppose that by a pleasure he does not mean, as his words imply, that which produces pleasure and the pleasure produced. Let us suppose him to mean that there are various kinds of pleasure, in the sense in which there are various kinds of colour—blue, red, green, etc. Even, in this case, if we are to say that our end is colour alone, then, although it is impossible we should have colour, without having some particular colour, yet the particular colour we must have, is only a *means* to our having colour, if colour is really our end. And if colour is our only possible end, as Mill says pleasure is, then there can be no possible reason for preferring one colour to another, red, for instance, to blue, except that the one is more of a colour than the other. Yet this is what Mill is attempting to hold with regard to pleasures.

Well, this is enough for to-day. I must leave the discussion of Prof. Sidgwick's Hedonism till next time. That discussion will depend entirely on this same distinction between means and ends; and it is perhaps as well that you should have a week to think over it. You will see that I have departed from the plan sketched in my Syllabus. That is partly due to our outstanding trouble about

Naturalism; but I think it is no disadvantage. I shall be able to deal with all the points I have promised to discuss just as conveniently in my next lecture. I must ask you therefore to wait till then for my attempt to refute Intuitionistic or ethical Hedonism, and for my discussion of the respective merits of Egoism with Utilitarianism.

LECTURE IV

Hedonism Continued

In my last lecture I began the discussion of Hedonism. Hedonism, I said, was the name given to the ethical doctrine that pleasure alone is good as an end or for its own sake; the doctrine that all other things are merely good as *means* to pleasure, or in so far as they are causes of which pleasure is the effect. I pointed out with regard to this doctrine, first of all, that it is sometimes supported by the naturalistic fallacy. In Mill, for instance, whose book called *Utilitarianism* I took as representative of hedonistic views in general, the 'desirable', which for him is equivalent to 'the good', is taken to *mean* what can be desired. The, test, again, of what can be desired, is, according to Mill, what actually is desired: if, therefore, he says, we can find some one thing which is always and alone desired, that thing will necessarily be the only thing that is desirable, the only thing that is good as an end. In this argument the naturalistic fallacy is plainly involved. That fallacy, I explained, consists in the contention that good *means* nothing but some simple or complex notion, that can be defined in terms of natural qualities. In Mill's case, good is thus supposed to *mean* simply what is desired; and what is desired is something which can thus be defined in natural terms. Mill tells us that we ought to desire something (an ethical proposition), because we actually do desire it; but, if his contention that 'I ought to desire' means nothing but 'I do desire' were true, then he is only entitled to say 'We do desire so and so because we do desire it'; and that is not an ethical proposition at all; it is a mere tautology. The whole object of Mill's book is

65

to help us to discover what we ought to do; but, in fact, by attempting to define the meaning of this 'ought', he has completely debarred himself from ever fulfilling that object: he has confined himself to telling us what we do do.

Mill's first argument then is that, because good means desired, therefore the desired is good; but having thus arrived at an ethical conclusion, by denying that any ethical conclusion is possible, he still needs another argument to make his conclusion a basis for Hedonism. He has to prove that we always do desire pleasure or freedom from pain, and that we never desire anything else whatever. This second doctrine, which Professor Sidgwick has called Psychological Hedonism, I accordingly discussed. I pointed out how obviously untrue it is that we never desire anything but pleasure; and how there is not a shadow of ground for saying even that, whenever we desire anything, we always desire pleasure *as well as* that thing. I attributed the obstinate belief in these untruths partly to a confusion between the cause of desire and the object of desire. It may, I said, be true that desire can never occur unless it be preceded by some *actual* pleasure; but even if this is true, it obviously gives no ground for saying that the object of desire is always some *future* pleasure. By the object of desire is meant that, of which the idea causes desire in us; it is some pleasure, which we anticipate, some pleasure which we have not got, which is the object of desire, whenever we do desire pleasure. And any actual pleasure which may be excited by the idea of this anticipated pleasure, is obviously not the same pleasure as that anticipated pleasure, of which only the idea is actual. This actual pleasure is not what we want; what we want is always something which we have not got; and to say that pleasure always causes us to want is quite a different thing from saying that what we want is always pleasure.

Mill, we saw, admits all this. He insists that we do *actually* desire other things than pleasure, and yet he says we do *really* desire nothing else. He tries to explain away this contradiction, by confusing together two notions, which he has before so carefully distinguished, the notions of means and of end. He now says that a means to an end is the same thing as a part of that end. This fallacy I begged you carefully to notice, as our ultimate decision with regard to Hedonism will mainly turn upon it.

Well, having thus dismissed the two steps of Mill's naturalistic argument for Hedonism, I pointed out that we had come to a turning point in our ethical method. We have now to consider ethical principles of which no direct *proof* can be given. We can, as Mill says, only present considerations capable of determining the intellect to accept or reject these principles. Such a principle is the hedonistic one that 'Pleasure alone is good as an end'. We have only proved so far that the naturalistic fallacy can not shew this principle to be true. But the principle may be true for all that, and nobody can *prove* either that is it true or that it is false. I, for instance, say that 'Pleasure is not the only good thing' and some-one else says that 'Pleasure is the only good thing': and neither of us can possibly prove that the other is wrong: no *reasons* can be given for either principle, because it is ultimate.

Well, somebody said last time that this was a very unsatisfactory state of things. So it is; but I wish you to understand a distinction between two different reasons, which may be given for calling it unsatisfactory. Is it unsatisfactory because our principle cannot be proved? Or is it unsatisfactory merely because we do not agree with one another about it? I am inclined to think that the latter is the chief reason. For the mere fact that in certain cases proof is impossible, does not usually give us the least uneasiness. For instance, nobody can prove that this is a chair beside me: yet I do not suppose that you are much dis-satisfied for that reason. We all agree that it is a chair, and that is enough to content us, although it is quite possible we may be wrong. A madman, of course, might come in and say that it is not a chair but an elephant. We could not prove that he was wrong, and the fact that he did not agree with us might then begin to make us uneasy. Much more then, shall we be uneasy, if someone, who we do not think to be mad, disagrees with us. We shall try to argue with him, and we shall probably be content if we lead him to agree with us, although we shall not have proved our point. We can only persuade him by shewing him that our view is consistent with some thing else which he holds to be true, whereas his original view is contradictory to it. But it will be impossible to prove that that something else, which we both agree to be true, is really so: we shall be satisfied to have settled the matter in dispute by means of it, merely because we are agreed on it. In short our dissatisfaction in these cases is almost always of the type felt by the poor lunatic in the story. "I said the world was mad" says he "and the world said that I was mad; and, confound it, they outvoted me". It is I say almost always such a disagreement, and not the impossibility of proof, which makes us call the state of things unsatisfactory. For, indeed, who can prove that proof itself is a warrant of truth? We are all agreed that the laws of logic are true, and therefore we accept a result which is proved by their means; but such a proof is satisfactory to us only because we are all so fully agreed that it is a warrant of truth. And yet we cannot, by the nature of the case, prove that we are right in having so agreed.

Accordingly, I do not think we need be much distressed by our admission that we cannot prove whether pleasure alone is good or not. We may be able to arrive at an agreement notwithstanding; and if so, I think it will be satisfactory. And yet I am not very sanguine about our prospects of such satisfaction. Ethics, and philosophy in general, have always been in a peculiarly unsatisfactory state. There has been no agreement about them, as there is about these chairs and lights and benches. I should therefore, be a fool if I hoped to settle one great point of controversy, now and once for all. It is extremely improbable I shall convince you in this lecture. It would be highly presumptuous even to hope that in the end, say two or three centuries hence, it will be agreed that pleasure is not the sole good. Philosophical questions are so difficult, the problems they raise are so complex, that no one can fairly expect, now, any more than in the past, to win more than a very limited assent. And yet I confess that the considerations which I am about to present appear to me to be absolutely convincing. I do think that they *ought* to convince you, if only I can put them well. In any case, I can but try. I *shall* try now to put an end to that unsatisfactory state of things, which was disclosed in last week's discussion. I shall try to make you agree with me that the fundamental principle of Hedonism is very like an absurdity, by shewing you what it must mean, if it is clearly thought out, and how that clear meaning is in conflict with other beliefs of yours, which I hope you will not so easily give up.

Well, then, our question is: Is pleasure alone good as an end? I began the discussion of this question last time by pointing out that, if you say 'pleasure', you must mean 'pleasure': you must mean some one thing common to all different 'pleasures', some one thing, which may exist in different degrees, but which cannot differ in *kind*. I pointed out that, if you say, as Mill does, that quality of pleasure is to be taken into account, then you are no longer holding that pleasure *alone* is good as an end, since you imply that something else, something which is *not* present in all pleasures, is *also* good as an end. I took an illustration from colour, which I wish you to remember, since it expresses my point in its most acute form. I pointed out that if you say 'Colour alone is good as an end,' then you can give no possible reason for preferring one colour to another. Your only standard of good and bad will then be 'colour'; and since red and blue both conform equally to this, the only standard, you can have no other whereby to judge whether red is better than blue. It is true that you cannot have colour unless you also have one or all of the particular colours: they, therefore, if colour is the end, will all be good as means, but none of them can be better than another even as a means, far less can anyone of them be regarded as an end in itself. Just so with pleasure: If we do really mean 'Pleasure alone is good as an end,' then we must agree with Bentham that 'Quantity of pleasure being equal, pushpin is as good as poetry'. To have thus dismissed Mill's reference to quality of pleasure, is therefore to have made one step in the desired direction. You will now no longer be prevented from agreeing with me, by any idea that the hedonistic principle 'Pleasure alone is good as an end' is consistent with the view that one pleasure may be of a better quality than another. These two views, we have seen, are contradictory to one another. You must choose between them: and if you choose the latter, then you must give up the principle of Hedonism.

But, as I said, Professor Sidgwick has seen that they are inconsistent. He has seen that he must choose between them. He has chosen. He has rejected the test by quality of pleasure, and has accepted the hedonistic principle. He still maintains that 'Pleasure alone is good as an end.' I propose therefore to discuss the considerations which he has offered in order to convince us. I shall hope by that discussion to remove some more of such prejudices and misunderstandings as might prevent you from agreeing with me. If I can shew you that some of the considerations which Professor Sidgwick uses are such as we need by no means agree with, and that others are actually rather in my favour than in his, we may have again advanced a few steps nearer to the unanimity which we desire.

That part of Prof. Sidgwick's argument with which I shall deal first occupies only a very small space in his book. A much greater space is taken up by attempts to shew that the application of hedonistic principle yields results not unlike the ordinary judgments of common sense. To this part I shall return later. What I wish to consider first is how he really does conceive the hedonistic principle—whether after all, he is a hedonist: for undoubtedly the results of his application of his principle must depend largely on what the principle is that he applies.

The passages in the *Methods of Ethics* to which I shall now invite your attention are to be found in Book I.ch.ix. § 4 (pp. 113–15) and in Book III.ch.xiv.3–5. (pp. 396–407).[1]

The first of these two passages runs as follows:

§ 4. It remains to consider by what standard the value of conduct or character, thus intuitively judged to be good in itself, is to be coordinated and compared with that of other good things. I shall not now attempt to establish such a standard; but a little reflection may enable us to limit

1. Moore refers to this passage by page numbers. The quoted material has been added to the text. Henry Sidgwick, *The Methods of Ethics* (London: Macmillan and Company, 1893), pp. 113–15.

considerably the range of comparison for which it is required. For I think that if we consider carefully such permanent results as are commonly judged to be good, other than qualities of human beings, we can find nothing that, on reflection, appears to possess this quality of goodness out of relation to human existence, or at least to some consciousness or feeling.

For example, we commonly judge some inanimate objects, scenes, &c. to be good as possessing beauty, and others bad from ugliness: still no one would consider it rational to aim at the production of beauty in external nature, apart from any possible contemplation of it by human beings. In fact when beauty is maintained to be objective, it is not commonly meant that it exists as beauty out of relation to any mind whatsoever: but only that there is some standard of beauty valid for all minds.

It may however be said that beauty and other results commonly judged to be good, though we do not conceive them to exist out of relation to human beings (or at least minds of some kind), are yet so far separable as ends from the human beings on whom their existence depends, that their realization may conceivably come into competition with the perfection or happiness of these beings. Thus, though beautiful things cannot be thought worth producing except as possible objects of contemplation, still a man may devote himself to their production without any consideration of the persons who are to contemplate them. Similarly knowledge is a good which cannot exist except in minds: and yet one may be more interested in the development of knowledge than in its possession by any particular minds; and may take the former as an ultimate end without regarding the latter.

Still, as soon as the alternatives are clearly apprehended, it will, I think, be generally held that beauty, knowledge, and other ideal goods, as well as all external material things, are only reasonably to be sought by men in so far as they conduce either (1) to Happiness or (2) to the Perfection or Excellence of human existence. I say "human," for though most utilitarians consider the pleasure (and freedom from pain) of the inferior animals to be included in the Happiness which they take as the right and proper end of conduct, no one seems to contend that we ought to aim at perfecting brutes, except as a means to our ends, or at least as objects of scientific or aesthetic contemplation for us. Nor, again, can we include, as a practical end, the existence of beings above the human. We certainly apply the idea of Good to the Divine Existence, just as we do to His work, and indeed in a preeminent manner: and when it is said that "we should do all things to the glory of God," it may seem to be implied that the existence of God is made better by our glorifying Him. Still this inference when explicitly drawn appears somewhat impious; and theologians generally recoil from it, and refrain from using the notion of a possible addition to the Goodness of the Divine existence as a ground of human duty. Nor can the influence of our actions on other extra-human intelligences besides the Divine be at present made matter of scientific discussion.

I shall therefore confidently lay down, that if there be any Good other than Happiness to be sought by man, as an ultimate practical end, it can only be the Goodness, Perfection, or Excellence of Human Existence. How far this notion includes more than Virtue, what its precise relation to Pleasure is, and to what method we shall be logically led if we accept it as fundamental, are questions which we shall more conveniently discuss after the detailed examination of these two other notions, in which we shall be engaged in the two following Books.

You see that in this passage, Prof. Sidgwick tries to limit the range of objects among which the ultimate end may be found. He does not yet say what that end is, but he does exclude from it everything but certain characters of Human Existence. And the possible ends which he thus excludes, do not again come up for consideration. They are put out of court once for all by this passage and by this passage only. Now is this exclusion justified?

I cannot think it is. 'No-one' says Prof. Sidgwick, 'would consider it rational to aim at the production of beauty in external nature, apart from any possible contemplation of it by human beings'. Well, I may say at once, that I, for one, do consider this rational; and let us see if I cannot get any one to agree with me. Consider what this admission really means. It entitles us to put the following case. Let us imagine one world exceedingly beautiful. Imagine it as beautiful as you can; put into it whatever on this earth you most admire—mountains, rivers, the sea; trees, and sunsets, stars and moon. Imagine these all combined in the most exquisite proportions, so that no-one thing jars against another, but each contributes to increase the beauty of the whole. And then imagine the ugliest world you can possibly conceive. Imagine it simply one heap of filth, containing everything that is most disgusting to us, for whatever reason, and the whole, as far as may be, without one redeeming feature. Such a pair of worlds we are entitled to compare: they fall within Prof. Sidgwick's meaning, and the comparison is highly relevant to it. The only thing we are not entitled to imagine is that any human being ever has lived or ever, by any possibility, *can*, live in either, can ever see and enjoy the beauty of the one or hate the foulness of the other. Well, even so, supposing them quite apart from any possible contemplation by human beings; still, is it irrational to hold that it is better than the beautiful world should exist, rather than the one which is ugly? Would it not be well in any case, to do what we could to produce it rather than the other? Certainly I cannot help thinking that it would; and I hope that some of you may agree with me in this extreme instance. The instance is extreme. It is highly improbable, not to say, impossible, that we should ever have such a choice before us. But an extreme instance is enough for our purpose. If in any imaginable case you do admit that the existence of a more beautiful thing is better in itself than that of one more ugly, quite apart from its effects on any human feeling, then Prof. Sidgwick's principle has broken down. Then we shall have to include in our ultimate end something beyond the limits of human existence. I admit, of course, that our beautiful world would be better still, if there were human beings in it to contemplate and enjoy its beauty. But that admission makes nothing against my point. It you have once admitted that the beautiful world *in itself* is better than the ugly, then it follows, that however many beings may enjoy it, and however much better their enjoyment may be than it is itself, yet its mere existence adds *something* to the goodness of the whole: it is not only a means to our end, but also itself a part thereof.

Well, in the second passage to which I referred you above, Professor Sidgwick returns from the discussion of Virtue and Pleasure, with which he has meanwhile been engaged, to consider what among the parts of Human Existence to which, as we saw, he has limited the ultimate end, can really be considered as such end. What I have just said, of course, appears to me to destroy the force of this part of his argument too. If, as I think, other things than any part of Human Existence, can be ends-in-themselves, then Prof. Sidgwick cannot claim to have discussed the Summum Bonum, when he has merely determined what parts of Human Existence are in themselves desirable. But in this discussion, too, he seems to me to make a similar error, which is important enough to be noticed for its own sake.

'It may be said,' says Prof. Sidgwick (p. 400),

that we may . . . regard cognition of Truth, contemplation of Beauty, Free or Virtuous action, as in some measure preferable alternatives to Pleasure or Happiness—even though we admit that Happiness must be included as a part of Ultimate Good. . . . I think, however, that this view ought not to commend itself to the sober judgment of reflective persons. In order to shew this, I must ask the reader to use the same twofold procedure that I before requested him to employ in considering the absolute and independent validity of common moral precepts. I appeal firstly to his intuitive judgment after due consideration of the question when fairly placed before it: and secondly to a comprehensive comparison of the ordinary judgments of mankind. As regards the first argument, to me at least it seems clear after reflection that these objective relations of the conscious subject, when distinguished from the consciousness accompanying and resulting from them, are not ultimately and intrinsically desirable; any more than material or other objects are, when considered apart from any relation to conscious existence. Admitting that we have actual experience of such preferences as have just been described, of which the ultimate object is something that is not merely consciousness: it still seems to me that when (to use Butler's phrase) we "sit down in a cool hour," we can only justify to ourselves the importance that we attach to any of these objects by considering its conduciveness, in one way or another, to the happiness of sentient beings.

The second argument, that refers to the common sense of mankind, obviously cannot be made completely cogent; since, as above stated, several cultivated persons do habitually judge that knowledge, art, &c.,—not to speak of Virtue—are ends independently of the pleasure derived from them. But we may urge not only that all these elements of "ideal good" are productive of pleasure in various ways; but also that they seem to obtain the commendation of Common Sense, roughly speaking, in proportion to the degree of this productiveness. This seems obviously true of Beauty; and will hardly be denied in respect of any kind of social ideal: it is paradoxical to maintain that any degree of Freedom, or any form of social order, would still be commonly regarded as desirable even if we were certain that it had no tendency to promote the general happiness. The case of Knowledge is rather more complex; but certainly Common Sense is most impressed with the value of knowledge, when its 'fruitfulness' has been demonstrated. It is, however, aware that experience has frequently shewn how knowledge, long fruitless, may become unexpectedly fruitful, and how light may be shed on one part of the field of knowledge from another apparently remote: and even if any particular branch of scientific pursuit could be shewn to be devoid of even this indirect utility, it would still deserve some respect on utilitarian

grounds; both as furnishing to the inquirer the refined and innocent pleasures of curiosity, and because the intellectual disposition which it exhibits
and sustains is likely on the whole to produce fruitful knowledge. Still in
cases approximating to this last, Common Sense is somewhat disposed to
complain of the misdirection of valuable effort; so that the meed of honour
commonly paid to Science seems to be graduated, though perhaps uncon-
sciously, by a tolerably exact utilitarian scale. Certainly the moment the
legitimacy of any branch of scientific inquiry is seriously disputed, as in the
recent case of vivisection, the controversy on both sides is generally conducted on an avowedly utilitarian basis.

The case of Virtue requires special consideration: since the encouragement in each other of virtuous impulses and dispositions is a main aim of
men's ordinary moral discourse; so that even to raise the question whether
this encouragement can go too far has a paradoxical air. Still, our experience
includes rare and exceptional cases in which the concentration of effort on
the cultivation of virtue has seemed to have effects adverse to general
happiness, through being intensified to the point of moral fanaticism, and so
involving a neglect of other conditions of happiness. If, then, we admit as
actual or possible such 'infelicific' effects of the cultivation of Virtue, I think
we shall also generally admit that, in the case supposed, conduciveness to
general happiness should be the criterion for deciding how far the cultivation of Virtue should be carried.[2]

There we have Professor Sidgwick's argument completed. We
ought not, he thinks, to aim at knowing the Truth, or at contemplating beauty, except insofar as such knowledge or such contemplation contribute to increase the pleasure or to diminish the
pain of sentient beings. Pleasure alone is good for its own sake:
knowledge of the Truth is good only as a means to pleasure.

I want you to consider what this means. What is pleasure? It is
certainly something of which we may be conscious, and something, as most psychologists would admit, which may be in our
minds even though we are not conscious of it. But the existence of
sub-conscious pleasure is not essential to my point. What I wish to
ask is this: Can you really say that you value pleasure, except in so
far as you are conscious of it? Would you think that the attainment
of pleasure, of which you never were and never could be con-

2. Moore again refers to this passage by page numbers. The quoted material has been
added to the text. Henry Sidgwick, *The Methods of Ethics* (London: Macmillan and Company, 1893), pp. 400–402.

scious, was something to be aimed at for its own sake? It may be impossible that such pleasure should ever exist, that it should ever be thus divorced from consciousness; although there is certainly much reason to believe that it is not only possible but very common. But even supposing that it were impossible, that is quite irrelevant. Our question is: Is it the pleasure, as distinct from the consciousness of it, that you set value on? Do you think the pleasure valuable in itself, or do you insist that, if you are to think the pleasure good, you must have consciousness of it too?

This consideration is very well put by Socrates in Plato's dialogue *Philebus*.[3]

'Would *you* accept, Protarchus' says Socrates 'to live your whole life in the enjoyment of the greatest pleasures?' 'Of course I would' says Protarchus.

Socrates: Then would you think you needed anything else besides, if you possessed this one blessing in completeness?

Protarchus: Certainly not.

Socrates: Consider what you are saying. You would not need to be wise and intelligent and reasonable, nor anything like this? Would you not even care to keep your sight?

Protarchus: Why should I? I suppose I should have all I want, if I was pleased.

Socrates: Well, then, supposing you lived so, you would enjoy always throughout your life the greatest pleasure?

Protarchus: Of course.

Socrates: But, on the other hand, inasmuch as you would *not* possess intelligence and memory and knowledge and true opinion, you would, in the first place, necessarily be without the knowledge, whether you were pleased or not. For you would be devoid of any kind of wisdom. You admit this?

Protarchus: I do. The consequence is absolutely necessary.

Socrates: Well, then, besides this, not having memory you must also be unable to remember even that you ever were pleased; of the pleasure which falls upon you at the moment not the least vestige must afterwards remain. And again, not having true opinion, you cannot think that you are pleased when you are; and, being bereft of your reasoning faculties, you cannot even

3. Moore's marginal note cites *Philebus* 21A. Again, there is every reason to believe the translation is Moore's.

have the power to reckon that you will be pleased in future. You must live the life of an oyster, or of some other of those living creatures, whose home is the seas and whose souls are concealed in shelly bodies. Is all this so, or can we think otherwise than this?

Protarchus: How can we?

Socrates: Well then, can we think such a life desirable?

Protarchus: Socrates, your reasoning has left me utterly dumb.

Socrates, you see, persuades Protarchus that Hedonism is absurd. If you are really going to maintain that pleasure alone is good as an end, you must maintain that it is good, whether you are conscious of it or not. You must declare it reasonable to take as your ideal (an unattainable ideal it may be) that you should be as happy as possible, on condition that you never know and never can know that you are happy. You must be willing to sell in exchange for the mere happiness every vestige of knowledge, both in yourself and in others, both of happiness itself and of every other thing. Can you really still disagree with me, and declare it obvious that this is reasonable? That pleasure alone is good as an end?

You see, the case is just like that of the colours, only, as yet, not nearly so strong. It is far more possible that we should some day be able to produce the intensest pleasure, without any consciousness that it is there, than that we should be able to produce mere colour, without its being any particular colour. Pleasure and consciousness can be far more easily distinguished from one another, than colour from the particular colours. And yet even if this were not so, we should be bound to distinguish them if we really wished to declare pleasure alone to be our ultimate end. Even if consciousness were an inseparable accompaniment of pleasure, a *sine qua non* of its existence, yet, if pleasure is the only end, we are bound to call consciousness a mere *means* to it, in any intelligible sense that can be given to the word *means*. And if, on the other hand, as I hope you now think, the pleasure would be comparatively valueless without the consciousness, then we are bound to say that pleasure is *not* the only end, that some consciousness at least must be included with it as a veritable part of the end. You see, our question now is solely what the end is: it is quite another question how far we must take account in our conduct, whether the end be practicable or not. When we come to consider *that*, you will see that I do not so much differ from the Utilitarians: I do not much disagree with their practical results. What I do disagree with is the reasons that they give for them. In so far as their reason is that 'Pleasure alone is good as an end' I do think they are *absolutely* wrong; and it is with the reasons that we are concerned in any scientific Ethics.

Well then, this is my objection to Prof. Sidgwick. I think he is confusing means and end. He treats of pleasure as if it were an element in human consciousness; and by so treating it he obscures the fact that it is distinguishable from all other elements, and that we must not think of them, when we profess to think of pleasure only. His arguments only tend to shew that a certain quantity of pleasure must be included in the ultimate end, a proposition which I do not dispute. But he thinks they shew that pleasure is the sole end: and that contention, I hold to be based on a confusion between means and end, and to appear as a naked absurdity, when that confusion is once dissipated.

And we are entitled to push the Hedonists to a still greater absurdity, if this is not enough. They are bound, by the terms of their claim, to maintain even that *nonexistent* pleasure is good; nay that it is the sole good, that it makes no difference to its goodness, whether it exist or not. For can we not distinguish pleasure from existence? Do not other things exist besides pleasure? Do we not mean something more when we say 'Pleasure exists' than when we merely say 'Pleasure'? If so, then, when we say 'Pleasure is good and the sole good', then we ought to mean, 'Pleasure, whether it exists or not, is good and the sole good': just as when we say Twice two is four, we do mean that this is true, whether two and four exist or not. But I do not wish to press this claim against the Hedonists. I do not imagine that any of them would seriously maintain that non-existent pleasure is the sole good. I am willing they should accept my amendment to their original resolution, the amendment that the word 'existent be inserted before the word pleasure, wherever it occurs'. But even so I do maintain that their resolution is absurd. It still omits that consciousness of pleasure, which appears to me so much to heighten its value; not to mention many other constituents of the ideal, which I shall presently propose.

So much for pure Hedonism. We must now go on to consider the two most common professedly hedonistic doctrines—the doctrine of Egoism and the doctrine of Utilitarianism.

Egoism is the doctrine which holds that we ought each of us to pursue our own greatest happiness as our ultimate end. The doctrine will, of course, admit that sometimes the best means to this end, will be to give pleasure to others: we shall, for instance, by so doing, procure for ourselves the pleasures of sympathy, of freedom from interference, even of self-esteem; and these pleasures, which may procure, by sometimes aiming directly at the happiness of other persons, may be greater than any we could otherwise secure. Egoism in this sense, must therefore carefully be distinguished from Egoism in another sense, the sense in which Altruism is its proper object. Egoism, as commonly opposed to Altruism, is apt to denote merely selfishness. In this sense, a man is an egoist, if all his actions are actually directed towards gaining pleasure for himself; whether he holds that he ought to act so, because he will thereby obtain for himself the greatest possible happiness on the whole, or not. Egoism may accordingly be used to denote the theory that we should always aim at getting pleasure for ourselves, *because*, that is the best *means* to the ultimate end, whether the ultimate end be our own greatest pleasure or not. Altruism, on the contrary, as I believe it was used by M. Comte, denotes the theory that we ought always to aim at other people's happiness, on the ground that this is the best means of securing our own as well as theirs. Accordingly an Egoist, in the sense in which I am now going to talk of Egoism, an Egoist, who holds that his own greatest happiness is the ultimate end for him may at the same time be an altruist: he may hold that he ought to 'love his neighbour', as the best means to being happy himself. And conversely an egoist, in the other sense, may at the same time be a utilitarian. He may hold that he ought always to direct his efforts towards getting pleasure for himself on the ground that he is thereby most likely to increase the general sum of happiness.

I shall say more later about this second kind of Egoism, this anti-altruistic Egoism, this Egoism as a doctrine of means. What I am now concerned with is that utterly distinct kind of Egoism, which holds that each man ought rationally to hold: My own greatest happiness is the only good thing there is; my actions can only be good as means, in so far as they help to win me this. This is a doctrine which is not much held by writers nowadays. It is a doctrine that was largely held by English hedonists in the 17th and 18th centuries: it is, for example, at the bottom of Hobbes' Ethics. But even the English school appear to have made one step forward in the present century: they are most of them now-a-days Utilitarians. They do recognise that if my own happiness is good, it seems strange that other people's happiness should not be good too. In fact, this is all I have to say about the doctrine. I cannot see the shadow of a reason why I should think my happiness to be the sole good, simply because it is mine. I can see many causes why I should think so. I am naturally much more likely to think my own happiness important; it affects me more than other people's, because I am not by any means a perfect creature and have many unreasonable feelings. But all this is not to the point: the question is, Have I any *reason* to think it true that my happiness is the sole good? If I admit that my happiness is a good, is it not reasonable to admit that other people's is so also? It makes a difference to *me* that it is mine, but does it make any difference to the truth? Well, Prof. Sidgwick thinks it does: and I never could make out why. He does think that Egoism in this naked form is reasonable. He thinks it reasonable for me to say that My happiness is the sole good, because it is mine. Surely one might as well say: I am the only man there is, because I am I. But then Prof. Sidgwick *also* recognises that Utilitarianism is reasonable. I am not quite sure whether he sees that the two doctrines are absolutely contradictory: that, if one is true, the other must be false. What he is more concerned with is the point that these two ends do not necessarily coincide: that there seems no reason for thinking that if I have my own greatest happiness, everybody else will necessarily have theirs. This difficulty he fully admits: he admits that if you adopt one of these two ends, it will not necessarily be reasonable to do the things as if you adopt the other; though, in general, he thinks it will. This is a serious practical difficulty; and you will find how serious he thinks it by looking at his last chapter. But I confess it seems to me not half so serious as the absolute contradiction between the ends: only, as I have said, I see no reason for thinking the egoistic principle a true one. And, if that is so, both the contradiction and the practical difficulty disappear.

But I wish to say a few words about the *causes* why Egoism is sometimes accepted. I think there is no reasonable cause for holding it; but it may be helpful to point out some confusions which may make us think it reasonable.

First of all, then, we know Mill said: 'Each person, so far as he believes it to be attainable, desires his own happiness' (p. 53). Mill, indeed, offers this as a reason why the general happiness is desirable. We have seen that to regard it as such, involves, in the first place, the naturalistic fallacy. But moreover, even if that fallacy were not a fallacy, it would rather be a reason for Egoism, than for Utilitarianism. Mill has been severely criticised already on this point, both by Prof. Sidgwick and by Mr. Bradley. There is, in fact, no logical means of passing from this proposition to Utilitarianism. Mill's argument is as follows: A man desires his own happiness; therefore his own happiness is desirable. Further a man desires nothing but his own happiness; therefore his own happiness is alone desirable. Well that sounds like the principle of Egoism. We have, of course, to remember, that everybody, according to Mill, so desires his own happiness: and then it will follow that everybody's happiness is alone desirable. That is simply a contradiction in terms. Just consider what it means. Each man's happiness is the only thing desirable: several different things are each of them the only thing desirable. This result, which does logically follow from Mill's argument, is not Egoism and it is not

Utilitarianism. It is simply an absurdity appearing to partake of the characters of both. Why I have discussed it here is that it serves to illustrate the fact that any Naturalistic Hedonism, such as Mill's, may cause us to think Egoism plausible. It caused him to think Utilitarianism plausible; but as a matter of fact it gives just as good ground for Egoism. Mr. Bradley, I believe, thinks it gives better. And it is this naturalism which as I believe is largely responsible for Egoism. Of course, a naturalist might hold that what we aimed at was simply 'pleasure' not our own pleasure; and that, always assuming the naturalistic fallacy, would give an unobjectionable ground for Utilitarianism. But more commonly he will hold that it is his own pleasure he desires, or at least will confuse this with the other; and then he may be led to adopt Egoism rather than Utilitarianism.

The second cause I have to give why Egoism should be thought reasonable, is simply its confusion with that other kind of Egoism—egoism as a doctrine of means. You see this second Egoism has a right to say: You ought to pursue your own happiness, sometimes at all events, it may even say always. And when we find it saying this we are apt to forget its proviso: But only as a means to something else. The fact is we are in an imperfect state[,] we cannot get the ideal all at once. And hence it is often our bounden duty, we often *absolutely 'ought'* to do things which are good only or chiefly as means: we have to do the best we can, what is absolutely 'right', but not what is absolutely good. Of this I shall say more hereafter. I only mention it here, because I think it is much more plausible to say that we ought to pursue our only pleasure as a means than as an end, and that this doctrine, through confusion, lends some of its plausibility to the utterly different doctrine of Egoism proper: My own greatest pleasure is the only good thing.

So much for Egoism. I wish only to remark in passing, that the name is a bad one. According to its original meaning, a meaning which is not likely to be soon forgotten, it ought to apply quite as much to any doctrine holding that anything of my own, not only my own pleasure, was the sole good thing. I might be called an Egoist, for example, for holding that my own perfection was the only thing worth aiming at for its own sake. But the name is not so used: it has been confined to a form of Hedonism and we must accept that restriction, only taking care that the name does not mislead us in judging of the thing. A similar criticism will apply to Utilitarianism, as a name for the doctrine to which we now must pass. What is useful means properly merely what is a means to good. And the utilitarian, when he insists on the importance of utility, might naturally be understood to mean that the goodness of conduct must be judged simply according to the degree in which it is good as a means. This doctrine in itself I should think to be objectionable, since I do hold that conduct, in part at least, may be not only a means but also a part of the end. But utilitarianism, as it is actually used, denotes a doctrine more objectionable still. It asserts nothing to be good, even as a means, unless it is a means to pleasure; or rather not to pleasure, for that as we have seen, must stand for non-existent pleasure, but to the greatest happiness of the greatest number. Utilitarianism is therefore, fundamentally not a doctrine concerning the useful, but concerning that to which all that is useful must be a means. This is the doctrine we have now to consider.

The greatest happiness of the greatest number! I have said that this doctrine is to be preferred to egoism, simply because, if one man's happiness is good, there seems no possible reason why another man's happiness if it be as great, should not be equally good. I have also tried to shew that in so far as both of them profess to be based on the principle that pleasure alone is good, they are based on an absurdity. For pleasure might conceivably be isolated from all that now accompanies it: it might conceivably exist apart from any consciousness apart from any mind or living body, it might exist simply as pleasure, per se, in fabulous quantities, or it might not exist at all; and it would follow from the utilitarian principle that, if the pleasure thus existent or not existent, were greater than what is likely to exist in human or other living souls: we ought to aim at it. The utilitarian principle involves all this: it regards the soul itself, with all its loves and hates, its knowledge and its passions; all beauty too, music and poetry and painting, the beauties of nature and of the human body, as so many mere adjuncts, mere means to pleasure, absolutely worthless in themselves. I cannot think this is ideal. But utilitarianism as commonly held does not include [*sic.*]; its supporters are not logical enough to draw the fair conclusions from its acknowledged principle. They do hold, though they themselves deny it, that what they regard as their end, is not mere quantity of pleasure but quantity of pleasure in human souls. The only point I want now to make is that even so, even granting that their ideal is not, so they say, pleasure, but pleasure plus a human mind, yet their ideal is more like a society of four-footed swine, than of the best men that we know. This is a point on which there seems unlikely to be any certainty for a long time to come. It hangs on this question: Are the pleasures of men, such as we would wish to be, superior in duration and intensity, to those which Mill calls the lower pleasures, the pleasures of sensual indulgence for example? Prof. Sidgwick thinks they are, as Bentham also thought: he did not think apparently that pushpin should take the place of poetry: the quantity of pleasure was not equal. This is a matter upon which everybody must judge for himself. For myself, I certainly think the quantity of pleasure is not equal: judging from my own experience I should say that the sensual and lower pleasures had greatly the advantage. The question of duration is so largely mixed up with the question, what is possible, that it cannot be well discussed here; it does depend so largely upon circumstances. But the question of intensity is clearer, and a careful consideration of it may tend to diminish any prepossession you may have in favour of this or any other Hedonism. Should you not judge that certain sensual pleasures were far more intense, than any intellectual or aesthetic pleasure? Than the pleasure of discovery, for example, or the pleasures of music and reading? And let me guard against one misapprehension. You must not take into account, the pleasure, you get in the latter case, from the thought that you are doing what you ought to do, from the thought that your pleasure is a right one. For that moral pleasure ought, *ex hypothesi*, to be transferred to the sensual indulgences, if they in themselves are more intense; and there seems no doubt that in the end it might be so, and thus might add to the total quantity of pleasure enjoyed through them.

But this is a complicated matter. We shall return to it later, when we consider what is practicable. All the other objections which I intended to urge against Utilitarianism, will also be more properly put off till then. I can, at present, only raise this doubt. Are not the swinish pleasures more intense? Are they not superior by the 'quantity of pleasure' standard?

LECTURE V

Some Main Forms of
Metaphysical Ethics

Before I begin the discussion of what I have called 'Metaphysical Ethics' I am anxious to recapitulate the main points in my treatment of Hedonism.

By Hedonism I mean the doctrine that pleasure alone (or freedom from pain) is good as an end. The doctrine that pleasure, *among other things*, is good as an end, is not Hedonism; and I have not disputed its truth. Nor again is the doctrine that other things, beside pleasure, are good as means, at all inconsistent with Hedonism: the Hedonist is not bound to maintain that 'Pleasure alone is good',—if under good he includes, as we generally do, what is good as means to an end, *as well as* the end itself. In attacking Hedonism, I am therefore simply and solely attacking the doctrine that 'Pleasure *alone* is good as an end or in itself': I am not attacking the doctrine that 'pleasure *is* good as an end or in itself', nor am I attacking any doctrine whatever as to what are the best means we can take in order to obtain pleasure or any other end. Hedonists do, in general, recommend a course of conduct which is very similar to that which I should recommend. I do not quarrel with them about their practical conclusions, I quarrel only with the reasons that they give for their conclusions; and I do emphatically deny that the correctness of their conclusions is any ground for inferring the correctness of their principles. A correct conclusion may always be obtained by fallacious reasoning; and the good life or virtuous maxims of a hedonist afford absolutely no presumption that his ethical philosophy is also good. It is his ethical philosophy alone with which I am concerned; what I dispute is the excellence of his reasoning, not the excellence of his character as a man or even as moral teacher. You may think that my dispute is unimportant, but that is no ground for thinking that I am not in the right. What I am concerned with is knowledge only—that you should think correctly and so far arrive at some truth, however unimportant: I do not say that such knowledge will make you more useful members of society. If you do not care for knowledge for its own sake, then I have nothing to say to you; only, pray, do not think that your lack of interest in what I have to say is any ground for holding it untrue.

Well, I pointed out first of all that this hedonistic principle 'Pleasure alone is good as an end' may be supported by what I have called the naturalistic fallacy. It may be said, as Mill says, that 'good' *means* merely what we desire or want; and that since what we want or desire is only pleasure, therefore pleasure alone is good. I insisted that this reasoning, at all events, can give no ground for thinking the hedonistic principle to be true. It is a way of reasoning which is used in support of other ethical doctrines besides Hedonism, and it is universally fallacious. For if good *means* nothing else than what it is asserted to mean in the major premise, then the conclusion cannot be an ethical principle at all. In Mill's hedonistic argument, for example, the only conclusion to which he is entitled is that pleasure is the only thing that we desire; and hence he is no nearer at the end of it than he was at the beginning to proving that pleasure is the only good thing. Nevertheless I think that fallacy is the chief cause why the principle of Hedonism is held to be true. It is so natural to think that 'good' means simply what we want, and to neglect the obvious fact that we sometimes want things which we cannot think to be good. People find a great difficulty in seeing that good can mean anything at all, unless it means something else than merely 'good'. Hence any doctrine which professes that it does mean something else has always a great chance of being accepted by them; much more so, if it be the doctrine that that something else is what we want or what we like. For, in ordinary speech, 'I want this', 'I like this', 'I care about this' are constantly used as equivalents to 'I think this good.'

However, I admitted and insisted, that the principle of Hedonism, might be true, even though it was supported by the naturalistic fallacy. But if it is true, it must be possible to find some other reason for it than this fallacious one. Well, the doctrine which I called Intuitionistic Hedonism, asserts it simply on the ground that it is self-evident. This is Prof. Sidgwick's doctrine. He holds that you cannot deduce this principle from any other proposition; (that you cannot so deduce it follows indeed from the meaning of good); but he thinks that you still can argue for it, by means, namely, of distinguishing it from other propositions with which it is commonly confused. I quite accept this method as the only method by which this or any other ethical principle can be proved. The proof cannot be strict; it can only be, in Mill's words, the presenting of 'considerations capable of determining the intellect to accept or reject the principle in question'. It was, then, a proof of this kind which was the main object of my last lecture. I attempted to distinguish the hedonistic principle from other principles with which it might be confused. I thought that Professor Sidgwick had after all confused it with something else; that his reasoning was therefore fallacious. It seemed that when he thought he was considering the question 'Is pleasure alone good as an end?' he was really considering the question 'Is pleasure, together with some consciousness both of itself and other things, alone good as an end?' Though, therefore, he might have presented considerations capable of determining the intellect to accept the latter proposition, he had not thereby, as he seemed to think, convinced us of the hedonistic principle. He seemed to imply that since pleasure is actually inseparable from some sort of accompanying consciousness, therefore that consciousness may be assumed to be a part of the pleasure and of the end, instead of being regarded as a mere means thereto. He seemed to commit the fallacy of confusing means and ends.

In fact, however, I first disputed the contention that everything but some state of consciousness must be excluded from the end. It seemed to me that, to take one instance only, that which was more beautiful must in itself be considered better than that which was more ugly, whether any-one were ever to be conscious of its beauty or not. It is, indeed, unlikely that in any actual choice we might have to make, it would be our duty to prefer one course of action on this ground alone—that it made the world more beautiful. In any actual choice we should have to consider the possible effects of our action upon conscious beings, and among these possible effects there are always some, I think, which ought to be preferred to the existence of mere beauty. But this only means that in our present state, in which but a very small portion of the good is attainable, the pursuit of beauty for its own sake must always be postponed to the pursuit of some greater good, which is equally attainable. But it is enough for my purpose, if it be admitted that, *supposing* no greater good were at all attainable, then beauty must in itself be regarded as a greater good than ugliness; if it be admitted that, in that case, we should not be left without any reason for preferring one course of action to another, we should not be left without any duty whatever, but that it would then be our positive duty to make the world more beautiful, so far as we were able, since nothing better than beauty could then result from our efforts. If this be once admitted, then it follows that beauty must itself be regarded as a part of the ultimate end, as a part of the *summum bonum*, and not as a mere means to its own effects on any conscious being.[1]

Again, I think this same position results from another consideration, which I did not mention last time, but which will be more fully developed in Lecture VIII with regard to another instance. If

1. There is a marginal note to "Sidgwick's Death of Pleasure, p. 128." In fact, however, Sidgwick does not discuss the "death of pleasure" here or elsewhere in *The Methods of Ethics*. What Sidgwick actually discusses on p. 128 is the definition of pleasure. Professor J. B. Schneewind has suggested (private correspondence, September 14, 1989) that an error may have occurred in the typescript of *The Elements*. Because the original was handwritten, the transcriber might have misread (or mistranscribed) 'death' for 'defn.' There seems to be no other way to account for Moore's marginal note in this case. As Professor Schneewind states, "Otherwise I give up."

it be granted, as many would be inclined to grant, that the contemplation of beauty, at least, is better than the contemplation of ugliness; if, for instance, the pleasure resulting from such contemplation is held to be what Mill would call a 'higher' pleasure, than that which may be derived from contemplating ugliness, then I think it must follow that beauty is also in itself better than ugliness. For whenever we contemplate a thing, then there is in us and in that thing something in common. In so far as we are really contemplating a beautiful thing, the qualities, which in it are beautiful, are also present in our contemplation. Such, at least, is the commonly accepted view. And however that may be the presence of these qualities is certainly the only thing which can distinguish the contemplation of beauty from the contemplation of ugliness, if these two contemplations be considered in themselves, apart from the different states of feeling which they may excite. But, in that case, the contemplation of beauty can only be better than its opposite, in virtue of those very same qualities which are also present in the beautiful object. It is they and they only which give to it its value; and they must of necessity bring the same value to anything in which they are present, and hence to the beautiful object. It would thus appear that we cannot consistently maintain even that the contemplation of beauty is better in itself than the contemplation of ugliness, that it is a higher pleasure, unless we allow that beauty alone, whether it be contemplated or not, is also better than ugliness.

But even if you will not admit this, if you will not admit that beauty is good as an end, and not merely as a means to something else, yet my case against Hedonism is by no means exhausted. My strongest plea still remains to be submitted to you. It is this that, even should we allow that nothing which is not in the mind, can have a value in itself, yet we cannot hold without absurdity that pleasure, alone of mental things, is good. I insisted last time that to say this implies that pleasure is the only thing we ought to aim at, even if we never could be conscious of it: that our consciousness of pleasure adds nothing to its value, but that the pleasure alone, if only there were enough of it, would be just as good, even if nobody were or ever could be conscious of it. I do not know that I can present the absurdity of this conclusion in any stronger light than that in which I tried to present it last time. I can only beg you to give it your serious consideration: not to decide upon it lightly, nor until you are quite sure that you mean what you say; until you are quite sure that you would sacrifice all consciousness of pleasure, if only the pleasure itself might thereby be increased. But I do wish to answer an objection which was suggested by someone who seemed disinclined to go to such a length of paradox as this. It was suggested, that even though it would be absurd to regard pleasure, of which no-one ever could be conscious, as the only proper end of action, and that though this, in strictness, is involved in the Hedonistic principle, yet that principle might by a slight modification be altered so as to avoid this absurdity. Why, it may be asked, should not the consciousness of pleasure be held to be the only good? I admit that, if this were so, hedonistic Ethics would, roughly, and in the main be justified. All previous systems, that I know of, would indeed, by such a modification be rendered hopelessly inexact and unscientific; but still there would be more justification for them than I am inclined to admit. I wish, therefore, to give what answer I can to this objection. In the first place, then, if this view be held, some value for its own sake is allowed to consciousness. We are necessarily bound to hold that consciousness, by itself, is good as an end, although we maintain that as consciousness of pleasure, its value is indefinitely increased. From this it follows, that in case increase of pleasure should be unattainable, it would still be our duty to increase consciousness for its own sake; and that even where as is now the case, an increase of both seems possible, we should always have to consider in what proportions each ought to stand to the other; and, in some cases, it would certainly be necessary to aim at increasing consciousness alone, because a greater part of our end might be thus realised, than could be realised, if in every case we were bound to consider the effects of our action on pleasure as well as on consciousness. This consideration is very damaging to the simplicity of method, on which hedonists are wont to pride themselves. And at the same time it shews how their arguments are fallacious. For, if, as now they do, they always consider only the increase of pleasure, among the possible effects of action, then, although they always think of it as accompanied by some amount of consciousness, yet, as they do not also take into account that amount, the results will be wrong from the point of view of the end which we are now considering. For from that point of view the amount of consciousness is quite as important as the amount of pleasure, and, by merely assuring some amount of consciousness, while they consider the particular amount of pleasure only, their calculations will not obtain the right result. This then is what I meant by maintaining that their formula by itself must lead to fallacies. Granted that in that formula they do think of some consciousness, yet, by not considering its amount, they are led to false results. In order to establish their principle, they require us to include quantity of consciousness along with quantity of pleasure; but in order to deduce their results, they assume only a fixed quantity of consciousness, and gauge the value of a particular end by the quantity of pleasure only.

But, apart from this, I think it absurd to hold that consciousness of pleasure, in however great quantities both may be present can constitute the whole end. The passage I quoted from Plato's *Philebus* holds against this supposition also. For, even so, we should not be able to remember or anticipate pleasure. For that purpose we should need to be conscious of something else besides, namely of the lapse of time. And consider how blank our whole life would be. We could not be conscious of one another, nor of any external world. All that we commonly regard as a source of pleasure, the pleasures of sight and hearing, and of mutual sympathy, must be absolutely excluded from us. We should only have the pleasure which is its effect, without those things which the hedonist regards as mere means to it. And I can only ask, with Socrates, would you be willing consciously to enjoy the very greatest pleasure, on condition that you remained entirely without these other ingredients which we commonly consider as constituting our pleasures? Without even the consciousness that you were you? Must you not rather think that some of these things, at least, are parts of the end and not mere means? That what you really care for is 'pleasures' and not mere quantity of pleasure?

Well, I went on to consider Egoism and Utilitarianism. The distinctions which I made between two kinds of Egoism and between Utilitarianism and Altruism I have not now space to repeat; they will receive [it] in later lectures. But I wish to emphasize the fact that neither of them can be regarded as pure Hedonism.

Both presuppose, in their very nature, not only consciousness of pleasure, as well as pleasure, but also, as essential to the end, the distinction between me and you, between my consciousness and pleasure, and your consciousness and pleasure. Why, indeed, the greatest happiness *of the greatest number?* Would the Utilitarian not think it equally desirable, if as great a quantity of pleasure and of consciousness, could all be concentrated in a single consciousness? His words seem to imply that he would not. But, if he would, then in his formula for the end he is including something which must be a mere means; and he is so far liable to be led astray.

One more point. Suppose the utilitarian urges that though not itself the sole good, yet quantity of pleasure is a criterion of this. Then, in order to establish this, he must first find out what the sole good is, which as yet he has refused to do. And next he must prove that quantity of pleasure is always in direct proportion to the degree of this sole good. And if he can do this, of what use is his criterion? For then, *ex hypothesi*, he will know both what is the end and what will lead to it; and if he does know this, then he can deduce his rules of conduct directly without any reference to pleasure. And against the view that quantity of pleasure is even a criterion of the good, I urged one consideration last time, which I think is not without importance. It is indeed only one consideration: it cannot be decisive by itself: I was, therefore, perhaps unwise to mention it, since it is not, in this respect, on a level with my other arguments, which, if true, are all decisive. This consideration concerns intensity of pleasure. At least a part of any hedonistic argument, which wishes to escape the reproach of advocating 'swinish' pleasures, must consist in shewing that what Professor Sidgwick calls 'the most refined and subtle intellectual and emotional gratifications' are more intense, in respect of pleasure, than 'the coarser and more definite sensual enjoyments.'[2] For there certainly seems no possible means of shewing that the one kind *can* be more intense than the other: mere possibilities are too indefinite to save Utilitarianism. The question can only be of the shortest road, under actual conditions, of attaining a maximum of pleasure. And this question must largely depend, on whether, as we are actually constituted, we do get more intense pleasure from the one source than the other. Professor Sidgwick seems to consider this an open question. I admit that the answer to it will differ largely with different individuals. But I do think that, if quantity of pleasure be distinguished carefully from quantity of excitement, quantity of desire, quantity of emotion and quantity of self-approbation, with none of which is it in direct proportion; then most people would judge that sensual indulgences do produce a decidedly greater quantity of mere pleasure, than the so-called higher pleasures. If this be so, then so far that would be a reason for a consistent Utilitarianism to recommend conduct tending to increase the quantity of these lower pleasures rather than that of the higher. What other practical considerations might tend to

2. Moore's marginal notes cite "p. 128, 402" of Sidgwick's *The Methods of Ethics*. The quoted material, however, is taken exclusively from p. 128. The larger context of Sidgwick's discussion is suggested by the following: "Shall we then say that there is a measurable quality of feeling expressed by the word 'pleasure', which is independent of its relation to volition, and strictly undefinable from its simplicity?—like the quality of feeling expressed by 'sweet', of which also we are conscious in varying degrees of intensity. This seems to be the view of some writers: but, for my own part, when I reflect on the notion of pleasure—using the term in the comprehensive sense which I have adopted, to include the most refined and subtle intellectual and emotional gratifications, no less than the coarser and more definite sensual enjoyments,—the only common quality that I can find in the feelings so designated seems to be that expressed by the general term 'good' or 'desirable'." (*The Methods of Ethics*, pp. 127–28). The apparent reference to p. 402 reads as follows: "The term Pleasure is not commonly used so as to include clearly *all* kinds of consciousness which we desire to retain or reproduce: in ordinary usage it suggests too prominently the coarser and commoner kinds of such feelings; and it is difficult even for those who are trying to use it scientifically to free their minds altogether from the associations of ordinary usage, and to mean by Pleasure only Desirable Consciousness or Feeling of whatever kind."

modify this result I must leave to be discussed later. But the actual greater intensity of sensual pleasures, if it be admitted, seems by itself to establish a plausible case for Carlyle's description of Utilitarianism as 'Pig-philosophy'. When to this is added the certain truth, that utilitarians, taken at their word, must admit that our consciousness of pleasure gives us no advantage, except as a means, over the four-footed swine, the plausibility of this attack which Mill resents so gravely and Herbert Spencer so furiously, is still further heightened. In any case, I wish to close this discussion of Hedonism, by reading you the passage in question. It is certainly very amusing, and, as I am inclined to think, contains no less truth than the drier discussions of *Utilitarianism* and the *Data of Ethics*.[3]

A singular piece of scribble, in Sauerteig's hand, bearing marks of haste and almost of rage (for the words, abbreviated to the bone, tumble about as if in battle on the paper), occurs to me at this moment, entitled *Schwein'sche Weltansicht [Pig Philosophy]*; and I will try to decipher and translate it.

If the inestimable talent of Literature should, in these swift days of progress, be extended to the brute creation, having fairly taken-in all the human, so that swine and oxen could communicate to us on paper what they thought of the Universe, there might curious results, not uninstructive to some of us, ensue. Supposing swine (I mean fourfooted swine), of sensibility and superior logical parts, had attained such culture; and could, after survey and reflection, jot-down for us their notion of the Universe, and of their interests and duties there,—might it not well interest a discerning public, perhaps in unexpected ways, and give a stimulus to the languishing book-trade? The votes of all creatures, it is understood at present, ought to be had; that you may "legislate" for them with better insight. "How can you govern a thing," say many, "without first asking its vote?" Unless, indeed, you already chance to know its vote,—and even something more, namely, what you are to think of its vote; what *it*

3. Moore here makes the following citation: "Latter Day Pamphlets: VIII. Jesuitism. pp. 268–70. Rule 13." The reference is to an essay by Thomas Carlyle. The mention of "Rule 13" is ambiguous. It could mean that Moore stopped reading from Carlyle *before* he read this Rule, or that he stopped *after* he had finished reading it. The Rule is included here, along with an introductory paragraph in which Carlyle sets his satirical stage. The passage is from Thomas Carlyle's *Collected Works*, "Latter-Day Pamphlets," edited by Thomas Carlyle (London: Chapman and Hall, 1850), pp. 378–81.

wants by its vote; and, still more important, what Nature wants, which latter, at the end of the account, is the only thing that will be got!—Pig Propositions, in a rough form, are somewhat as follows:

1. The Universe, so far as sane conjecture can go, is an immeasurable Swine's-trough, consisting of solid and liquid, and of other contrasts and kinds;—especially consisting of attainable and unattainable, the latter in immensely greater quantities for most pigs.

2. Moral evil is unattainability of Pig's-wash: moral good, attainability of ditto.

3. "What is Paradise, or the State of Innocence?" Paradise, called also State of Innocence, Age of Gold, and other names, *was* (according to Pigs of weak judgment) unlimited attainability of Pig's-wash; perfect fulfilment of one's wishes, so that the Pig's imagination could not outrun reality: a fable and an impossibility, as Pigs of sense now see.

4. "Define the Whole Duty of Pigs." It is the mission of universal Pighood, and the duty of all Pigs, at all times, to diminish the quantity of unattainable and increase that of attainable. All knowledge and device and effort ought to be directed thither and thither only; Pig Science, Pig Enthusiasm and Devotion have this one aim. It is the Whole Duty of Pigs.

5. Pig Poetry ought to consist of universal recognition of the excellence of Pig's-wash and ground barley, and the felicity of Pigs whose trough is in order, and who have had enough: Hrumph!

6. The Pig knows the weather; he ought to look out what kind of weather it will be.

7. "Who made the Pig?" Unknown;—perhaps the Pork-butcher?

8. "Have you Law and Justice in Pigdom?" Pigs of observation have discerned that there is, or was once supposed to be, a thing called justice. Undeniably at least there is a sentiment in Pig-nature called indignation, revenge, &c., which, if one Pig provoke another, comes out in a more or less destructive manner: hence laws are necessary, amazing quantities of laws. For quarrelling is attended with loss of blood, of life, at any rate with frightful effusion of the general stock of Hog's-wash, and ruin (temporary ruin) to large sections of the universal Swine's-trough: wherefore let justice be observed, that so quarrelling be avoided.

97

9. "What is justice?" Your own share of the general Swine's-trough, not any portion of my share.

10. "But what is 'my' share?" Ah! there in fact lies the grand difficulty; upon which Pig science, meditating this long while, can settle absolutely nothing. My share—hrumph!—my share is, on the whole, whatever I can contrive to get without being hanged or sent to the hulks. For there are gibbets, treadmills, I need not tell you, and rules which Lawyers have prescribed.

11. "Who are Lawyers?" Servants of God, appointed revealers of the oracles of God, who read-off to us from day to day what is the eternal Commandment of God in reference to the mutual claims of his creatures in this world.

12. "Where do they find that written?" In Coke upon Lyttelton.

13. "Who made Coke?" Unknown: the maker of Coke's wig is discoverable.—"What became of Coke?" Died.—"And then?" Went to the undertaker; went to the——

But we must pull up: Sauerteig's fierce humour, confounding ever farther in his haste the fourfooted with the twofooted animal, rushes into wilder and wilder forms of satirical torch-dancing, and threatens to end in a universal Rape of the Wigs, which in a person of his character looks ominous and dangerous.

It is now high time we should turn to Metaphysical Ethics. I do not know what notion you will attach to the word Metaphysical. It is perhaps most commonly used now-a-days as a term of reproach. But I do not use it in that sense. On the contrary, the doctrines which I am about to discuss are the doctrines of a class of philosophers of whom I should wish to speak, in the terms which Aristotle used of Plato and Platonists, as pre-eminently φίλοι ″ανδρες— men whose reputation is particularly dear to me. These are men, who, however rashly they may have proclaimed for truth what was only a matter of belief, have at least done an inestimable service to philosophy, in pointing out what a gross assumption it is that nothing is real but what we can touch and see and feel. It is for this reason that their ethical doctrines may be put into a class by themselves as opposed to those which I have so far been discussing. They all, in their discussion of ultimate good, make use of certain conceptions as to what may be called a super-sensible reality, where other men use only the conception of nature.

I must try to explain briefly wherein this conception of reality differs from that of nature. I will be necessary to discuss this matter much more fully, if I ever come to deal with Kant, but I hope I may be able to make the distinction clear, if not complete even now.

By nature I do mean and have meant that which is the subject-matter of the natural sciences and also of psychology. It may be said to include all that has existed, does exist, or will exist in time. The natural sciences are distinguished from psychology, in that that with which they deal has existed, does exist, or will exist in space also. But the subject-matter of both alike is marked out by this[,] that it is in time. If you will consider whether any object is of such a nature that it may be said to exist now, to have existed, or to be about to exist, then you may know that that object is a natural object, and that nothing, of which this is not true, is a natural object. Thus for instance, of our minds we should say that they did exist yesterday, that they do exist today, and probably will exist in a minute or two. We shall say that we had thoughts yesterday, which have ceased to exist now, although their effects may remain: and in so far as those thoughts did exist, they too are natural objects.

There is, indeed, I think no difficulty about the 'Objects' themselves, in the sense in which I have used the term. You will easily be able to say which of them are natural, and which (if any) are not natural. But when we begin to consider the properties of objects, then I fear the problem is more difficult. Which among the properties of natural objects, are natural properties and which are not? For I do not deny that good is a property of certain natural objects: certain of them, I think, *are* good; and yet I have said that 'good' itself is not a natural property. Well, my test for these too, also concerns their existence in time. Can we conceive of 'good' as existing *by itself* in time, and not merely as a property of some natural object? For myself, I cannot so conceive it, whereas with the greater number of properties of objects—those which I call the natural properties—their existence does seem to me to be independent of the existence of those objects. They are, in fact, rather parts of which the object is made up than mere predicates

99

which attach to it. If they were all taken away, no object would be left, not even a bare substance: for they are in themselves substantial and give to the object all the substance that it has. But this is not so with good. If indeed good were a feeling, as some would have us believe, then it would exist in time. But that is why to call it so is to commit the naturalistic fallacy. It will always remain pertinent to ask, whether the feeling itself is good; and if so, then good cannot itself be identical with any feeling.

So much then for nature and for natural properties. But the philosophers, whom I have called pre-eminently metaphysical are those who have recognised most clearly that not everything which is belongs to nature. Good does not stand alone in this respect. Take, for instance, numbers. It is quite certain that two natural objects may exist. But it is equally certain that two itself does not exist and never can. Two and two are four. But that does not mean that either two or four exist. Yet it certainly means *something*. Two *is* somehow, although it does not exist. And so with good and with many other concepts. Of *all* concepts, indeed, it is true that they *are* whether they exist or no. But there is a clear and precise distinction between those which also can and do exist in time, and those which cannot.

Well then, the metaphysical philosophers have recognised this peculiar kind of being which belongs to concepts as such; whereas English philosophers have hardly ever recognised it at all. And that, I think, is the great merit of metaphysicians. They have proved it is not true that nothing *is* but that which we can touch and see and feel, even though it may be true that nothing else exists. This, I think, is the chief significance of Plato's doctrine of Ideas, of which you all have heard. They are not ideas in the sense in which we commonly use the word. The Greek word for them is εἶδος or ἰδέα which just means 'form'. And they are what I have called concepts, something which *is* whether it exists or not, the only thing which can be known with absolute precision.

But neither Plato nor the other metaphysicians have been content with this. They have also wished to assert of certain concepts, not only that they are but that they do exist, and exist not in space and time, but in another world which is not temporal but eternal. And this other world has been called reality, as opposed to nature, which is condemned as mere appearance. The arguments for the existence of this other world, this truly real world, are too long and complicated for me to discuss them here. I can only say that none of them appear to be convincing. The most convincing appear to me to rest on the confusion of these very notions of being and existence, which metaphysics has once for all distinguished. Such is the ontological argument, both in the old form, which Kant refuted, and in the new form which Hegel gave to it. But though I think the metaphysicians have not proved that their real world, their Absolute, actually exists, yet I think they have proved abundantly that it is possible. There may be such a world, although I cannot say there is. And what I am now concerned with is the question: Supposing there is one, what bearing can it have on Ethics?

Now it seems to me that many metaphysical writers have committed a fallacy similar to that which I have called the naturalistic fallacy, in dealing with this question. They hold that reality must be good, and that not simply for any definite reasons they can give, but because if it were not good, it would not be reality. Thus the Stoics held that to be good, *meant* simply to live in accordance with nature. I need hardly say that by nature (φύσις) they did not mean what I have so called. They did not commit so gross a fallacy as that which I have hitherto discussed. They meant some sort of ideal world, which could not be identified with this one: something like what Plato meant when he spoke of his ideas as 'fixed in Nature'. But they did regard it as not an open question whether this ideal world was good. Their reasons for holding it existed was not that it was good, and yet they would have thought it meaningless to ask whether it was good or not. This is my chief contention against their Ethics. With regard to anything which can be defined in other ways, as Nature could with them, it can never be meaningless to ask whether or not it is also good.

And the same criticism holds of Spinoza. His first principle of Ethics was that we should try to unite ourselves by the intellectual love of God, with his Absolute Substance. Perfection he held, was merely a relative term, appropriate to finite beings. One man might be more perfect than another and therefore better. But of God the same could not be said. There could be no end outside himself since he included all that was even conceivable; hence it must be meaningless to ask whether he himself were good or bad.

Now this result like that of the Stoics, seems to rest largely on a confusion as to the meaning of end. If we take it to be the essence of end that it should be merely something conceivable as apart from what exists, as are the ends of conscious action: then indeed, if God exists and includes all that is conceivable, there can be no good outside of him, in reference to which he may be judged. But that is not the sense of end as it is used in Ethics. In Ethics it merely denotes one sort of conceivable thing, that namely which is also good; and in that case it will be as full of meaning to say that God is good, as to say that he is the *eus realis suum* or most real being.

Proof then must be given that a real world is good, even after it is proved that a real world exists. But no such proof is offered. And, even if we had it, what would be its bearing upon Ethics? 'Conform to reality' would be our maxim, as it was Spinoza's. This maxim, I admit would not be meaningless in this case, as it is in ordinary Naturalism: for reality is at least defined as something different from nature. But how can we apply it? In order to do so, it must be possible to see that certain natural objects are more like reality, or in the Hegelian phrase, 'manifest it more' than certain others. But if we can see that, then we can also see directly that they are also better for the same reasons for which we hold that reality is better than nature; and the reference to reality is thus quite useless. Or else we may hold as seems to me to be necessary, that reality cannot manifest itself more in one part of nature than another, and then we shall either be logical, and admit that we need some other guide for action, than reality—something to discriminate be-tween one natural object and another: or else we may be illogical, and, holding that whatever is is right, become fatalists: not seeing that by our omission to choose in certain matters, we are ourselves altering the course of nature as much as if we made a positive choice, and that our omission is therefore as much in need of justification as our action. Such fatalistic conclusions were actually drawn by the Stoics: they are the root of much of their asceticism. And yet there is no real reason for them in their doctrine. Either their doctrine must imply our knowledge that some things in nature are better than others, in which case that is the reason for action and omission or else it implies that nothing in this world is better than any other, and in that case, if we are to choose at all, we must find some other reason for our choice than the ideal of natural life.

The same dilemma will apply to the doctrine of modern Hegelians and to Kant. Of Kant's I shall have more to say in later lectures; but Hegel will not recur again. Hegel undoubtedly held that in the state we see morality objectified. That may be so; but if it is, what earthly use is that for Ethics? Either the state and the social duties which it brings along with it, are to be supported because they are good; and in that case we shall be able to prove they are good, as easily as we can prove first that reality is good, and then that the state is a manifestation of reality. Or else they are to be supported, merely because they are there. But in that case crime and antisocial instincts are also there, and we have an equal reason to aim at them.

And still another objection applies to the morals of self-realisation. Either we are to realise ourselves, in virtue of some metaphysical proof that ourselves are the same with all reality. But in that case the old dilemma applies: either there is no practical guidance in the maxim, or else we could prove at once that the self is good. Or else the phrase will mislead us into thinking that our self is after all not the same as all reality. And then, under cover of the pretence that we are pursuing what is real, we shall be aiming at something which is indeed a part of ourselves but which is by no means that in virtue of which our self is held to be real.

I have treated these metaphysical doctrines very briefly and I fear not very clearly. They are, I think, of greater value than may appear from what I have said. But their value, I hold, is chiefly metaphysical and not ethical. As attempts to prove that the world

103

is good, they cannot be overrated. But in Ethics it must be assumed that all things are not equally good. The metaphysical doctrine, therefore, even if it be true, must be useless for ethical purposes. I may take a future opportunity of saying more on this subject if any of you have anything to ask or to suggest.

LECTURE VI

Ethics in Relation to Conduct

In the present lecture we have again to take a great step in ethical method. My discussion hitherto has fallen under two main heads. Under the first, I tried to shew what 'good'—the adjective 'good'—*means*. This appeared to be the first point to be settled in any treatment of Ethics, that should aim at being systematic. It is necessary we should know this, should know what good means, before we can go on to consider what is good—what things or qualities or concepts are good. It is necessary we should know it for two reasons. The first reason is that 'good' is the notion upon which all Ethics depends. We cannot hope to understand what we mean, when we say that this is good or that is good, until we understand quite clearly, not only what 'this' is or 'that' is, which the natural sciences and philosophy can tell us, but also what is meant by calling them good, a matter which is reserved for Ethics only. Unless we are quite clear on this point, our ethical reasoning will be always apt to be fallacious. We shall think that we are proving that a thing is 'good', when we are really only proving that it is something else; since unless we know what 'good' means, unless we know what is meant by that notion in itself, as distinct from what is meant by any other notion, we shall not be able to tell when we are dealing with it and when we are dealing with something else, which is perhaps like it, but yet not the same. And the second reason why we should settle first of all this question 'What good means?' is a reason of method. It is this that we can never know, on what evidence an ethical proposition rests, until we know the nature of the notion which makes the proposition ethical. We cannot tell what is possible, by way of proof, in favour of one judgment that 'This or that is good', or against another judgment 'That this or that is bad', until we have recognised what the nature of such propositions must always be. In fact, it follows from the meaning of good and bad, that such propositions are all of them, in Kant's words, synthetic: they all must rest in the end, upon some proposition which must be simply accepted or rejected, which cannot be logically deduced from any other proposition. This result, which follows from our first investigation, may be otherwise expressed by saying that the fundamental principle of Ethics must be self-evident. But I am anxious that you should not misunderstand this expression. The expression 'self-evident' means properly that the proposition so-called is evident or true, *by itself* alone, that it is not an inference from some proposition other than *itself*. The expression does *not* mean that the proposition is true, because it is evident to you or me or all mankind, because in other words, it appears to us to be true. That a proposition appears to be true can never be a valid argument that true it really is. By saying that a proposition is self-evident, we mean emphatically that its appearing so to us, is not the reason why it is true: for we mean that it has absolutely no reason. It would not be a self-evident proposition, if we could say of it: I cannot think otherwise and therefore it is true. For then its evidence or proof would not lie in itself, but in something else, namely our conviction of it. That it appears true to us may indeed be the *cause* of our asserting it, or the reason why we think and say that it is true: but a reason in this sense is something utterly different from a logical reason, or reason why something is true. Moreover, it is obviously not a reason of the same thing. The *evidence* of a proposition to us is only a reason for our holding it to be true: whereas a logical reason, or reason in the sense in which self-evident propositions have no reason, is a reason why the proposition must be true, not why we hold it so to be. Again that a proposition is evident to us may not only be the reason why we do think it or affirm it, it may even be a *reason* why we ought to think it or affirm it. But a reason in this sense too is not a logical reason for the truth of the proposition, though it is a logical reason for the rightness of holding the proposition. In our common language, however, these three meanings of 'reason' are constantly confused, whenever we say 'I have a reason for thinking that true'. But it is absolutely essential, if you are to get clear notions about Ethics or, indeed, about any other, especially any philosophical study that you should distinguish them. Pray, therefore, when I talk of Intuitionistic Hedonism, do not understand me to imply that my denial that 'Pleasure is the only good' is *based* on my Intuition of its falsehood. My Intuition of its falsehood is indeed my *reason* for holding and declaring it untrue; it is indeed the only valid reason for so doing. But that is just because there is *no* logical reason for it; because there is no proper evidence or reason of its falsehood except itself alone. It is untrue, because it is untrue, and there is no other reason: but I declare it untrue, because its untruth is evident to me, and I hold that that is a sufficient reason for my opinion. You must not therefore look on Intuition, as if it were an alternative to reasoning. Nothing whatever can take the place of *reasons* for the truth of any proposition: intuition can only furnish a reason for holding any proposition to be untrue: this however it must do when any proposition is self-evident, when, in fact, there are no reasons which prove its truth.

So much, then, for the first step in our ethical method, the step which established that good is good and nothing else whatever, and that Naturalism was a fallacy. A second step was taken when we began to consider proposed self-evident principles of Ethics. In this second division, resting on our result that good means good, we began the discussion of proportions asserting that such and such a thing or quality or concept was good. Of such a kind was the principle of Intuitionistic or Ethical Hedonism—the principle that 'Pleasure alone is good'. Following the method established by our first discussion, I claimed that the untruth of this proposition was self-evident. I could do nothing to *prove* that it was untrue; I could only point out as clearly as possible what it means, and how it contradicts other propositions which appear to be equally true.

My only object in all this was, necessarily, to convince you. But even if I did convince you, that does not prove that we are right. It justifies us in *holding* that we are so; but nevertheless we may be wrong. On one thing, however, we may justly pride ourselves. It is that we have had a better chance of answering our question rightly, than Bentham or Mill or Sidgwick or others who have contradicted us. For we have *proved* that these have never even asked themselves the question which they professed to answer. They have confused it with another question: small wonder, therefore, if their answer is different to ours. We must be quite sure that the same question has been put, before we trouble ourselves at the different answers that are given to it. For all we know, the whole world would agree with us, if they could once clearly understand the question upon which we want their votes. Certain it is, that in all those cases where we found a difference of opinion, we found also that the question had *not* been clearly understood. Though, therefore, we cannot prove that we are right, yet we have reason to believe that everybody, unless he is mistaken as to what he thinks, will think the same as we. It is as with a sum in mathematics. If we find a gross and palpable error in the calculations, we are not surprised or troubled, that the person who made this mistake has reached a different result from ours. We think he will admit that his result is wrong, if his mistake is pointed out to him. For instance if a man has to add up $5 + 7 + 9$, we should not wonder that he made the result to be 34, if he started by making $5 + 7 = 25$. And so in Ethics, if we find, as we did, that 'desirable' is confused with 'desired', or that 'end' is confused with 'means', we need not be disconcerted that those who have committed these mistakes, do not agree with us. The only difference is that in Ethics, owing to the intricacy of its subject-matter, it is far more difficult to persuade any one either that he has made a mistake or that that mistake affects his result.

In the second division of my subject, therefore, I only discussed one principle, the principle of Hedonism. The dismissal of that principle, however, accounts for half, or more than half, the Ethical systems that ever have been held. Of such importance is

Pleasure in the history of Ethics. Still there are other rival systems, which we ought to notice, and I am bound myself to say what I propose to substitute for pleasure, as furnishing the fundamental principle of Ethics. Before however I proceed to treat these matters, I think it desirable to discuss the third great division of ethical enquiry. This third division is the subject of this Lecture. We shall find that its discussion throws much light even on the importance of Pleasure; and still more upon other proposed ends—virtue, for instance, which has been pleasure's great rival. The confusion of the question which we are now about to discuss, with the question of the end, which we have hitherto discussed, is, I think, largely responsible for the divergent opinions which previous ethical philosophers have expressed.

What then is this third great division? I have called this Lecture 'Ethics in relation to conduct.' And that title shews very well the *importance* of the discussion upon which we are now entering. It is a discussion that is absolutely necessary before we can determine how we ought to act. But it may be more precisely defined as a discussion of what is good as means. Just as our second division dealt with what was good as an end, so this must deal with what is good as means. That distinction is an absolutely precise one. It is as precise as the distinction between our first step and our second—between the enquiry 'what good means' and the enquiry 'what is good'. And every possible ethical question must fall under one or other of these three heads or under all at once. If you can clearly distinguish them, and keep them before your minds, you will know the method by which an answer is to be sought to any question whatever in which the terms 'good' or 'right' or 'ought' occur.

Everything that is good is good either as an end or as a means; and a means is only good according as it is a means to a good end. What is good as a means is simply what is a means to a good end; and it will hardly be denied that part of our conduct at all events is simply good as such a means, even if part is also good as an end. It is therefore essential that we should discover what is meant by a means. And this I now propose we should discuss. The word 'means', as perhaps you know, denotes originally what is in the middle. We still use the singular 'mean', in this sense, as when, in Euclid we talk of the mean between two extremes. It is an open question, whether, in the ethical sense also, we ought not to use the singular, and talk about a mean, and not as I have done, about a means. This form of the singular has been used in this century by Coleridge and by John Stuart Mill. But I am inclined to think that in both cases it was for pedantic reasons: both knew the original usage and wished to revive it. For the other usage is certainly much the commoner: so much so that it sounds strange and outlandish to ask if virtue, for instance, is a mean. Foreover to one acquainted with the history of Ethics, this would suggest the Aristotelian doctrine that virtue is essentially a mean between two extremes; and that is quite another question. But most of all do I think it desirable that 'a means' should be our singular in this ethical sense, because that usage will suggest a difference of meaning—a difference of meaning which, as I shall now try to shew you, is of the last importance.

Well, 'means' originally meant 'things in the middle'; and how does it pass from this to its present sense? The history is, I think, not uninstructive. A man may be said to have an end or aim or object, when he has in his mind the idea of something, which he desires to bring about. My end, in these lectures, for instance, or part of it, is to convince you: I have the idea of convincing you before my mind, and I desire that you should be convinced. But when I try to bring about this end, I have to perform many intervening actions: a number of steps must come *in the middle* between my desire and the realisation of its object. I must, for instance, take the trouble to write all these lectures down; a thing which I by no means desire for its own sake, but on the contrary find very irksome. And yet this and many other steps are necessary, if the object of my desire is to be brought about: they must come *between* my purpose and its fulfilment, because it is impossible to convince a person, by simply desiring to convince him, without in any way communicating with him. It is, therefore, plain how 'means' comes to be used in contra-distinction to 'end' as the object of desire. It does denote the middle terms or actions, which must come to pass, before the end itself is brought about. It denotes the chain of events connecting the idea of the end, with the actual existence of the end.

So much, I hope, is plain; but, in order that we may go further towards defining the ethical sense of 'means', we must consider the notion of 'end'. 'End', as you are well aware, means properly the extreme or last of something. It may mean the extreme or last in any series—the end of a line for example—but the usage which is relevant for us is that in which it denotes the last or latest thing in time. Thus the end of the world denotes its latest moment; and the end of this lecture, denotes the moment when it will cease to be delivered. But we have just seen that 'end' is also used to denote the 'object of desire': in this sense the end of this lecture is to make you understand the relation between end and means; and that end may persist long after the lecture has ceased to be delivered, or, on the other hand, it may not come about until long after that time. These two meanings of 'end' are therefore obviously not the same, and it is important you should understand the relation that there is between them.

Let us consider the use where 'end' means object of desire, for that is the most complicated. The object of desire is the thing or event which is desired. End, in this sense, denotes something which is not actual, when it is desired. It is something which may or may not come to pass in the future, but which in any case is not actual at the moment of desire. I have indeed the idea of it, while I do desire it: the idea of it is actual in my mind simultaneously with my desire. But that idea is not my end. My end is that of which the idea is, and therefore something not yet actual. Suppose for instance I desire to eat an apple; I have an idea of eating the apple, and yet the apple is not yet eaten. My object is to eat it; the eating of it is my end, and yet the eating of it is nothing actual; it does not yet exist. But, suppose my desire takes effect: suppose I do eat the apple. Then my end has been realised: the eating of the apple is no longer something not actual, it is something which does actually exist, or has already ceased to be. Now was that actual eating still my end? We saw that the eating was my end, before the eating was actual; and is it still my end after the eating is over, has ceased to be actual? You see it is the same *thing* after and before. It is the eating by me of a particular apple, and that is one and the same thing, whether it has existed, does exist, or will exist, or whether it never has existed, does not now exist, and never will exist. The fact that I desire it seems to make us call it an end; and yet this fact seems to make no difference whatever to what it is in itself: anything whatever may be an end in this sense, and whatever it is, it is the same whether it be an end or not.

Well, I think this analysis shews us one reason why the object of desire has been called 'an end'. It is in fact that the realisation, the coming to pass of that object, does generally put an end to the desire: the existence of the object is actually the end of the desire. But this, we can see, is not by any means always true. As in most cases, the name points only to something which is very common, not to anything which is absolutely precise and universal. For in the first place, I may not know that the object of my desire has been realised. I may still go on desiring it, although it is actually there; and thus, from ignorance, the realisation of its object is often not the end of a desire. And, in the second place, an end may be put to my desire by other things than the realisation of its object: I may see for instance that it is foolish to expect it will be realised, or my attention may be engaged by something else and I may forget it altogether. If, therefore, we want a precise definition for 'end' in this sense, we must say that it denotes anything whatever which ever stands in a definite relation to our desires— the relation of being the *object of the idea* which causes our desire. 'End' is thus to be defined merely by this relation to desire: it implies no intrinsic property whatever of the object in question, nor does it stand in any necessary relation to 'end', as that which is latest in time.

But how does this analysis bear on the relation of end to means? In a most important manner: for 'means' is not a precise correlative to 'end' as the object of desire. To mean by 'end' the object of desire is to give to 'end' a perfectly definite psychological meaning: but there is no definite and precise sense of 'means' to correspond to this. For we should, if we wished this correspondence, intend by *means*, what we *think* to be means to the realisation of our end. But merely to say this is to refute the supposition. For everybody understands the difference between what we think to be the means and what actually are such. By *'means'* we understand what actually *will* bring our end to pass; or if it has come to pass, that, which actually caused it to occur: we do not mean what the agent, at the time when he desired, his 'end' desired as means thereto. For we constantly say: 'He knew what he wanted, but he was mistaken as to the means'. The means a man meant to take are not what we mean by the *means* to his end: whereas his end does mean that which he meant to get.

What then is meant by means? I can find no meaning in it, but simply cause, or, in the plural, chain of causes. And this meaning obviously corresponds to that meaning of 'end', whereby it stands for that which is latest in time. An effect is necessarily subsequent to its cause. Everything is a cause of something and everything is also an effect. Anything whatever may therefore be an 'end' in this sense—the sense of 'effect'; and all its causes are ipso facto means to it. Every effect must also, no doubt, be a cause; every end is also a means to something else. But yet the distinction is perfectly precise. It is as precise as the distinction between before and after. Everything is an effect, because its causes have preceded it; it is a cause, because its effects will follow it. The terms are purely relative; but the relation they denote is perfectly definite and precise. A thing is an effect or end, in relation to that which precedes it; it is a cause or means, in relation to that which follows it. The thing is the same whether it be preceded or be followed; but its relation to that which precedes it is obviously different from its relation to that which follows. And there is perhaps no relation which is more definite and more easy to understand than are these two.

But though every cause must precede its effect, and every effect must follow its cause, and though this temporal relation is enough to distinguish effect from cause, yet not everything which precedes another is also that other's cause. It is indeed necessary to suppose that no single event could ever be what it is, unless the whole arrangement of the world, in the moment which preceded it, had also been what it was. But it is also necessary to suppose, that if you take any single thing or event, you will also find some other single thing or event, or at all events some *finite* combination of such, which does precede it whenever it occurs. And this is what we commonly mean by its cause; this, which is only a part of the whole state of things, which has preceded it, just as itself is only a part of the whole state of things which is simultaneous with it. The difference between these two notions, the notion of that finite group which invariably precedes any finite effect, and the notion of the sum of things which is also necessary to the occurrence of that same effect, may be easily marked by the use of the common terms 'cause' for the first and 'necessary condition' for the second. If, therefore, we adopt these terms, and then say that 'means' are nothing but 'causes', we must be understood not to include under 'means' mere necessary conditions. And this, I think, is how the word is generally used. But we shall presently find reason to extend it.

So far, however, what is our result? We have found a precise meaning for means, but one that will not accurately correspond to that precise meaning of end, in which it denotes an object of desire. 'End' we saw, in this sense denotes something, which is the same, whether it exists or not. Moreover the same thing may exist, and in one case be an end, because it happens also to have been desired, and yet in another be not an end but merely an effect. To be an end in this sense is no intrinsic property of anything: it denotes merely a definite relation to desire. Our 'end', in this sense, may be something which never will exist; it may be something utterly impossible according to the laws of nature, although *ex hypothesi* it cannot be something inconceivable. And in this case, if it be impossible according to the laws of nature, then there will be no means to it. Nothing can cause it: that is what we mean by calling it impossible; and therefore here is an end without means.

On the other hand, if it be possible, then *ex hypothesi*, some part of its complete cause must exist. But only if it is actually realised, can we say that there were really the means of realising it. Only in this case, which is frequently not fulfilled, has the end its corresponding means. And the fact that this which was realised was an end, has nothing to do with the fact that there were means to it. There must have been means to everything which happens, whether it is an end or not.

The correspondence between end and means in this sense is therefore by no means close. But we have still to take the greatest step of all; to observe that sense of 'end' in which it denotes no longer something merely relative, but an *intrinsic property* of that which is an end. Between this sense of end and means we shall find an accurate correspondence: here at last the relation becomes truly significant as something distinct from that of mere cause and effect. This is the sense in which end denotes that which is good in itself. In this sense, if a thing is an end, then it is always an end: if it is good, it is always good; and not by any means everything is an end in this sense. End no longer denotes something merely relative, it is no longer possible that a thing should suddenly become an end, simply by being desired; nor is it possible that the same thing should at one time be an end and at another not an end. Here at last we have something definitive: end is equivalent to 'rational end'.

This is the sense in which we ask 'What is the end of life?' We do not mean by that 'how will it turn out?', 'What will be its effects?', but rather how ought it to turn out, what is the use of it, what is it there *for*, what good is it? And this sense may be seen underlying its use, almost everywhere in Ethics. This is in fact its ethical use; just as its use as object of desire was psychological; and its use as effect was its one and only meaning in physics or biology. All these three are perfectly distinct. The same thing may indeed be all the three at once; but also a thing may be any of them, without being either of the others. They must not therefore be confused. It is of the utmost importance we should not suppose that because a thing is end in one of these senses, therefore it is end in both or either of the other senses too. And yet this confusion has been made in Ethics *almost invariably.*

I must plead guilty to having implied it in my language already. What did I mean by 'good as an end?' I did not mean a good that is actually desired; I did not mean a good which can be desired; I did not mean a good effect: I meant simply a good which ought to be desired; and that means simply a good which is good. What is good, *as an end,* or in other words, *if it be our object of desire,* is good whether it be our end or not; and nothing is added to the notion, when we say good as an end. The expression is useful only in contra-distinction to 'good as a means'. We use it because *the word good* is applied both to what is good in itself, and to that which is a mere means to this. But in fact, that a thing is a means to good, gives it no intrinsic property of its own. 'Good as a means' means nothing but 'a means to good'. The only intrinsic difference is in the end and not in the means. Wherefore to call a thing 'good as an end' is simply tautological. It means 'good in itself'; and everything, which is good at all, which has any intrinsic property, distinguishing it as good from other things, is 'good in itself'. What is only 'good as a means' is not good at all. To call it so is simply a concession to common usage, and can only lead to confusion in Ethics. And similarly what *is* good at all, is necessarily an end. Not an end as that which is actually desired, but as that which ought to be desired, which it is good to desire. And a thing is good to desire only because it is good in itself.

And the same confusion may be observed from another side in the use of End. The question 'What is the ultimate end?' is commonly taken as equivalent to the question 'What is the Summum Bonum?' But either these two things mean precisely the same, or there is no connection between them. For if we mean what is the world ultimately coming to; then there is no reason to believe that it is *ultimately* coming to anything whatever. So far as we can see, it must go on for ever. And the question what is the Summum Bonum is plainly a different one from this. Or if we mean what is that which I or you or most people *ultimately* desire; what is that which people always regard as the effect they want, and never as a mere means to something else they want? Then our first answer must be: Different people so desire different things; and our second answer will be: And some of these ultimate ends are good and some of them are bad. This therefore is obviously not the Summum Bonum. Thus there remains no alternative but that, if the two questions have any connection at all, the 'ultimate end' must simply mean the Summum Bonum, or that which is absolutely good; and the other meanings of 'end' are quite irrelevant.

If we take 'end' then in this sense as simply meaning 'the good' or that which is good; what are we to say of 'means'? Well, if we wish to say that everything is either good or bad, or else a 'means' to these as is commonly done in Ethics; then we must use 'means' to include not only causes proper but every kind of necessary condition; not only those which precede, but also those which accompany the end, along with every necessary consequence. This use is certainly convenient. Some word is wanted to denote in Ethics everything, so far as it is not in itself either good or bad; and means can well be made to serve for this. I have used it in this way in criticising Mill and Sidgwick, and I shall continue so to use it.

But in relation to conduct it is means as cause, whether it be also good or bad or neither, with which we are chiefly concerned. The question of conduct is how ought we to act. That is a question which constantly arises and it is the business of Ethics to answer it; not indeed, as I explained, in each absolutely particular case, but certainly in the form of general rules. And this question always involves two separate ones. In the first place, what is good? And in the second place, what will bring about this which is good, what are the means thereto? These two questions must be asked and answered separately, and both must be asked and answered in any question of conduct. For though in some cases, perhaps, the answer to the first will tell us that certain kinds of conduct themselves are good; yet even in these cases the conduct will also have effects, it will also be a means to something else, and the goodness or badness of that something else will have to be taken into account in our judgment of the conduct.

I shall consider in my eighth lecture how far conduct may be good in itself. My present business is with conduct as a means. We have I say, when we ask how ought I to act? to consider first what ought to be brought about? and next how, if at all, *can* that result be brought about? And first it is obvious that much which is good, cannot be brought about at all. We cannot make the whole world perfect by to-morrow. We have to consider, therefore, when we have decided what is good, how much of it is possible. And this consideration involves a compromise. Either we may choose, what is less good, but is more likely to be brought about; or else we may choose what is much more good, but is much less likely to be brought about. Each of these choices seems to be equally rational. We have to balance degrees of goodness against degrees of probability. And it is obvious that we can be certain of neither side.

But when we have decided this question as best we can; when we have decided what we ought to aim at: it may still be asked why should I take steps to bring this about? The answer to this question is twofold. In the first place we must answer because this ought to be; and in the second place, because you ought always to do that which is a means to what ought to be. This second principle is a principle that is absolutely necessary to give a reason for conduct. It seems to me to be self-evident; but there is no means of proving it from the first. That which ought to be certainly ought to be, and it is simply absurd to talk of any other reason why it should be. But it does not follow from this that that which will cause it, as a means to it also ought to be, though certainly no other reason can be given. If you are to give a reason for acting in one way rather than in another, you must accept the principle that that which is a means to good, ought to be done. But it may be held without a logical contradiction that no reason at all can be given: that there is no reason for doing one thing rather than another, except in so far as the action itself is good.

If, however, we accept this principle, then the method of deciding on our conduct is plain enough, but it is also plain how difficult that decision is. For we have still to consider what means will bring our end to pass; and also what, of these, are possible. Thus the consideration of means is necessary in a threefold way, before we can decide the rules of conduct. First we must decide how far the good itself is possible; we must balance its degree against the degree of probability that it will be realised. Then we must decide what are the means which lead to it; and again which of these and, how far, they are possible. And it is obvious that to answer any of these questions completely demands the completion of all the natural sciences, besides psychology and sociology. These, therefore, all are necessary to Ethics in so far as Ethics is to give rules of conduct. Ethics cannot be complete without them. But I wish to insist that it is only in this way that they are necessary. Ethics has a question of its own which none of them can answer, the question what is good. The naturalistic fallacy is committed, when they are supposed to give an answer to this question. And against that procedure no protest can be too strong. But when this question has once been answered, when Ethics has settled what is good, what is the end, then every science must be allowed full play. Then, in considering the means to the end, we have questions which only they can answer. And it is in this way that such attempts as Mr. Spencer's have their value for Ethics. His theory of the correspondence between increase of pleasure and increase of life, would, if it were true, have great importance for Ethics. Not because it can ever tell us, as he thinks it can, what ought to be, but because it can tell us what is likely to be, and because we have to take account of this in considering how we ought to act.

But what more can we say about the rules of conduct? We can answer a question about them which has certainly given much trouble in the history of Ethics. We can say that conduct ought certainly to be consistent. If you ought to do a thing at one time, it is quite certain that you ought to do the same thing under the same circumstances at another time. For in the first place the good is fixed. If it is once good, then it is always good, and nothing can make a change in this respect. But so too the means are fixed. The means of bringing the good about are merely causes, and the same cause must always have the same effect. So that if two cases of conduct are really the same, then they will always have the same effect; and if that effect was good once then so it must be always. The difficulty in this question arises merely in finding out when the *conduct* in question is the same. For conduct is a very complex thing. All the circumstances which influence the results of our action, must be included in it; and it is very rarely that we can get an exact repetition of a case, with all the elements which constitute its goodness and its badness still the same. It is impossible therefore to draw from this rule of consistency any such conclusion as Kant drew: for instance, the absoluteness of the rule 'Thou shalt not lie'. This principle that consistency is necessary gives no justification for such a table as the Ten Commandments. Yet nevertheless it is true that conduct to be good must be consistent, and this truth is one of our chief means of judging whether it be good or bad, since it alone allows us to compare one case with others.

Action, therefore, must conform to all these conditions, in order that it may be rational, in one sense of the term. It will be right and rational, if it is the best means to the best and that it is possible to attain. It will then be absolutely *right*: but it will not be absolutely good, for it may not even be good at all, since it may be a *mere* means. But it is obviously impossible for us to fulfil all these conditions; the sciences are not complete, nor do we know what the good is. If therefore we do call actions rational and right we must mean something else than this. We are apt to mean in fact that the person acted up to his lights, that he did the best he knew. We may add to this that what he did was also the best *we know*: otherwise our definition becomes obviously paradoxical. But still it can be held: we shall consider its truth in Lecture VIII. Meanwhile, we have only pointed out what conditions an action must fulfil, if it is to be rational and right in that which has been called the 'external sense'. We cannot *know* that any action is right even in this sense: but we certainly must form our opinion on this point, as I shall even in order to decide whether the action is right or rational from the point of view of motive. This, therefore, is essential to any right action whatsoever. This method and all the difficulties it involves, we must accept.

LECTURE VII

Free Will

I wish to introduce the subject of this lecture, the subject of Free Will, by explaining to you in what way it has a bearing upon Ethics. Its only importance is, in my opinion, connected with that branch of ethical enquiry, to which I introduced you last time; which I described as the third great step in ethical method. It is in considering what means there are of bringing the good to pass, that we need to settle the question of Free Will. If there be any Free Will, then it is obviously one of the causes we have to reckon with, in considering how much good is possible. Free Will will be a means to good; and it is as claiming to be such we must consider it.

I discussed last time what could be meant by 'end' and 'means'. I decided that 'end' in Ethics, must be taken to mean simply and solely what is good. It cannot, without great danger of confusion, be used also to denote that which, in psychology, it must denote, namely that of which the idea moves us to action, or that which is the object of desire. These two meanings of 'end', I showed, are utterly distinct. Whenever we speak of taking something as our end, then we are using end in the psychological sense: that which we so take may be anything whatever, it may be something very bad indeed; and it can cease to be an end, without ceasing to be the same thing as it was. But if a thing is an ethical end, if it is good in itself, then it must always be an end. It is an end, whether we take it for our psychological end or not. Its being an end is wholly independent of our choices and desires.

'Means' then was to be opposed to end in this sense. Anything whatever which is connected by natural laws with an ethical end, may be called a means to such end. Everything in the world, therefore, which is not good in itself, must be called in Ethics a mere means; and ends themselves must also in this sense be means to other ends. Everything whatever, whether it be an end or not, is therefore a means; but only certain things are also ends, and those which are not ends are *merely* means.

Now the second department of our ethical method was concerned with the inquiry, What things are ends? That inquiry we left unfinished, only attempting to dispose of the very common theory that pleasure was the only such thing, the only end in itself. We left it, for the time, in order to consider what was the ethical importance of means to good. This importance lay in this; that not everything which is an end is possible. We have, therefore, in answering the question of conduct 'What ought we to do?' to consider not only what is good, but what is possible. The necessity of this inquiry made, at one jump, the whole of Natural Science relevant to Ethics. The Sciences must help us to decide what are the different degrees of probability that various alternative goods will come to pass, and we shall have to weigh these degrees of probability against the various degrees of goodness of the ends in question, choosing for our aim either a greater good, that is proportionately less probable, or a lesser good, that is proportionately more probable. We shall, in short, have to take as our *psychological end* either a better ethical end, that is less probable, or a worse ethical end that is more probable. And when we have thus settled our psychological end, by bringing science to the aid of Ethics, I would have you note that we shall already have determined, what means we must take to reach it. For these must have already been considered, in determining the probability of our end—that end which is now both end as good, and end as aim of action—which is, in fact, simply the best possible. That right conduct consists in doing these things which have thus been found to be the means to good, will then follow from the principle of conduct—the principle that we ought to *do* that which is a means to what ought to be.

Well, then, the relevance of Free Will to Ethics is its relevance to the question what is the best possible; or we may also say to the question what is a means to the best possible. For the best possible is *an* ethical end; and it is also *the* psychological end, at which, as Ethics tells us, we ought to aim. The question of Free Will is not, therefore, essentially more important to Ethics than any question as to what are the causes of events. It seems however, to deserve a special lecture for the following reasons. The question of what events our choice is cause, what can be done *because* we will it, must enter into any estimate of conduct whatsoever, whether our ethical end be some effect within our minds or some external effect. Psychology, for this reason, has a closer connection with Ethics, than have any of the other Natural Sciences: some psychological laws must be known before any question of conduct whatsoever can be settled, whereas physical laws are relevant only to a part of such questions. But again there are special reasons why the question of Free Will should be singled out from among other psychological questions, as of greater importance for Ethics. One of these is that this question again must always enter into any question of conduct whatsoever, whereas other psychological laws are not relevant to *every* such question: will is the first link in any chain of causes constituting deliberate conduct, and though other links in the chain may vary, *it* must be always there. A second reason is that this is one of the most obscure points in psychology, just as psychology itself is more obscure than any of the natural sciences.

This question of Free Will is indeed so obscure that all psychologists are not agreed whether it is even a psychological question. They would say that psychology must assume that some mental events are caused—that it can indeed only deal with such; but nevertheless they would not be prepared to hold that all mental events must be so caused: there is room, they might say, for Free Will, for all that we psychologists can tell; we will accept its existence as a fact, if the metaphysicians can prove it to us. But finally, and this is my chief reason, we must discuss Free Will, simply because it has been so much discussed in modern Ethics. So many modern systems have thought Free Will essential, in one way or another, that I must give my reasons for the very modest place which I assign it. Many have said: If there is no Free Will, then there can be no Ethics: and they say this, it appears, for three main reasons. They may have confused Fatalism with Determinism: that is an error which I shall discuss to-day. Or they may hold that the peculiar goodness, which they find in the agent himself, in his character and disposition, as distinguished from his actions, is due to his possession of Free Will: that is a question which I shall discuss next time. Or finally they may declare that the connection between Free Will and Ethics is more fundamental still. Such is the view of Kant; and this I shall discuss *at once*. For this is a discussion which stands over from my lecture on Metaphysical Ethics: I promised to discuss it then, but had not time. I wish to discuss it now because I hope I can put my objections to Metaphysical Ethics in general, more clearly in this definite case, than perhaps I put them then. And also it is necessary that Kant's position in defence of Freedom should be demolished, before I proceed to the substance of this lecture—my arguments in favour of Determinism. For Kant holds that his view of Freedom is not inconsistent with Determinism. If that were so, in proving Determinism, I should not be disproving freedom. I shall try, therefore, at once to shew you briefly (1) that it is inconsistent with Determinism (2) that in any case it can have no bearing upon Ethics, except as means.

Kant, you may know, takes as the fundamental principle of Ethics, what he calls The Categorical Imperative. This principle is: 'Act only on that maxim whereby thou canst at the same time will that it should become a universal law'. I dare say you cannot see at once what all this means. Well, I cannot discuss it fully now: that I shall have to do next term. But what it comes to is this: Never think that you ought to do a thing, unless it is true that everybody else, in like circumstances ought to do the same. The meaning of that, I hope, is plain enough. This principle merely asserts that what is good once is good always; that you ought to act consistently. And this, as I explained last time, is a direct deduction from the principle which I regarded as the first step in Ethics: the principle that Good is good, and nothing else whatever. I can find nothing more than this in Kant's Categorical Imperative; but this, I think, is true, and most important.

But what, you may well ask, has this to do with Freedom? Kant thinks the connection is as follows. This principle, you see, asserts that something ought to be done; though it does not tell us what. Now Kant thinks it would be absurd, if not untrue, to tell us that we ought to do something which we couldn't do. If you ought, he says, it follows that you can. And that you ought, is certain: that is the principle of morals. Therefore it is also certain that you can. But, he admits, although you can, you don't. The moral law commands things which don't happen, and which perhaps even, will never happen. When, therefore, he says 'you can obey it', he does not mean that it is possible according to natural laws; but he does mean that you are *free* to do it. You must have a kind of freedom, in virtue of which you can do what is naturally impossible.

But Kant goes further than this. He says: If such freedom could be shewn to be impossible, then there could be no Ethics. And note what this implies: It would not, he says, be true that you ought to do a thing, if you could not do it. Freedom is, in short, the ground of the possibility of the moral law: if there is no freedom, then there is no moral law. And that, I contend, involves the metaphysical form of the naturalistic fallacy. It is only because we are free, that anything is good. That is what Kant says. And it is the naturalistic fallacy whenever you assert that anything is good for any other reason, then because it is good. Kant does here assert that something is good, not because it is good, but because we are free.

You see the fallacy here is very subtle; and for that reason it serves as an excellent example of the form it takes in metaphysicians generally—Spinoza for example. I want, if possible, to make you understand quite clearly what that form is; what is the source of the fallacy among these thinkers, who do not take the gross and unreflective view that everything that is is something 'natural'.

Let us then reconsider Kant's argument, with a view to diagnose this 'last infirmity of noble minds'. Kant starts, we have seen, by asserting the principle which is the opposite and refutation of the naturalistic argument. His Categorical Imperative amounts to the assertion that Good is good. And he also says that we know this to be true. We know that we ought to do something. But, he says, if we ought, we can. Therefore, we ought not, unless we can. Therefore the fact that we can, is the reason why we ought.

I think you will admit this reasoning is logically very plausible. You may indeed dispute the premiss that If we ought, we can: I am not just now concerned with that. What I am concerned with is the pure logic of the matter: and I think it is not so strange that a man who could appeal to such a chain of argument as this should have been misled by it into a fallacy—not so strange as that Mill should have been misled by the verbal analogy between 'desirable' and 'visible'. The mistake is much less obvious in Kant. Yet there is a mistake; and I must try to point it out.

The reasoning in question runs: If we ought, we can. Therefore we ought not, unless we can. Therefore the fact that we can is the reason why we ought. Now the second of these three propositions follows, in a sense, from the premiss. It is true that *we* ought not, unless we can, in the sense that we can have no duties, unless we exist to have them. But even this proposition is not true in the sense that we *ought* not, unless we can: something certainly ought to be, whether it exists or not; in fact when we say it ought we very generally imply that it does not exist. It is therefore true that we are under an ethical obligation, even if we do not exist; though it is not true that we can be said to have a duty. And in our third proposition, through this ambiguity in the second, the true meaning of that is dropped, and only the false meaning is retained. To say that 'The fact that we can, is the reason why we ought' implies that there is no other reason: and that is absolutely false. The fact is Kant has supposed he can assert a distinction between two kinds of reason—the *ratio cognoscendi* or reason of knowing and the *ratio essendi* or reason of being. This distinction is what he shares with other metaphysicians; with Spinoza and with Hegel. The Categorical Imperative or Moral Law he admits to be the *ratio cognoscendi* of morality and freedom equally; but he thinks it must itself have a *ratio essendi*, and this is freedom: Freedom is the *ratio essendi* of the Moral Law, although the Moral Law is the *ratio cognoscendi* of Freedom. But what is the *ratio essendi?* It is a mixture of the *ratio cognoscendi* with something very different—the notion of *cause*. In so far, then, as the *ratio essendi* means the *ratio cognoscendi,* his conclusion is obviously fallacious: he then asserts that two different things, freedom and the moral law, are each of them the *ratio cognoscendi* of the other; and that can never be true. But if he means by *ratio essendi* merely cause, then indeed it is true that you can infer from the existence of an effect, to the existence of a cause, and vice versa, with equal certainty. But it is not true that Kant or any other metaphysicians have meant by *ratio essendi* merely cause. They have indeed used it in a way which can only be justified if it is a cause. But they have also ascribed to it other properties, the properties of a logical reason, which it cannot have if it is a cause. And therefore their reasoning is distinctly fallacious. They have assumed that nothing can be true, except because something else *exists*. And this is false: a logical reason must be true, whether anything exists or not; and of such a kind is the moral law. It is only true that the existence of a cause depends on the existence of its effect and vice versa; but that is just because each of them is an existent. A logical reason is not always an existent; the moral law, for instance, is not: and, not being so, it can never depend upon any existent. It can have no *ratio essendi;* it is only we who have the *ratio essendi,* and that purely in the sense of cause. Kant's fallacy was not to distinguish in his if we ought we can, that part of it, whereby it applies to what exists, from that part of it which is true, quite apart from existence. The fact is that if 'ought' implies 'can', then if anything existent 'ought', it also 'can'. You can therefore infer from the fact that any existent can, that it 'ought' and vice versa but you cannot infer that 'ought' has no meaning unless it goes with 'can'. It will be true that the same existent will be both; but it will not be true that one will not be true, unless the other is so.

So much then for Kant's attempt to make morality depend on Freedom: we have still to see whether his freedom is or is not inconsistent with determinism. Well, as I pointed out, Kant does insist that what is naturally impossible is, according to his Freedom, possible. Now what I have to say is that this is either contradictory, or else it gives no ground for asserting freedom. Possibility, so far as I can see, has just two senses, which it is most important to distinguish, but which leave room for no third. Either by possible you mean logically possible; and in this case anything whatever is possible, which is not self-contradictory. Or else by possible you mean naturally possible, possible according to natural laws; and I must try to make you understand what natural possibility may be. We might say it is just possible that this house will fall down within the next half hour. We know it either will fall down or it will not; and we know also that whether it will or not, depends on causes already in existence. What we do not know is what all those causes are. We do not know, for instance, whether there be not an anarchist coming with a bomb; and we do not know whether, if there is, there is anything that will necessarily stop him or lead to the discovery of the bomb. We can therefore name certain causes which would infallibly lead to an explosion of the Settlement; but we cannot be certain whether those causes do exist or not. Now anything, where this is the case, is naturally possible. It is possible because certain of the conditions necessary for its happening do exist: as for instance that this house is standing, which it must be if it is to fall. And it is possible because certain causes, if they do exist, will certainly produce its fall. But when the next half hour has passed, then, if the settlement has not fallen in, it will no longer be naturally possible that it should have fallen in. We can indeed say that it is possible certain events did happen in the past; but that is only when we do not know whether they did happen or not, and because we do know of certain effects which, along with others we do not know, would certainly have been results of that event. But, if the event is known to have happened, then there is no longer question of a possibility that it should not have happened: if it happened, it happened necessarily. We can indeed say 'it was possible that it should not have happened' meaning 'we do not know what were the causes which made it necessary': but we cannot say 'it is possible that it should not have happened' because we do know that it was necessary. We can, moreover, isolate any chain of past events, and say of them 'it is possible that this should have happened so': but then we mean mere logical possibility; we mean that that chain of events does not contain any internal contradiction against natural laws; we must hold at the same time, that if it did happen otherwise, then it was necessary, and necessary because of some external cause, which we have not included in our chain.

Well, then, when Kant says of any past event, that it was possible, although it did not happen; and of any future event, that it is possible, although it will not happen; and both these things he does say: he cannot consistently mean that there was any cause, sufficient by itself to result in that event, nor yet, that, in the future there will be such a cause. And yet by Freedom he does mean such a cause. He can only consistently mean that the event is logically possible: and in that case there is no reason to ascribe it to a cause. When he does ascribe it to a cause, then he is confusing, as we saw he did above, *cause* with *reason*. Logical possibility depends only on a *reason*: a thing is logically possible, merely for the reason that it is not self-contradictory. But, if a *cause* is assigned as reason for a possibility, then that implies indeed that the thing in question is not *self-contradictory*; but it implies also that it is positively consistent with something other than itself, namely its cause: and in order that it may be so consistent, the cause must be connected with it by some natural law; which Kant admits is not here the case. If, then, Freedom is a cause, then it is inconsistent with Determinism; and if it is not a cause, then it is not freedom. Kant's Pure Will, which is free, if it can exist, is not a reason for anything but must be a mere cause; but if it can not exist, then it is simply misleading to call it Will.

129

So much then for Kantian Freedom. What I have now to do is to convince you, if I can, that Determinism holds. And here the argument is Kant's.

I have spoken of the laws of nature, as determining what is naturally possible. Now some of you may doubt, whether I was justified in laying such stress on them. It is a view, too commonly held now-a-days and that chiefly by partisans of natural science, that natural laws are mere hypotheses: that it is possible they should be suspended any day. Some even hold that there are no laws at all: that we merely see what happens and describe it; that this is all that Science has to do.

Now these are rank absurdities and based, as might be supposed, upon confusion. I must try to make distinct the questions which are thus confused.

It is one thing to hold that a thing must have a cause; and it is quite another thing to hold that we know what its cause is. Now natural laws consist of statements that such a thing is the cause of such another thing. They do imply then that we know what a thing's cause is. And in this they may always be mistaken. There is always some probability that they have not hit the thing precisely, which is the cause; and in this sense they cannot claim to be quite certain. But what is certain, is that, if they are true, then they are necessary: if true in one case, then always true. For this conclusion hangs on the utterly different principle, that every event must have a cause. And by a cause we mean some particular thing, which always must precede it whenever it occurs. That everything must have some other thing connected with it in that manner is the principle of causality. The object of science is to discover what in each case that thing may be; and in this it may always be mistaken. But if it has once discovered truly, then it has discovered once for all: it is absolute nonsense to say that the law is hypothetical, in the sense that at some other time the thing in question may have a different cause.

That this is so is what Kant tried to prove against Hume. And I think he proved it absolutely. I must try to represent to you what the proof is. For its certainty is absolutely necessary to our ethical doctrine of means; consequently also to our doctrine of Free Will. And I will take an instance of psychological causation, such as Kant did not take, in order to obviate the possible objection that though this may be true in the world of matter, it yet is not true in the world of mind.

The proof consists in this. All those who hold that the principle of causality is not true, do yet hold that we know what happens under our inspection: that some statements with regard to such events are true. It is, therefore, sufficient we should shew that the principle of causality is as certain as the occurrence of any particular event whatever. And this is amply shewn, if we can point out that the truth of the principle is *implied* in the truth of every single event.

Let us, therefore, take some single mental event. I look into my mind and say that I have an idea of this room, and of a paper from which I seem to be reading. Those ideas are occuring in my mind. And it may be said that nothing can be more certain than this. Even if I were subject to an hallucination, and no such room or paper were really here, still it would be true that I had the ideas of room and paper in my mind. If some statements of this kind, statements about what is in my mind, are not true, then what indeed can be? Yes, but let us look into these statements. I have an idea of this paper. Yes, but now it is gone. I have still an idea of this paper, but it is not the same idea that I had a moment ago. Well, but did I really have it? I have one now, and yet not now, for that is already gone; and indeed I can never find I have it now, for no sooner do I say 'I have it now', than it is gone and some other has succeeded it. Well, then, what is it that I say is so true and so certain? Is it statements about ideas, which are in my mind now, or about those which were there just now? It may be an hallucination now, this idea I have that I had them just now. But what of that hallucination? Perhaps I had it, when I said I had it; but it is not there now; something else has succeeded it: an idea that it was or was not an hallucination, which may itself be or be not an hallucination. I never can tell which, for the moment I begin to think about it, there it is gone again, and the only idea which I do have is something different.

What are we to say then? We cannot even think what is in our minds at the moment, without implying that we know with equal certainty what was there just before. But how can we know this? We remember it, you say: and remembrance of what is *just* past, i[s] as certain as perception of what is now present. But how do I know that that which I remember *is* just past? Only certainly, if I can assume, that what is just past produces always a present effect, which is different from that produced by what is not just past. I may indeed be mistaken in any particular instance; but it is meaningless to say so, unless it was a particular instance, unless it was different from another instance and had a different cause. Here, therefore, we have a crucial example. I cannot get so far as to make any statement whatsoever, even about what is in my mind, without implying that, if that is true, then it is true that there are invariable laws of mental procedure. Even to admit that one such statement may be possibly mistaken, is to admit that others, which equally involve the causal principle, are not so mistaken. I cannot even be mistaken about what happens to me, unless the causal principle is true. And this is so in *any* instance we can take. It cannot be true that any event at all is happening, unless it is true that that event has had a cause, and not any random cause, but one particular cause, which always precedes it, whenever it may happen. We may know what the event is and yet not know what its cause was; but if it is an event at all, then we know it must have had a cause.

And now let us see how wantonly the assumption of Free Will offends against this principle. Free Will presumes to offer itself as an alternative to Determinism. Determinism is the theory that everything which we ever do or ever can do must have its cause; and this cause again its cause; and so till we come back to causes now existing. It follows then that if we knew precisely all the causes which now are in existence, and also all the natural laws which tell us what the effects of each must be; then we should be able to predict with perfect certainty, what each of us or any one, will ever do. This Kant admits in so many words. The possibility of absolute prediction follows with perfect certainty from the truth of the principle of causality. We are far enough indeed from knowing all the causes now existent, and from knowing all the natural laws which would tell us their effects. But, if we knew, then indeed there would be no question of conduct. It would be senseless to ask What ought we to do? For though the question What is good? would still be open, the question What is possible? would have disappeared. It would have been answered by the certainty: that *this* is necessary; that this is what we shall do, whether it is good or not.

All this, then, the doctrine of Free Will denies. It holds that some of our actions are such that they could not be predicted, however complete our knowledge. The will, it says, is cause of certain actions; and is itself uncaused. Something, therefore, happens sometimes, which is uncaused, although it is itself a natural cause of that which follows it. It holds, therefore, that free will is limited. It can do certain things, but not do others. No one, for instance, that I know of has maintained that if we willed it, we could at this moment jump to the moon. Though the believers in Christian Science seem to go very far in this direction. But nobody can go the whole way. No-one can believe that the power of Free Will is absolutely unlimited. Every one must admit that some one event, in any case is naturally caused. And the point I wish to make is that if one event is caused, then all must be; that if you hold Free Will, then you must contradict yourself. If there is Free Will at all, then no reason can be given why it should not be absolutely unlimited, and that it is so, no one consistently can hold.

For, if you once admit, that one kind of event is uncaused, then you must admit you cannot tell under what circumstances it will occur. For if you can tell, then you are admitting that you know the causes, of that which *ex hypothesi* is uncaused. But if you can't tell, then it may occur at any moment: absolutely everything may be an uncaused event, and to admit this is contradictory to the admission that any one event is caused. If any one event is caused then it cannot be possible that it should be uncaused; and yet, if any one event is uncaused, then it is possible that *any* event may be: and here is contradiction.

But in general the supporters of Free Will do not attack this argument. They rely on what they would call their positive argument that Free Will is a fact, irrespective of whether it is contradictory to any other fact or not. This positive argument is their consciousness that they *can* choose to do what is right, when any question what they are to do arises.

Now let us consider of what they thus profess to be conscious. They are conscious, they say, that they can choose to do a certain action. Now do they mean by that, that if they choose, then they *will* do it? Hardly this, for though they have chosen, they may be prevented from carrying out their choice by external force for instance. They may be shot, before the thing is done. But, then, they can mean only that they know that they can choose. Well, what have we to say to that? If I have an idea before my mind, it is generally possible that I should choose it. But what if I forget it, before I have chosen, as very often happens? Can I choose it then? I think we must admit I can't. And moreover, can I choose a thing, which never even occurs to me? I cannot certainly till it occurs to me: so that in this, in the occurrence of the idea of the proposed action, we have one indispensable condition of choice. Our choice even is not absolutely free.

But suppose I have the idea before my mind. Then it is asserted I feel that I can choose it. But does that argue freedom? What do I mean by saying that I can choose it? That *I* shall be the cause of the choice if it occurs? But who am I to be the cause of choice? Will not the choice itself be equally a part of me? And is not the idea which is to be the object of my choice, also such a part? If I say then that I can choose, I mean by *I*, myself, nothing but a part of me. And, if it is only a part of me that will be cause of choice, then we have still to discover which part. And if the champion of Free Will can tell us which part, then perhaps we shall agree with him that that part of him will cause his choice. It may be a part which we already know to be a cause of similar choices, and of which indeed we also know the causes.

But the final question is, after all, what is meant by this I *can*. What is meant by saying that the choice is possible? Hardly that it is logically possible. That it is that we can admit; but that is not in opposition to our determinist contention, that what he will do can be predicted. We mean then only that it is naturally possible, possible according to natural laws. But this a choice must always be. We can never be perfectly sure that we know all the causes, which govern its occurrence, nor yet what their effects must be. It is always possible according to natural laws that such and such a choice will be made by you or me. It may be exceedingly improbable; and if it is not made then we shall know it was not possible. But beforehand we can never say that it is absolutely impossible. And the question is: Are we ever conscious of more than this? Are we ever conscious of any part about our moral choices, except that the right one is just possible, that it *may* happen? If not then this consciousness, so far from being in favour of Free Will, is dead against it. It presupposes that the reason why such and such a choice is possible, is just this that there are causes for it, but we do not know whether those causes are complete. We cannot even say that it is possible, unless we mean that it could be predicted, if only we knew more about ourselves than we do know.

And now I wish to point out how positively contrary to morality this assumption of Free Will is. It is not only absurd; it also leads to what is bad. We are all, I hope, inclined to think this in such a case as that of Christian Science. But the evil consequences are general. In proportion as the doctrine is carried to its logical consequences (fortunately it never can be that completely) in that proportion it involves the refusal to allow that one course of conduct is more improbable, less likely to be carried out than another. People will always be trying to do a certain thing which they think right, however improbable is their success, on the ground that it is possible and equally possible with that which they think less right. The holding of Free Will does certainly lead to this deplorable waste of effort. The person who holds it cannot consistently allow that one good thing is either more or less possible for him than another. He will not therefore aim at the best possible as we have defined it—at the best possible which is the only *right* aim of conduct. He will aim at the best, irrespective of its degree of probability; and thus will attain a much less quantity of good, than was attainable for him.

And then as to the bad effects that are alleged against Determinism. They all proceed from the confusion of this true scientific doctrine, with that other false ethical doctrine, that is known as Fatalism. The fatalist says I will not choose, because what will happen, will happen, whether I choose or not. But to say this is to contradict Determinism. According to Determinism, it cannot be that the same will happen, whether I choose or not. My choice must necessarily have some effect. And so indeed has the fatalist's refusal to choose. It has the effect of leading to quiescence, where a choice might have led to fruitful action. It is irrational, because it is a contradiction to Determinism, and it leads to quiescence,[1] just in so far as it does not recognise the truths which the determinist must recognise.

Determinism, however, will still be met by the argument from moral responsibility. It is commonly held that if all our bad actions were inevitable, we cannot be considered responsible for them. Such questions are asked as 'Why should I be sorry I did that? On your theory I was not responsible for it!' And again the rationality of punishment is thought to depend on responsibility: vindictive punishment seems plainly to require it; and it may even be said that it is no use to apply correction or remonstrance to any[2] plausible agent. The meaning of responsibility would seem generally to be furnished by such instances as these; and it is certainly owing to an apparent difficulty of justifying the common practices of repentance, punishment, etc., without responsibility, that most people are so loathe to surrender their belief in freedom. If,

1. There is a blank space in the text between the words "leads to" and "just in so far," so we again are left with the task of completing the sentence. Given the structure of the previous sentence ("It has the effect of leading to quiescence") and that of the one under examination ("and it leads to . . ."), I have followed Professor Andrews Reath's suggestion and inserted the word 'quiescence.'

2. There is a blank space in the text between the words "remonstrance to" and "plausible agent." The word "any" has been inserted, as this seems to convey Moore's meaning.

therefore, we can succeed in such a justification, that seems the most that can still be done towards refuting this argument.

First, then, with regard to repentance. Is it absurd to repent of an action, when I could not have done anything else? It is not absurd, in the first instance, because the action was bad. It may reasonably be maintained that sorrow is a feeling appropriate to anything that is bad whether in me or in the world: that it is a good thing in itself to feel sorrow in contemplating such things. But it may be said that this feeling is not specifically repentance; and that the reduction of our own actions to precisely the same level as any external events is just what refutes our theory, since it leaves no ground for the distinction of repentance from a proper sorrow in general. Something more is then needed for the specification of repentance. But this, I think, can easily be found. For, repentance is only felt for actions of our own *such* as we have no grounds for thinking to be inevitable. The past action towards which our repentance is directed was indeed inevitable. But it belongs to a class of actions which we have reason to think may be avoided; and our repentance is due to a combination of the feelings appropriate to such actions in general, with the sorrow that is felt for any bad action that has existed. That the action, of which we repent, belongs to a perfectly specific class, seems quite enough to account for the specification of the feeling. And repentance can also be justified by its utility. To have this feeling towards a past action of the class named, is a factor towards the prevention of the recurrence of members of the class. This would not be so, if the action was of a class seemingly inevitable. And accordingly repentance in some cases, where the person repenting wrongly supposes he can avoid actions such as he repents, of that he is likely to repeat them, sorrow for things beyond our control, has been severely reprobated by some moralists. But even here the direct judgment that sorrow is appropriate to such actions, combined with the impossibility of knowing how far they are unavoidable or like to recur, will often suffice to justify the feeling.

Similarly in the case of punishment, vindictive punishment can only be justified by the direct judgment that pain is appropriate to the person who has done certain things. Such a judgment may be mistaken, but there seems no means of proving it so. Whereas corrective punishment is justified by its utility. The difficulty felt in accepting this argument from utility seems largely to rest on the common confusion of fatalism with determinism. The fatalist is unable to see how, in general, if a thing is predetermined, it can be affected by what is done now. It is obvious, of course, that what is done now is itself part of what determines the future. But, then, what is done now is itself similarly predetermined; and it seems, therefore, absurd to say 'Do this rather than that', since, whatever you say, one or the other or neither will be done. That it is difficult clearly to think out this problem may be conceded. But, what is generally not noticed, is that the mere occurrence of the idea of an action is itself a cause, which, in conjunction with others, will produce the action—that it may always be said to have a tendency to produce it. Hence corrective punishment, as addressed to a responsible agent, differs from the punishment of a dog, in that it associates the idea of omitting a specific action with the idea of the action itself, and the former idea tends to prevent the action of the latter on its recurrence. In general, I cannot choose that it shall occur to me to choose that original choice; but if it does occur to me to choose that I should make some other choice, that occurrence will tend to produce the second choice.

LECTURE VIII

The Ethics of the Inner Life

My business to-day is to make some remarks about that special kind of goodness, which is commonly distinguished from all others as peculiarly *moral* goodness. Many people, indeed have been inclined to say that this kind of goodness by itself forms the whole subject-matter of Ethics. The Stoics, for instance, when they said that virtue, and virtue only, was truly good, seem to have meant by virtue a goodness of this kind; and a similar view appears in the doctrine of those Christian sects, who have claimed that we are saved by faith alone and not by works. Kant again, would seem to favour the same doctrine, when he says 'There is no conceivable thing in the world, nay nothing even outside the world, that could be accounted good without restriction, save only a *good will*';[1] and this, I understand, is also the main drift of a much more modern writer, a writer not unknown in England,—Dr. Martineau,[2] who holds that the essence of goodness lies only in our motives. This view, as I said, is consecrated in our common language. It is this that we imply when we talk of moral goodness, as if nothing were moral except these inner qualities of men. We imply the same, when we call a man pre-eminently 'good', not because he does great deeds or manifests great powers, but because (as we say) he

1. Moore here offers what seems to be his own translation of the opening section of the First Section of Kant's *Grundlegung zur Metaphysik der Sitten,* first published in 1785.

2. The reference is to James Martineau (1805–1900), the influential English philosopher and Unitarian. His most important works are *Types of Ethical Theory* (Oxford: Oxford University Press, 1885) and *The Seat of Authority in Religion* (London: Longmans, Green & Company, 1890).

tries to *do his duty*; The same too is implied when, we distinguish the 'wicked' from the merely 'bad'. This, finally, this emphasizing of a state of mind, as against mere actions or external objects, would seem to be the chief thing which distinguishes the Christian view of life, from the Ethics of the best Greek period, of Plato and of Aristotle.

This Christian view of Ethics is what I have called the Ethics of the Inner Life. It is difficult to find a name, which will cover all the different theories which I have just mentioned. But this, I hope, may pass. The essence of these theories appears to be in this that what they praise is something mental—something indeed not *merely* mental, but implying actual consciousness, in the narrower sense of the word. Though, therefore they do not praise everything which is inner, inner or in the mind; yet they are distinguished by the fact that they will praise nothing *outer*, nothing in external nature. Some of them, the Stoics and Kant, for instance, would seem even to dispute, whether anything that is in *space* can be so much as a means to good. To most Christians, however, this would seem paradoxical. They would allow that rewards and punishments, good houses and good food, were means to good; and yet they would deny that any such things could be good in themselves. Such we saw, seemed to be the view even of Professor Sidgwick. He, indeed, retains the distinction in question, when he distinguishes 'external' from 'internal' 'rightness'.[3] An action, he thinks, is externally right, when its external effect is a means to greatest happiness; it is internally right also only as a means; but in this case the goodness of the agent's conscious purpose is a part of

---

3. Moore refers to Sidgwick's distinction between 'internal' and 'external' rightness, citing p. 207. In fact Sidgwick does not make or discuss this distinction either here or throughout *The Methods of Ethics*. What he actually discusses is the difference between formal and material rightness, and though he uses the word 'internal' in footnote 1, on p. 207, he does not express himself in the way Moore would have us believe. In private correspondence (September 14, 1989) Professor J. B. Schneewind has suggested that "Moore just misrecollected" Sidgwick's actual language. Footnote 1 reads as follows: "I do not myself usually employ the antithesis of Form and Matter in philosophical exposition, as it appears to me open to the charge of obscurity and ambiguity. In the present case we may interpret 'formal rightness' as denoting at once a *universal* and *essential*, and a *subjective* or *internal* condition of the rightness of actions."

the means and this makes the action right *internally*. It is with those who take this 'conscious purpose', which Sidgwick regards only as an 'internal means' to good, as being in some form or other, the one and only end, that I have now to deal. I shall try to shew, that this extreme view—the view that makes such a state of mind, the *only* good—is obviously absurd, however willing we may be to allow that such a state of mind is much better than most other things.

Plato, I said, would seem to represent the contrary mode of thought. It is true he always says that the goods of the soul are far the best, if not the only, goods. And to this view of his, the exaggerated Stoic doctrine is certainly largely due. And Stoicism again had a great influence upon Christian doctrine. But nevertheless Plato seems inclined to represent the goodness of the soul as consisting merely in the contemplation of what is good and beautiful, whether in external nature, or in another soul. It is good, he says, that the soul should contemplate the good; but it is not necessary that it should also know that it is contemplating. This further refinement of internality the greater inwardness expressed by self-consciousness as opposed to single consciousness, is foreign to his thought. He does not distinguish what is *good* from what is *moral*, nor what is *bad* from what is *wicked*.

One may say, perhaps, that he regards the good, even the good of the soul *objectively*; whereas this goodness that I mean to talk of, the goodness of the inner life is something *subjective*.

But yet, with all this, you may well complain that you do not yet understand what this *internal* or *moral* goodness is. It is not all that is mental; it is not even every mental *good*: it is not, finally, even every *conscious* mental good. And there is, I think, a very good reason, why you should not understand. For, I really think it does mean nothing definite. It is impossible to define this mental good, without becoming paradoxical. It is only possible to give it a supreme value, so long as our thought is in confusion. It is this confusion which I must try to dispel. But the matter is very complicated. I can only deal with it in its general outlines; and it is very likely that I may omit to mention some particular form of this doctrine, which may commend itself to you. In such an event I can only beg you to make for yourselves the necessary application of my general principles.

Let us return to the consideration of Christian morality. It is often thought, I believe, that the essential character of this morality was anticipated in the Jewish prophets. You will all remember passages from the Old Testament, similar in their drift to the following from Hosea (6.6): 'I desired mercy, and not sacrifice; and the knowledge of God more than burnt offerings.'⁴ The very first chapter of Isaiah enlarges on this doctrine. 'I delight not in the blood of the bullocks, or of lambs, or of he-goats' (Isaiah, 1.11); and then 'Cease to do evil, learn to do well; seek judgment, relieve the oppressed, judge the fatherless, plead for the widow' (Isaiah, 1.17). And this is also certainly the teaching of the epistle of St. James, the epistle of 'works'. 'Pure religion and undefiled before God and the Father is this, To visit the fatherless and widows in their affliction, and to keep himself unspotted before the world' (James 1.27). But I would have you notice that it is just for doing no more than this that Christ *blames* the Pharisees. 'I fast twice in the week, I give tithes of all I possess', says the Pharisee in the famous parable (Luke, 18.12). The Pharisees therefore did not only offer sacrifice; they also practised mercy. It was essential with them to give alms to the poor. And thus they had already made that progress in morality which is advocated by the prophets. But Christ demands of them something more than this: 'Ye make clean' says he 'the outside of the cup and of the platter, but within they are full of extortion and excess' (Matthew, 23.25). By this, I think, we are to understand, that though their outward actions were just and orderly, yet they *desired* to be unjust and vicious. And it is a better desire, a love of what is good, for its own sake, that Christ is recommending to them. No doubt he does also repeat the exhortations of the prophets. In the immediate context of this passage, we find him saying: 'Ye pay tithe of mint and anise and cummin,

4. Moore is not consistent in how he cites his biblical references. Sometimes they are given in the margin, sometimes in the body of the text, and sometimes not at all. In what follows they are inserted in the body of the text. All are taken from the King James translation.

and have omitted the weightier matters of the law, judgment, mercy and faith: these ought ye to have done, and not to leave the other undone' (Matthew, 23.23). Christ does therefore mingle the old with the new; but I would have you notice what there is in his teaching that is quite new, what in it can not be found in the Old Testament. This new element is his praise of the inner disposition, from which good actions may proceed—of the Sermon on the Mount. The famous 'Blessings' in the fifth chapter of St. Matthew, are almost all of them concerned with a man's character, not with his outward actions[,] with what he *is* and not with what he does. And that this is the tendency of Christ's teaching is rendered indubitable by what immediately follows (21, 22). 'Ye have heard that it was said by them of old time, Thou shalt not kill; and whosoever shall kill shall be in danger of the judgment; but I say unto you, That whosoever *is angry* with his brother without a cause, shall be in danger of the judgment' (Matthew, 5.21, 22, emphasis added). And then again 'Ye have heard that it was said by them of old time, Thou shalt not commit adultery: but I say unto you, That whosoever looketh on a woman to lust after her hath committed adultery with her already in his heart' (Matthew, 5.27, 28). In these two instances, what I have been calling the inwardness of the morality is unmistakeable. We are told that to be angry without a cause is as bad as to commit murder. No example could well be stronger than this. And it is the more remarkable that the very next verses betray that confusion of thought, which is inevitable in those who advocate this kind of Morals. 'And' Christ goes on 'whosoever shall say to his brother Raca! shall be in danger of the council: but whosoever shall say, Thou fool! shall be in danger of hell fire' (Matthew, 5.22). Here is a very sudden change of front. We were told that the feeling of anger was as bad as the act of murder; and now we hear that the act of speech is worse than either! Here Christ is merely insisting on the badness of a *different kind of action*: he has already abandoned that point of view, which distinguishes him—the view that it is a man's inward feelings which constitute him good or bad. You may say, of course, that evil speaking is here condemned, because it is a sign of angry feelings.

But if it is condemned as a mere sign, surely the act of murder ought to be much more condemned? That a man should go as far as murder, is a much more trustworthy sign of angry feelings, than that he should merely use insulting language. If the angry feelings are as bad as murder, then they must be much worse than mere abuse. But here on the contrary abuse is held to be worse than they! We cannot therefore say that Christ's morality is clear and consistent. But yet it is true that he has insisted more than most on the goodness of the feelings which prompt to action; and on the worthlessness of mere actions, of whatever sort, without these feelings. The emphasizing of this view has certainly been the result of his teaching; so far as Christianity results at all from him. And it is the value of this view which we must now consider.

Well, let us examine the three steps of moral progress, which we have just been noticing. First came the belief in rites and cere-monies, as constituting moral duties; a view of morals, attacked by the Jewish prophets, still retained, along with a better view, by the Pharisees, and discarded almost completely by Christ. Then came the prophet's view that morality consists in doing good to those around us: in the performance of justice, the helping of the poor and needy, in short, in altruistic services. This is a view already recognised by the Pharisees; and just as they retained the older morality of ceremonial alongside of it, so this second view of morality, the view that was preached by the prophets and by John the Baptist, was retained by Christ and His disciples (by James, for instance as we saw), alongside of the third new view, which Christ himself had introduced. Now what are we to say of these first two views? It is obvious that in both these cases that which is recom-mended if good at all, is good only as a means—is, at best, nothing but a means to good. The Jewish ritual would seem, indeed, not even to have this value: we regard it, for the most part, as abso-lutely worthless. In respect of it the Jews were no better than their neighbours, who worshipped Baal and Moloch and Ashtaroth, with the greatest conscientiousness and punctuality. The superi-ority of the Jews lay just in this that they *also* recognised the duties of external conduct towards their neighbours, the duty of living a good life. The belief in ritual, for the most part, seems to us a mere superstition. Ritual is not in general, a means to good; in so far as it is so at all, as would be claimed, I suppose, by modern ritualists, it is so as a far more direct means to a much higher good, than are justice and benevolence. It may in fact, be a direct means to producing a good state of mind—the state of conscious worship of what in itself is good; whereas the practices of justice and benevolence are only means *directly* to happiness and comfort— things which are themselves for the most part means, necessary, perhaps, for the production of what is good in itself, but by no means always leading to it. But we shall hardly say that the superstitious practices of early nations were, in any large degree, productive of such contemplation of the good. They were on the whole inferior to justice and benevolence; they were causes of nothing very good, and can be excused only by necessity. The nations who performed and still perform them, could not have been persuaded to believe in what was a means to any great good. They could not be persuaded that justice and benevolence were such means: their belief in superstitious practices was nothing but a necessary stage in their development, necessary because of their incapability and ignorance. Their ritual and ceremonial *was* perhaps a means to good for them; it *was* a means to what little good they could attain: but for us, who can attain much more, it *is* no longer even a means; it is no longer *necessary*, because already so much more is *possible*.

But when we come to the third stage of moral teaching, the stage that is marked by Christ, what are we to say of this? I think we must say that what Christ recommends is still for the most part a mere means and not an end. There is no doubt in Him some recognition of what Plato would call 'goods of the soul'—mental states that are good in themselves, and are not merely means to something else. But Christ himself does certainly not distinguish between those mental states which are such goods, and those which are mere means. He is as inconsistent in this matter as in the matter of external and internal rightness. Just as we saw Him putting side by side the inner feeling, and the act to which it leads;

so in this case he puts side by side that which is good in itself, and that which is a means to other goods. The morals of Christianity in general seem to me certainly to emphasize those parts of our mental life, which are merely means to good. In this they differ markedly from Plato and from Aristotle, and even, though less markedly, from the Stoics. And this is why they have been so involved with the question of Free Will.

This tendency to recommend things which are mere means, appears quite plainly in the Sermon on the Mount. Christ gives some reason in each case for the goodness of the virtue which he recommends: and the reason is not that the virtue is good in itself, but that it will have a good effect. 'Blessed are the pure in heart: for they shall see God'. The inference is that you are to be pure in heart, *because* the effect of your purity will be, that you will see God. The seeing God alone is good as an end; the purity of heart is only recommended as a means thereto. And, in general, the end to be obtained is something less exalted still. 'Blessed are the merciful: for they shall obtain mercy'. To be merciful may here simply mean—to act mercifully. But if we take it, as is quite in accordance with Christ's other teaching, to mean the having of a certain kindly feeling; then here this feeling is plainly recommended, on the sole ground that its results will be an end of the same kind as could be obtained by mere external actions. And this, I think, has been the general line of Christian Ethics. It has recommended states of mind, of which the goodness lies merely in the fact that they are means to those same ends, to which justice and benevolence are also means. To have a certain disposition, for instance a liking for benevolence, is to be recommended chiefly, because, if you have it, you are likely to be more often and more benevolent, than if you do benevolent actions for any other reason. This view is actually expressed quite clearly by St. James, though there are many different inconsistencies in the immediate context. 'Faith' he says 'if it hath not works, is dead, being alone' (James, 2.17). That is to say, faith is only good as a means to works; only, if it bear fruit in works. It has no value in and by itself. But it is not necessary for my purpose that Christians should have consistently, or even ever recognised that what they praise, deserves praise only as a means. What I wish to point out is that what they praise does actually deserve praise chiefly as a means, and not as an end in itself. If it were possible, as it is certainly conceivable, that the works should be obtained as well without the faith, then the faith, if we take faith to stand for what I have called the inner life, would for the most part be utterly superfluous.

But it is to be expected that when a thing has been much praised at all, though in reality it is nothing but a means, it should come to be regarded as an end in itself. This happened with the Jewish ritual; it happened again with the Jewish almsgiving, which was first praised as better than the ritual; and it has happened again, finally, with the object of the Christian's moral approval. It has actually been held that a 'good disposition' is good in itself, and even the only good thing. This is the view we have now to consider. That a good disposition is the only thing good in itself. Such is the view of Kant: and we will try the case, in the form in which he gives it us.

I said just now that this Christian morality was closely connected with the doctrine of Free Will. In Kant this connection is particularly close and definite. In making it so close and definite, Kant seems to me to have singled out that element in Christians which is peculiarly paradoxical. He has singled out for praise, as the only end-in-itself, just that part of our mental life, which is most clearly a mere means. To take a famous instance, Kant quotes the famous command of Christ: Thou shalt love thy neighbour as thyself. This he says is a right command; it is our duty to love our neighbour as ourselves. But it is only true that we ought so to love our neighbours, if by 'Love' we understand a merely *practical* love. It is not, he says, necessary that we should have a feeling of love towards them; that which is our duty is merely to have a fixed resolution, a constant will, to do them good, whether we feel a strong desire to do them good for their sakes, or whether we do not. A desire to do them good because we love them, in the ordinary sense, is, he says, superfluous and worthless. Now I certainly do not believe that Christ meant this. I do think he meant to set a value on our mere feelings towards our fellow-men. But Kant is here emphasizing one aspect of Christ's teaching; an aspect which has shewn a great persistence in Christian civilisation, and which perhaps distinguishes it more clearly than any other trait from other civilisations. Christ is, I think, responsible for this view, owing to that confusion between means and end, which I have noticed in his teaching. Some of the inward goods he recommended were merely means to good results; others were in very truth what Plato calls the goods of the soul. But he recommended them, as if both were on the same level; and the greater practical importance of the former, has gradually led to that paradoxical distinction of them as the only goods, which we find carried to its highest pitch in this doctrine of Kant's. The other reasons which led Kant to adopt this doctrine, his conception of 'end', for example, and his absolute distinction between 'sensibility' and 'reason' I cannot discuss now. The latter especially has its roots in the fundamental principles of the Critical Philosophy. It is, I think, mistaken, and I shall discuss the mistake next term. All I can do now is to ask you to consider this doctrine, as a moral doctrine, on its own merits; to inquire whether you can really finally hold that this disposition of the will is the *only good*, or even so very great a good.

In order to put this question fairly before you—this question, to answer which is the main object of this lecture I shall now proceed to give you some sort of analysis of voluntary action. Such an analysis I had meant to give last time. It will find an even more appropriate place to-day.

I want to take an example of an action, the most perfectly virtuous we can imagine. I want to point out all the elements in such an action, to which I can assign a value; and to explain to you the degree and kind of goodness, which I would ascribe to each such element. It does not much matter, for my purpose, what the action is. Perhaps you will not think it very virtuous. I only ask you to *suppose* it so, while I point out the principles on which I think it must be judged. Those principles will also apply to any other action which you might take as the pattern of the virtuous. It is the principles with which I am concerned, and not the illustration.

Well, then, let us suppose that our model hero, has saved another man's life. Let us suppose that the man whom he has saved is peculiarly valuable: that he is both excellent in himself and capable of conferring the greatest benefits upon his kind, whether by his works in art or science, by his political reforms, or by his clear upholding of the principles of true morality. I want you to imagine such a man: a man of any kind which seems to you the most proper object of your hero-worship. And then you are to suppose that some one has saved his life. You are to consider the value of that action. You are to consider under what circumstances that action will bring the greatest credit to the hero who performs it.

Now it is obvious in the first place that he may do this action without either knowing what he does or whom the man is that he saves. He may, for instance, be hypnotised or intoxicated; may see some one struggling in the Thames; may be impelled by a pure instinct; and may succeed in saving him. Now, in this case, I do not think we should consider him so very great a hero: his merit would be about on a level with that of a Newfoundland dog, who has been trained to fetch things from the water. We should be inclined to say that it was by a mere chance that he performed an action so important. And yet the action is exceedingly important. It is, we have supposed, a means to about as much good as any human action can ever be. It has saved a life, which is supremely valuable, both in itself and as a means to further goods. We must I think admit that the action is extremely valuable and yet we certainly should not regard it as bringing much credit on the agent. It does not constitute him a hero.

But now suppose the agent does know what it is that he is doing. Suppose he is, as we should say, in the ordinary possession of his senses. He sees that some one is drowning, though he does not know who; and he jumps in and saves him, knowing that he risks perhaps his life, and at all events the catching of a very bad cold. We should certainly be inclined to allow him more merit in such a case, than if he were intoxicated. But, we must distinguish further. Suppose he knows, as well as any man can know that his own life is very valuable. Suppose he is a great man and he knows it; whereas he does not know that the drowning person is also a great man. Is it then right for him to risk his life? There is no doubt that if he does succeed, the consequences will be very good. But so they were in the drunkard's case; and we should now be in doubt whether there is more merit in this case and in that: it will even be disputed whether there is not much less; whether he did not do wrong, in preferring a doubtful good, the saving of an unknown person, to what is certainly great harm, the losing his own life, it being equally doubtful which event will actually happen.

But granting that he is right in this, that his action is really better than that of a Newfoundland dog, so far as his knowledge is concerned: yet we have still another question to consider. Suppose our hero is naturally brave; or that bravery has become with him habitual. That it is with him an easy matter to jump in and risk his life; and that not because he strongly feels the saving of the other to be preferable, but because the mere idea that there is a man drowning sets up in him a mechanical process, which leads him to jump in, but in which his conscious feelings play but little part. We should, I think, still hold him for a hero. Aristotle indeed would seem to think that the essence of virtue can be found in such an action: that virtue should be merely such a habit of doing things consciously, which in general lead to good results. But I am glad to say that a contrary view seems to me to be more prevalent. It would be commonly thought, as I think, that we can much improve on such a hero. But how do we improve him?

Well, let us suppose that courage is not with him habitual. Let us suppose that what is habitual with him is not a disposition to perform courageous actions, but a disposition to imagine to himself so strongly certain good results, that his desire for them leads him to action, despite all obstacles which it may offer. Now virtue of this sort is I think much better than that which Aristotle holds up for imitation. Our hero now feels strongly the goodness of a life that has been saved, and that is why he tries to save it. He may feel not a little distaste for the means which it is necessary to employ. He may shrink from risking his life. But his desire for the good that he imagines is so much stronger than his aversion to the risks and difficulties it involves, that nevertheless he does the action. In this I think he is much more a hero than if the action itself and not the feeling, were mechanically caused by the incident in question.

But at this level we must take into account two other elements that often will occur in voluntary action. These both concern our hero's knowledge. Suppose he knows how good the man whom he is saving is. Then I think that in proportion as that man is good, in that proportion our hero has the greater merit for feeling his goodness strongly. It is better that he should do the action, because he recognises how very good it is to save the life of such a man, than because he recognises the lesser good of saving any man whatever. This feeling, based on knowledge of a greater good, is a better cause of action; and this greater goodness, which he sees as possible, is a better motive for his action.

But the second point connected with his fuller knowledge concerns not his motive but his intention. Suppose he foresees with certainty, that if he succeeds in saving this man, yet he himself will die. That this *will* happen he can never absolutely know; but it may have the very greatest probability—a probability, much greater than that he will fail to save the man. Well, in this case, the loss of his own life will be part of his intention. This loss he will have foreseen, and will perform the action deliberately, knowing, as far as the future can be known, that it entails his death. His death, then, will be part of his intention, but not part of his motive. For we are assuming that he does not desire to die, for its own sake: that on the contrary, he both feels it good in itself, and does desire to live; only that he desires the life of the other man more strongly, and that is therefore the only motive of his action. Well what we have to consider is, how the having this intention affects the goodness of his action. This, I think, it may do in two ways. (1) Suppose that he is wrong in thinking that the other man's life is more valuable than his own. Then I think we shall hold that his action is not so good, if he intended to lose his life, as if he had not foreseen that he would lose it. We shall think that he would have been the better man, if he had realised the greater value of his own life, and if, to save it instead of the other man's, has thus become his motive. We shall condemn him more than if it had never occurred to him that he would lose his life, because he has now had the two alternatives before him, and has chosen the worse; because he has shown he has not proper feelings about what is good. But (2) Supposing he is right in feeling that his own life is more worthless than the other's, and yet that his own life is in itself a good, and a great good. Then I think we should completely applaud the man: he has done the best that was possible, knowing that it was the best, and because he knew it was the best. His action, too, will be completely right, but it will not be completely good. To be completely good, his own life as well as the other's should have been preserved. That both should be so was *ex hypothesi* impossible. We do not therefore blame the man; but we do and must blame the world. The man's action we say, was right both externally and internally. But the fact that he had the intention of doing something which in itself was bad, and the fact that that bad thing came to pass, do shew that this world is not completely good, nor yet the action which it rendered necessary.

But finally there is yet another element in some voluntary actions, of which we must take account—the element which Kant would single out for special praise. Our hero may not only feel the goodness of his end; he may not only do as lovers do, and save the man because he loves him. He may also have another feeling, the specifically moral feeling; that which is produced by the knowledge that the thing in question is good. I wish you to observe this distinction very carefully. It is one thing to have a feeling appropriate to the goodness of its object: it is one thing to love very much, that which is really good enough to deserve to be loved; this you may do without ever thinking that what you love is thus worthy to be loved: but it is quite another thing to know that a man is good, and to have the feeling excited by that knowledge. The distinction between these two, is most obvious, perhaps, from the case in which the latter occurs by itself. We often, as we say, know or feel that a thing is good, and yet feel no attraction towards it. In this case we should be said to exercise the 'moral sense'. But further, in those cases, where this perception of its goodness is the cause and only cause of a strong feeling towards the thing, when it actually does lead to such attraction, then we should be said to have a moral feeling or emotion. Now it is this, which according to Kant, alone can render an action internally right, or even right at all. Where this feeling is what leads to action, and where the goodness which excites it is the motive, there alone he would say, have we perfect virtue—a morally good man. Now it is the recognition of this element which I think peculiarly distinguishes Christian morals: it is this which Christianity served to bring into a prominence, which it never had even in Plato. Plato does not sufficiently distinguish between mere love of what is good, and that other love, the love that is due to knowledge that the thing is good. He does, I think mean both, but he lays the emphasis upon the first. Christ also, as we saw, meant both, but he lays emphasis upon the second. And it is this Christian emphasis which Kant has exaggerated into paradox.

Now let us review the various elements of goodness in an action, which we have traced in our heroic case. First of all the action may be successful, it may be a means to good: and this is undoubtedly I think a reason to commend it, as a means, though not for its own sake. But secondly the action may be due to a virtuous habit of action, such as Aristotle would commend. And why should we praise this virtuous habit? I can conceive no reason, but that it is a means and a surer means of producing many good results, than instinct or mere chance. But thirdly the action may be due to an appreciation of its good results—an appreciation varying in degree according both to the agent's knowledge of what the expected result is, and according to his susceptibility of feeling towards such result. Why are these two new elements good? The knowledge, I think, is something good in itself; and the having a proper feeling towards what is good is something much more indubitably good and better in itself. Here, therefore, I think we have got beyond mere means. We have got something, namely certain feelings of the agent, which are both a means and also an end in themselves. The occurrence of these feelings, no doubt, is equally with that of Aristotle's virtuous action, a result of habit: but the immense difference between the two lies in this, that here habit produces always something which is good in itself, whereas the Aristotelian virtue produced nothing but a means to good. And lastly the action may be due to a knowledge that a thing is good, to a perception of the moral sense. And to such perception, as knowledge, I must allow some goodness, for its own sake: in so far too, as it produces a strong feeling I would allow it more. But yet I think the value of both these elements lies chiefly in their being means. They are means to the formation of those virtuous habits, which Aristotle praises. The Christian cultivation of the moral sense has led chiefly to the formation of new habits of action. To have the habit of regarding things from a moral point of view is I think a most important means of bringing you to perform actions, which you would not otherwise perform. But when the habit of performing them has been acquired, then I think we may dispense almost entirely with the moral sense and feeling. It is a condition of progress and a safeguard, but only to a slight degree a good thing in itself. It is not a much better thing to act on principle, because you are conscious of the principle according to which such action is good, than to act so without such consciousness, because it is your habit or for any other reason. But it is very much better to act on principle, along with a sincere love for what is good. Such a love is one of the best things to which action can ever be a means. It is a very different thing from the merely moral feeling that is excited by the knowledge that the thing is good. It is that which is good about which we ought to feel strongly; not its goodness or the mere fact that it is good, distinguished from itself. And yet this latter has been elevated by Kant into the sole proper motive of action, and indeed along with the will which wills it into the only thing that is good in itself.

This extreme doctrine may I think be proved to be untrue. For let us admit that it is good to be moved to a certain action by the knowledge that that action is good. Then that motive and our will which is determined by it, cannot *ex hypothesi* be the only things that are good in themselves. For it is only because the action itself is good that its goodness can be a good motive for doing it. Unless the action was in itself better than another, then there could be no reason why the motive which leads to it should be better than the motive which leads to that other. But Kant does admit that the one motive is better than the other. He cannot therefore, without an absolute contradiction, deny that the one action in itself is also better than the other, nor hold that the motive is itself the only good thing! The motive may indeed be much better than the action; but unless the action in itself is better than other actions, that motive cannot be better than any other motive.

And again it is a frank impossibility that we should be moved to any action by the mere goodness of such action. In order that our action may take any particular direction, it is necessary that the idea of some particular direction should have a share in moving us. And we cannot act at all, without acting somehow, in some particular direction. In other words, therefore, there must be something in the action itself, something in Kant's phrase Bewegengrund ("a moving consideration")[5] which forms at least part of the motive in any possible action; hence also in any possible good action. And Kant will not admit that no good action is possible.

These two considerations seem to disprove the Kantian exaggeration of the Christian doctrine, both as a doctrine of ends and as a doctrine of means. And I think without entering into Kantian metaphysics, it will be instructive to discuss two of the reasons which led him to this view. The first is this. He alludes[6] to an old

---

5. There is a blank space in the text at this point, so we are left with the task of inferring what "Kant's phrase" might be. In private discussion Professor David Falk has suggested that the German word 'Bewegengrund,' which Kant uses to refer to "a moving (or motivating) consideration," most likely is what Moore had in mind.

6. The reference is to Kant's *Critique of Practical Reason*. See the translation by Lewis White Beck (Indianapolis: Bobbs-Merrill, 1959), pp. 27–28.

song, about a husband and wife who were always quarrelling, because each wanted to possess the same thing, which both could not possess at once.

O wundervolle Harmonie.

So it begins; translated into English doggerel

What a wonderous harmony!
What he wanteth, wanteth she.

And Kant goes on to instance the story of Francis I and the Emperor Charles V. "What my brother Charles wants" said Francis, "I want too". What they both wanted was the town of Milan. What Francis said, is, I think, a good joke, but it is so obviously nothing but a joke. Yet it seems to have misled Kant. It is obvious that for two people to have the same thing at the same time, if you mean by having a certain kind of possession, eating for instance, is quite impossible. But that does not prove, as Kant seems to think that there are no material objects whatever, the existence of which can be the motive of each of two different people. Kant seems to think that the only object which can be aimed at by us all at once, without producing quarrels, is just agreement with the moral law—which he calls something purely formal. But this is utterly untrue. Such an agreement if it can be an object to be aimed at cannot be purely formal, and many other material ends can also be pursued harmoniously.

The second reason which influenced Kant, and which I want to notice is connected with Free Will. I think he felt an objection to the theory that anything good could be a natural product. You see I have been bound to admit that what I think most good in action[,] namely the feeling of love for what is good, is after all a merely natural product, something which can be cultivated within certain limits, something which may be habitual to us. This fact would seem to many people to make against its worth. They would say with Kant: It is no merit in us to have such feelings; we are not responsible for them. They would therefore place their merit, in that for which they feel the most responsible. And this is just their momentary resolution. Of these they never know the causes. They never know whether it is possible or not that they will make a good resolution in any given case. Whereas their general disposition, their likes and dislikes, are something permanent, upon which they feel that they can calculate. These, therefore, they attribute to nature because they are so orderly. But if you look more carefully at your volitions, will you not see the same regularity there? Does any one of us think that the occurrence of the ideas upon which we may resolve, is in his own control? Does it not depend on a man's disposition and circumstances, whether the ideas of certain actions occur to him at all? It is only when they have occurred, that he feels himself free to choose them: he cannot choose that they should occur. But when they have occurred, then indeed it must seem always possible that he will act upon them. But not because he has free will. Merely because when an idea is once consciously before the mind, it is very difficult to know how much force it will exercise. That which it does exercise, will depend as we commonly recognise, partly on our disposition and our habits, but also partly on its own strength, which we cannot gauge immediately on inspection, and on other causes which we do not know. We therefore feel free with regard to these, because we do not know the rules of their procedure. But yet there must be rules, and if there are we should feel more respect for just this fact of our resolve, than for our more permanent feelings. Both alike are equally natural, and we are left simply to our unprejudiced judgment which of them is better. I think the Kantian view of merit must disappear, when once we have discussed the prejudice that the cause or its causes unexplained is therefore worthy of respect. This worship of free-will is a last relic of the savage's respect for what he does not understand.

I conclude then that the disposition to do what you think right, because you think it right is valuable as a means. The strong influence exercised by the idea that something is your duty; the way in which this idea will not let you rest until you do the thing in question: *all this* which may be described as the psychological obligation due to the idea of ethical obligation, is certainly valuable as a means. To feel this compulsion keenly is the mark of a conscientious man. But we must remember in estimating its value, that what we think in this way to be right is very apt to be wrong. And also that this feeling of compulsion, has very little value in itself, it only has, so far as in it is included something of that insight into what is good, that strong feeling of attraction towards it, which I have praised as the best of mental goods.

LECTURE IX

Practical Applications

In my last lecture I had already come to treat of the objects of our ordinary moral judgments. These are of such a complex nature that it is impossible to treat of them with such precision, as I endeavoured to bring into my earlier lectures. It is no longer possible to say of them: *This* is to be handled either so or so; there are no other alternatives. For now we have to ask the question: What, after all, is *this?* Till we have settled what it is, we cannot expect to be precise in our moral judgment of it. The fact is we are coming near to casuistry. We are treating of cases, such as do indeed frequently recur; which are therefore general enough to be included in a systematic Ethics; but which nevertheless have so many different aspects that it is difficult to decide with any certainty which aspect is predominant. And yet our moral judgment of the whole must depend upon a prior judgment of this question. It is therefore, at this stage, not possible to do more than distinguish as clearly as we can certain aspects of conduct or of character, and then to adjudge the relative values of each whether as means or ends. Thus, last time, when I spoke of Christian Morals, it must be understood that they serve only for an illustration. Whether the aspect which I distinguished in them, is really their predominant aspect, it was not my intention to decide. What I do insist on is that such a factor in conduct, as that which is called 'moral goodness', does very frequently occur, and that its value is very apt to be over-estimated. That a man should be moved to action, by his belief that the action in question is right, is certainly

159

not an uncommon case; and I think we are apt to think too highly of such a man. Christianity, I take it, has certainly tended to insist on the value of such a disposition, a disposition to act up to one's lights, whether this has or has not been its *chief* effect on moral judgments. And all that I maintain is that by insistence on the value of this disposition, our ethical views are apt to be perverted. It is, I think, of high value as a means; but by undiscriminating praise of it we are often led to think it far more of an end-in-itself than it can ever be. Even as a means I think it is generally over-estimated. The encouragement of a false feeling towards a certain motive of action I do therefore attribute to Christianity. I think that Christians are apt to have towards moral goodness or towards conscientiousness, feelings which are appropriate only to something much better than either. And to have this false feeling is I think an evil in itself, and partly even evil as a means. Moreover, in so far as it is false and common, it will mislead even ethical writers: Kant I think it has misled. I do not therefore attack Christian morals as a system; to be a system they do make no pretence, and the value they may have for practice is not much affected by the inconsistencies with which they swarm. But I do attack them as encouraging false feelings: feelings which may have had great value as a means, at the time when they were first preached, but which now, I think, have largely lost this value, while they never had that value as an end, with which they were also invested. For I must remind you that what is good as an end, is always equally good and cannot change its value; whereas the value of a thing as a means to good, may differ quite indefinitely according to the circumstances.

Well, I must continue again to-day to deal with matters which offer the same difficulties. I must try to distinguish certain elements in character and conduct, which I can represent to you only by illustrations which will never exactly fit the case. The relative values of these elements, as ends, I shall try to determine; but even this can only be done roughly. Their relative value as means it is still more hopeless to discuss exactly. This must depend upon their relative intensity, as well as on other circumstances, which will differ in every special case. But I should like it to be understood, that in talking of their value as mere means, I am talking only of their value now: that restriction will at least lessen my difficulties somewhat. I shall talk of them as means in the circumstances of modern civilisation, especially the civilisation of us here in England.

Well, first of all, I have promised to discuss a subject which is in some sort a continuation of last Thursday's lecture. I did then roughly identify 'internal goodness' with what in Christian writings is meant by 'faith'. And from this 'internal goodness', it must be understood, I am excluding those feelings, which are certainly internal or in the mind, but to which I would myself assign the very highest value as ends-in-themselves. I mean to exclude what last time I distinguished as in Plato's language, 'goods of the soul'. What I wish to consider is merely that internal state, which consists in the belief that such and such a thing is good or right, together with the feelings that may thereby be excited. If internal goodness be thus limited in meaning, then at once it is plain how much it has to do with 'faith' in the sense in which faith means belief.

But let us consider this connection much more closely. In the first place, one fact is plain, which I hardly touched on last time. Namely, that the insistence on the value of this inward state has a strong tendency to lead to Antinomianism. For it is obvious that a man's belief that such or such a thing is good may be a false one. He may have a most sincere belief that it is good to commit secret murders. And if we say that it is right to do what you think good, because you think it so, then, in so far as his belief leads him to commit murders, we shall be bound to judge his conduct right. Nay we shall judge it worse in him to abstain from secret murder, despite his conscientious conviction, than if he obeyed his conscience.

It is, I suppose, but rarely that such an extreme case as this does actually occur. But cases of the conscientious fanatic, in some form or other, are only too common. We all know how much harm may be done, in the sincere belief that it is right, and because of that belief. And if we hold Kant's view, then we must hold that the man who does it, is therein acting better than he who does the greatest good, from love of good alone. If we are to say that to do what you think good, because you think it good, is pre-eminently right, then we must not only justify but praise, the most extreme excesses of law-breaking. In order to avoid this paradox we must insist that any action to be completely right, must not only be what I or you think right but also what is really so.

But then, the question arises, suppose I cannot discover what is really right? I quite admit, for my part, that we never can be sure we have discovered it. And then the former difficulty would seem to recur. For the only guide I can have to what I ought to do, is still what I believe I ought to do. And this difficulty, I admit, cannot be entirely overcome. In great measure, however, it can be overcome, and that by the consideration whether the belief in question is a rational belief. For those who say the only test of rightness is that you should believe your action right, this escape is not similarly open. But if it be admitted that such a belief may be false, we thereby open the question how we are to know whether we should act on it or not. A rational belief is one which there are good reasons for holding; and if we insist that a man is not to act on his belief, unless it is thus rational, then, by that proviso, the dangers of Antinomianism are greatly lessened.

For now we have to ask not only: Do I believe that this is right? But also, Have I reason to believe it? And to answer this second question three considerations must be taken into the account. (1) It is plain that if one of our beliefs is inconsistent with another, then it cannot be rational to hold them both. And to have decided this will be already something. It will not, indeed, tell us which of them is true, or which it is rational to hold. But the man who recognises that he ought not to hold them both, will be less likely to act rashly on either one of them. He will be set thinking what reasons there may be for holding the one rather than the other. And these he may perhaps find under our second head. (2) This second way of determining whether your belief is rational is to consider how strongly, how intensely, you do hold it. People are apt to think that they believe a thing sufficiently to act on, when they are quite unaware how weak their belief in it is, when compared with their belief in other things. They do not know how easily they could be persuaded to abandon it. In order to discover whether it is rational they ought first to consider, how it will stand comparison in this point with their beliefs in what they see and hear. When once this comparison is instituted, it will be very hard not to lay great weight on the question whether other people do agree with us or not. We can not generally believe a thing so strongly when other people hold it to be false, as when they do agree with us about it. And in so far as we do not believe it strongly, we are the less justified in acting on it. Moreover in so far as the question before us is, whether we are to believe that a certain action is a means to certain definite results, we may justly allow great weight to the opinions of other persons, especially of experts, on the ground that their opinions are likely to be true. It is only on the question whether the effect, which they tell us will truly be produced, is a good one in itself, that we can allow no probability that they are right. On this question, the question of ends, we can I think allow no weight to their opinion, except that which it does naturally exercise, in determining the strength of our belief. And this for the following reason, which is the third we have to consider in deciding on the rationality of a belief. (3) This third consideration concerns the nature of moral beliefs in general, when by moral beliefs is meant the belief that such and such a thing is good in itself, the question what it is a means to, being utterly excluded for the time. We have to consider what can justify a belief that such or such a thing is good in and for itself, good as an end. And here at once appears the importance of the fact which I insisted on from the beginning of my lectures—the fact that these moral judgments are utterly independent of any other judgment whatsoever. We cannot assert the smallest probability, that our judgment is correct, on the ground that the doctrine of evolution is true, or that what we all desire is pleasure. The discarding of all naturalistic arguments involves this: That no decision with regard to what exists or happens, no decision as to the laws of happening, afford the slightest presumption that anything which thus exists or happens is good. The question whether it is good or not is an entirely new question: and no assertion that this or that is the tendency of human nature, or that this or that is necessary for the preservation of the state or of society, has any bearing on the moral question whatsoever. We have always still to ask is the tendency of human nature good? Is the state good? Those questions, as we saw, can never lose their meaning, as naturalistic writers would have us to believe. And they are the primary questions which Ethics has to answer. And, this being so, how, in the last resort, can we justify our answers to them? Only, as it seems to me, in the following way. We have to ask: Is it good to believe that this or that is good? And this is itself a moral question. We have to weigh the strength of our unproved belief that it is good to believe in an unproved moral judgment against that unproved moral judgment. If we do that, we have I think, the last and strongest test to which that unproved moral judgment can be submitted. It must itself be as strong as our belief that we ought not to act except upon conviction. We have to compare any particular conviction with this general conviction about the justification of convictions. Let us take an illustration. I have a conviction, let us suppose, that it is right to lie in certain circumstances. I want to test the rationality of that conviction, to find out whether I ought to act on it or not. Then I must ask: Am I convinced that it is right to act on such a conviction about which in itself I have some doubt? Our answer to this question will depend on the degree of doubt. We shall feel a doubt whether we ought to act on some convictions, about which in themselves we doubt. And according as the latter doubt is stronger than the former, we shall decide against it. We are bound, you see, to justify ourselves by some moral conviction, if we are to justify ourselves at all. The sceptically minded person may take the alternative of continuing his enquiries into moral subjects rather than acting in any other definite direction. And he can only do that rationally on the ground that to enquire seems more indubitably good to him than to act in any other way. This attitude I am quite ready to commend; I do not see that much harm can come from it: but I think there is very little danger that most of us would take this course. What I wish to insist on is that, when we have contemplated this alternative, and not till then, can we claim to be acting on a rational belief. If we have definitely rejected it, on comparison of it with the particular action we are considering, we shall have the strongest possible assurance that our belief in that particular action is rational. If, on the other hand we refuse to make this comparison, then we cannot claim that we are acting conscientiously in acting on our particular belief. Our action may indeed be externally right, but it will have but little claim to be also right internally.

Now these considerations are intended to shew that the ultimate question in deciding whether an act was conscientiously performed, is the question whether it was preceded by a conscientious intellectual enquiry. How very few actions, which claim internal rightness, can stand this test, is plain enough. There would have been but few Antinomians, had it once been plainly recognised, that moral goodness was not a mere question of belief but of rational belief, and how very hard this is to come at. In this form only, the form of rational belief, can the moral goodness, the 'faith' of Christianity be justified. It is a question not only of your feeling that such and such a thing is good, but of your feeling that this first feeling is justified, both on comparison with other feelings, and on comparison with your feeling about the need of justification. Christian faith is thus a difficult and rare virtue, not, as some have been apt to imagine, easy and universally provided.

Let us, then, finally reconsider the elements in rational belief. The ultimate and chief question about any belief is this: Is the object of it true? That I admit can never be said with certainty of any moral belief. There next arises the question: Is it good? For, if it is, then it can claim to be rational in another and subordinate sense. It is, as such, that Christian faith is praised. Well, it is plain, that this question too can not be answered with certainty, because the first one cannot. But here it is a question of degrees, and we can give certain tests by which one moral belief can be decided to be better than another. The first of these is this. Two contradictory beliefs cannot both be true. This will help us to condemn the 'faith' of many persons. A 'faith' which holds to contradictories cannot be completely 'good'. And by applying this test we can much improve our own faith. We shall probably find inconsistencies on divers points, and then it will be reasonable to suspend our judgment, to commit ourselves to neither, until we find some reason for preferring the one to other. The second great reason for holding one belief to be better than another, is that it is necessary. All beliefs, no doubt, that ever were held or ever will be held, must be, in one sense, necessary. The fact that they happen, proves that they could not have happened otherwise. But what we are here considering is what we think to be necessary, not what is so. It is no doubt also necessary that we should think necessary, what we do so think. But that we necessarily think it, is no proof that it itself is necessary. And the question is of reasons for believing that the latter is the case. The reasons in this case must chiefly be the comparison of our beliefs. If after turning over and over in our minds our different beliefs, we find that there is one which continues in unabated force, while the others grow weaker, then we have more reason to believe that that is necessary, than we have for believing that the others are so. In proportion therefore as we have done this, as we have decided on that belief which appears to us the strongest, will that belief be rational. It will be a better belief, because we shall know we can less help acting on it, whether we decide to do so or not. It will be necessary, and therefore justified as a means, whether it lead to good or not. And finally, suppose we cannot so decide whether one of our beliefs is better than another. Then we shall have to ask. Do I believe it better to give up the search, or to continue it? We must again turn these alternatives over in our mind, and if the latter seems to be the stronger, then we shall have a rational belief in the goodness of enquiry; and our continuance of it will be justified. But if we take the other alternative, and will give up the search, then two alternatives are possible. Either we may have decided that our belief in the goodness of some one particular action, is stronger than our belief in the goodness of enquiry; and then that action will be internally justified: we shall have a rational belief in the goodness of trusting to our instincts and our habits stronger than our belief in the goodness of enquiry; and then we shall be justified in trusting to our instincts. In this case we shall have a rational belief in our general procedure; but we shall not be able to claim that we have such a justification for our particular actions. We shall not be able to claim that our particular actions are internally right; we shall only be able to claim internal rightness for our decision that in them internal rightness is unnecessary. And this, I believe is the commonest case of all. This is the decision which I am most inclined to believe the best in general; but so always, be it understood, that in any particular case, the whole question may be raised again, and the strength of your belief, that that particular action is good, be weighed against the strength of your general belief in habit and in instinct.

And finally we shall justly attribute weight to the beliefs of other persons, according as we have reason to think that they have taken these precautions. In so far as we think they have considered our first question—the question whether their beliefs are inconsistent, we shall have reason to think that their opinions are actually truer than ours; and may assign to them so far the weight which we assign to the opinion of a man of science on a scientific question. But by far the greater influence which they may exert upon our own beliefs is that which is justified by the need we feel for agreeing with their opinions, right or wrong. We may safely calculate that, unless we believe a thing very strongly indeed ourselves, the fact that common sense does not agree with us, will reduce its strength below that of other beliefs, in which it does agree with us. The beliefs of other people should therefore be taken into account, when we are considering the necessity of our own. That they themselves have found their beliefs necessary will not in general be the case. And where it is the case that fact should influence us much less. It gives no shadow of presumption that their beliefs are true, and what is necessary for them will very often not be necessary for us. And finally we may attribute weight to common sense, on grounds like those on which we allowed it to our instinct: and our habits. We may believe so strongly that it is in general right, that that will justify us in acting on its maxims. On any of these three grounds our belief may be supported by its agreement with the beliefs of other men. But on just that ground on which the morality of common sense is most apt to be recommended, I think it cannot. That a certain moral opinion is the opinion of common sense is, I think, hardly any ground at all for thinking that opinion true. By this argument our beliefs cannot be justified. That common sense is likely to be right, just because it is common sense, is not to be admitted. With regard to means there is some reason in holding it is probably right. For its rightness on this point the evolution argument is strong. People who constantly made mistakes as to what was likely to happen, could not have survived. But in the matter of opinion as to what is good as an end, evolution indeed may shew that people on the whole are likely to agree. It may shew that common sense is strong. But it can never shew that common sense is right. For that purpose it must first be shewn that the course of evolution has on the whole tended to good. And then, if that be granted, it must be further shewn that the good it has attained is a large proportion of what is absolutely good. And this certainly no one need admit. That it is a large proportion of what is immediately attainable may be admitted. But to say that is to combine the question of means with that of end, to consider common opinion as to what is best possible, not simply as to what is best. On the former question we may admit great probability that common sense is right, but on the latter question, the only question we are now considering 'What is simply best?', I can see no ground for admitting any probability at all.

You will understand, I hope, what is my object in this discussion of rational belief. I have been considering it merely as a chief constituent in one particular state of mind, for which it is claimed that it is a great good. I have tried to make out under what conditions it is good to have a moral belief at all, because it has been held that to have such beliefs is the chief or only good there is. In answering this question I have of course been bound to consider ethical method in general. I claim, of course, that that is the method I have followed in these lectures, that the few beliefs on moral points which I have ventured to express, are rational beliefs. But it was not my object in the present discussion to defend my method. My object was to help myself to another rational belief on a particular ethical question—the question how far rational belief itself is good. I did condemn it last time, and do condemn it now, as little more than a means. The method by which I arrive at that conclusion, I have, by the way, exposed. And it is not, I confess, a very satisfactory method. But what I do claim is that none other is more satisfactory. Those who hold that faith or inward goodness is much better than I have made it out to be, cannot defend their view by any arguments more cogent. Any ethical view, no doubt, is a mere matter of faith, but that does not justify any one in saying that faith itself is better than other things which may likewise be objects of faith. Well, it is an object of my faith that faith itself, faith in the goodness of this or that, is but slightly an end in itself; that it is chiefly to be recommended as a means to good, and not to be much recommended even as such. That is the position for which I have been arguing.

And there is another particular ethical question, to which the same arguments may apply; the question which I have mentioned in the Syllabus, concerning religious belief. I think it will not be uninstructive to say something of this matter, if only because by another example of faith light may be thrown on my previous discussion of moral faith. I do not intend to discuss what direct arguments there may be for the truth of the objects of religious faith. If their truth can be proved, then faith in them is *ipso facto* justified. I shall not even try to shew, what seems to me quite certain, that religious doctrines can derive no more support from our every day beliefs about this world or from the systematised results of science, than these can give to moral doctrines. My arguments will only be addressed to those who are willing to admit that the facts which we believe about the world in which we live, about these lights and chairs and tables, give us no more ground for asserting even that God exists than they can give us for asserting that any one of these things is good in itself. I assume, then, that religious faith and moral faith are on a level in this one respect, that the truth of neither can possibly be proved by an inference from any scientific fact. I wish only to consider those arguments for religious faith which may be based simply on its existence (the existence of the faith, not of its objects) or on its goodness. Such arguments are, I think, quite frequently used; and I think it is plain that they are ethical arguments, that they can, therefore, properly be treated by a lecturer on Ethics.

Well, then, as to the existence of this faith, a direct faith in the super-natural, it cannot be denied that it exists. But its mere existence cannot be a complete justification for it. This you will remember was the plea, which made moral faith lend support to Antinomians. 'I believe that this is so', the Antinomian and Christian may say equally: 'and my mere belief is all I care about; I will not regard its nature or its consequences'. But it is certain that beliefs may differ very much in strength; and if religious belief is to lay claim to be rational or conscientious, then he who wishes to justify it, must subject it to that process, to which we have subjected moral faiths. He must see, if it retains its appearance of strength, when it is compared with other beliefs of his: and if it does still appear to do so, then no doubt his belief is justified by necessity—he cannot help believing it. But what I wish to point out is that on this head, moral belief has a necessary advantage over the religious. We saw that in its case, the last question we could ask was still a moral question: Is it good to believe that of which I am in doubt? Any decision, therefore, must imply some moral belief. If you decide at all, you must be deciding a moral question. So that here there would seem to be an absolute necessity for having *some* belief, though not for any particular belief. But with religious faith this is not so. Here the ultimate question is still a moral one—not therefore a question of the same kind as itself. You can without inconsistency decide against any religious belief whatever. To give it up does not involve the giving up of moral judgments. The question whether you should have religious faith is simply one among other particular moral questions. Religious faith, considered as a state of mind, must be weighed against other states of mind or external goods, both in itself and in its consequences. Particularly it is necessary to consider how far it is compatible with intellectual honesty, and which of these is the greater good. What the result of such comparison ought to be, must depend on the strength of the belief and many other circumstances. That the method I have given you is the one which ought to be applied in answering this problem, I do insist, but what the proper answer is, in one or in most cases, is quite a different question.

So much then for internal rightness and the difficulty of knowing what it is and when we have it. I wish now to turn to the consideration of external rightness. To consider particularly the views of those moralists who tell us certain rules of action, which we ought they say invariably to follow. Such for instance are the Ten Commandments. Even the best of these I hold are not without exceptions. But I shall take an instance, where the dispute is much more frequent and more serious. The supposed virtue of truth-speaking, the supposed vice of lying.

Is it always right to tell the truth? I think there is no question here as to whether this is a great good in itself. The question whether it is good or bad, must depend on its effects. These may be so much vaster for good or for evil, than any merit that may be supposed to lie in the mere utterance of truthful words. And, first of all, there occurs the well-known example, which is used I think by Plato and certainly quoted by Fichte. Supposing a madman with a sword in his hand is pursuing an innocent person. Suppose I know where the innocent person is hiding, and the madman asks me where it is. Ought I to tell him the truth or a lie? The ordinary compromise occurs to everyone. I will tell him neither. I will either evade the question, or I will give no answer at all. But I think it is plain what a shallow subterfuge this is. Suppose I do either of these things, then several things may happen. I may convince the madman that I do not know. This I suppose is what I should hope for. But in this case, have I not lied? I have certainly succeeded in conveying a false impression, and it must be obvious to everyone that this, and not the words we use, is the substance of a lie. But suppose the madman is not deceived by my silence or evasions. Then he will probably, as Fichte points out, be angry with me. He may kill me as well as the other person. Or even supposing he cannot find the other person, because I would not tell him, yet the loss of my own life may be a bad enough effect of my refusal to tell the plain truth. My life may even be of much more value than that other person's. So that I shall neither have told the truth nor yet have avoided the worst results. I shall both have dissembled and been killed.

But supposing I tell the truth quite boldly. Then one bad effect will be that he will kill the other person. But what will be the good effects? Well, say I have the approval of my own conscience. Here is certainly some good. My self-respect will help me to go on telling the truth and exercising other virtues. But yet there will remain the awkward question, Ought my conscience to approve my action? If the action was really bad, then my approval of myself will lead to my committing similar crimes in future. It will encourage me to do always what I think good; but what I think good will be sometimes right and sometimes wrong: in the most relevant case it will be wrong. So that, even if we admit that the effects on my own character are chiefly good, yet they are just as likely to be partly bad, and along with this evil there must be reckoned the death of that innocent man for which I am responsible.

But again it may be said, the effect of my truth-speaking may be to encourage that virtue in general. I may tell my friends and the madman may tell his, how openly I spoke the truth in defiance of unpleasant consequences. And here is certainly some good: for I grant that in general it has good effects to speak the truth, and the resolution of others always so to do, may be strengthened by my magnificent example. But then too it is possible that no one will ever hear of what I did. I may be too modest to speak of it myself, and the madman may forget it. Or else he may have killed me, for a joke, as soon as I have told it. I think it very doubtful whether my truth-speaking will have been a means to good in such a case as this.

But still it is another question whether I had reason to think that it would be so. I could not be expected to foresee all its consequences. I could only reckon up their probabilities, and the question may be Does probability always justify us in adhering to such a rule as this rule not to lie? I cannot think it does. For though I can reckon a certain probability that my action may be known, it well may be that it will not be approved. And then it may encourage other persons in doing likewise—in doing what themselves do not approve. Moreover if it was bad and yet is approved, then it will encourage other people to do similar bad things, and what is worse, to think them good meanwhile.

I think therefore we cannot hold that the universal rule Thou shalt not lie is always justified by its effects. It is true that when the effects of adherence to it are, as in this case, generally good, then that, for example's sake, both to ourselves and others, will justify adherence to it sometimes, even where the other effects in that particular case are bad. But this excuse will certainly not serve always. And the same strictures will apply to most other so-called virtues or vices. None of them, so far as they are mere means, like justice, charity, murder or theft, are always and without exception to be praised or blamed. We must ask first what the action is of which we speak. Whether for instance, lying is to create a false impression or to use words which do not correctly express the facts. Whether the public executioner or soldier is committing murder. And when we have thus settled on our definition of the vice or virtue, we must further try to consider whether most good will be done, if we support it now by our example, or if we aim at avoiding the other bad effects which will follow from our action in this instance.

And there is one general principle underlying all such instances which is of great importance. It is quite true that if the action is the same both in itself and its effects, then if we ought once to do it, we ought to do it always. But when we do an action, which is bad in this case, on the ground that actions, bearing the same name— actions which are in general good—will thereby be encouraged; then we assume that people will confuse our action, which is bad, with others which are good; that they will judge the action by its name or by some of its effects and not by all. And this in general may be assumed with safety. People do not distinguish when an action is really the same and when it is not. But this fact, you see, has a most damaging effect on the value of our test by consistency. For if in general people cannot tell when actions are really mutually consistent, then by telling them that they must act consistently, you will be encouraging them in doing things which they take to be consistent with other things they do but which may really be quite opposite in their effects.

And this I think is a very real danger. As soon as we begin to reflect on ethical questions, we see certain similarities between cases, which we thought to be different, and certain differences between cases, which we before held to be similar. Inasmuch therefore as we are led by the desire to be consistent, we shall be apt to reverse our former way of acting. We shall do things or omit them, because we can see or cannot see how they cohere with other of our principles. But what we see in this way is almost sure to be no test of the question whether they really do cohere or not. We shall omit some most important actions, which really are consistent with the rest, because we cannot see how they fit in to the general scheme. And conversely we shall do most harmful things, because we think we are driven to them by our principles.

For this reason my final advice for arriving at proper practical conclusions, is Do not live by theories or principles at all. Do not, as Emerson says, care, if you are inconsistent. But that not because consistency is not good; but because you are more likely really to obtain it, if you do not think about it. This view that you are more likely to hit the truth by an immediate judgment of the whole act, taken in the lump, than by spying for its agreement with your principles—this view I shall try to establish next time.

In the meantime I would wish to point out one other advantage which it has over principles—an advantage as a means. Those things of which we really see the good, which do appeal to us, are much more likely to be understood by us, than those whose goodness we merely infer. We shall both better understand the means to get them, and also shall pursue them with much greater ardour. This is the advantage which I take Egoism as doctrine of means, to have over Altruism. What directly concerns us we feel about more strongly, and can therefore attain it better; both because we are more eager for it, and because we understand its bearings. Against Altruism so far as it is based on these direct feelings, so far as it means doing good, to those in whom we already take a lively interest, I have nothing whatever to say. But if Altruism be elevated into a principle it must mean more than that, it must mean acting with some approach to universal charity; and this we shall only do because we think it right. It is Kant's 'practical love' over again.

Principle, therefore, is to be avoided both as a motive, from the internal point of view, and also as liable to lead us wrong externally. And this for the same reason in both cases. It must as principle apply to means as well as ends, and as applying to the former, must be comparatively worthless as an object of our feelings. And in external action it will lead us wrong, because questions of means are too intolerably complicated for us to hope to find the *true* principle they must fall under. But when we are considering ends alone, then these dangers do not occur. The more you think of them the better, both because in practice they cannot lead you wrong (being but rarely attainable) and because all the feelings they excite are goods in themselves; veritable goods of the soul.

LECTURE X

General Conclusions

Ladies and gentlemen, I have come to the end of this course on the Elements of Ethics. And yet I have told you scarcely anything, from which you could draw any inferences as to what you ought to do. I should, indeed, be very sorry if you did draw any such inference; I have failed in my object, if you think you can. For any answer to the practical question What ought I to do? involves, as I have pointed out not only a perfect knowledge of what would be best, if it did exist, but also a perfect answer to the question What means are there existing to bring that good about? The first of these questions, concerning knowledge of the end, cannot I think be fully answered; and the second, which involves the completion of every science, including such sciences as the psychology, both of psychologists so-called, and of those who are called novel-writers, and such sciences as sociology and anthropology, which are as yet in extreme infancy—this second question, I say, concerning means, is so obviously unanswerable now, that you would have a right to laugh at any one, who offered you an answer. The only inferences, therefore, which I would have you draw from what I have said, are these: That questions of conduct can not pretend to scientific answers; and secondly; What are the reasons why they cannot so pretend. It has been my object to shew you these two things. I shall hope you will have now some better notion as to how the study of Ethics is to be conducted. I have tried to furnish you with two or three main principles, which must be presupposed, if we are ever to get a scientific answer to any ethical question whatsoever. Ethical questions themselves are so numberless, that merely to know these principles can carry us but a little way towards answering even a few of them. But these principles are, I should claim, true; and so far it is good to know them. Moreover, I would also claim that they are a necessary framework for any scientific Ethics. And lastly I think it is no little good, that a knowledge of them should teach you to distrust any so-called system, which seems to disregard them, I do think there can be drawn from a knowledge of these principles, the inference that theories of conduct, which profess to tell you definitely what your conduct should be, are not to be believed. For this reason, if my last two lectures have seemed to give occasion for drawing inferences about your practice, I beg you to discount them. I trust I have said very little, even in them, which could give colour to any inferences you might draw; but what I *have* said in them, I hold, as I explained, to be much less precise and complete, than what I said in earlier lectures. They come much nearer to mere opinions of my own. Upon the necessity of those three great steps in ethical enquiry, which I at first explained to you, I do insist: I think that their necessity is demonstrable. But for these later lectures I have no great respect. What can be said in their defence, what can be said of rules of conduct, in the absence of scientific knowledge, I shall try to say to-day. That discussion will form one main part of the present lecture. I shall explain how near I think a man may come to laying down a general rule for conduct. But first I have to consider another question, a question which we put off for a time, when in the VIth. Lecture, we took our third great step, and plunged into the discussion of the principles of practice. This other question is the question of the End—the question falling under our second head. I shall now try to say what I have to say about it; and when I add to that my general discussion of the rules of conduct, I shall hope to have given to these lectures such completeness, as was possible, and to have left you in no doubt as to what, in the main, I meant to say in them.

First, then, as to The End or The Ideal. I have explained to you what I mean by 'end' in Ethics. I mean by it anything that is good in itself, anything that is not a mere cause or necessary condition of good. What is a mere cause or necessary condition of good things, is a mere means. It is not an end; and though what is an end, may and must in this world, also be a means, either to good or bad, yet some things may be mere means, may not be ends at all. I say 'may be'; for that anything at all is not an end, is open to some doubt. Everything, we know, *must* be a means, either to good or bad, but everything *may* also be an end: we cannot say it must be.

It *may* be for this reason. It is not a necessary presupposition of Ethics that anything whatever is either bad in itself, or even just indifferent. If anything is thus bad or just indifferent, then that thing is *ipso facto* not an end, it is not good in itself. But we can give a meaning to Ethics without supposing that there is anything not good. All that is necessary for an Ethics, and this is absolutely necessary, is that we should suppose that some things are *better* in themselves than others. Unless we do suppose this, we can give no meaning to the phrase that some things are better as mere means: unless some things are better than others in themselves, there can be nothing which we ought to do—no duty, no expediency, no prudence. But a thing, if it is a complex thing, may be better than another in two ways. It may be that some *parts* of the other are bad or indifferent in themselves; or else it may be merely that, though all its parts are positively good, yet some of them are less good than others. This latter alternative, I think, cannot be denied to be a possibility. It may be held that every difference in degree of goodness (and some such difference Ethics presupposes) depends only on a difference in degree of goodness among elements that all alike are positively good. This view, I say, is possible; it will give ground on which to base an Ethics. Nay, we may even go further than this and say that it is possible everything may be positively bad. With this view, too, we should have ground to base an Ethics, if only some of these bad things were worse than others. For then the things that were less bad, would be better than the others; and though none of them could be positively good, yet the mere fact that some were better, would give us something at which we could rationally aim.

179

But though both these views are possible, consistently with the existence of an Ethics, yet I think myself that neither of them is true. I think myself that some things, some elements or parts of things, are positively good, and that other things, some elements or parts of things are positively bad. And I believe that any one who examines what he thinks with care enough, will find he thinks with me. The one view, the view that nothing is positively bad, has indeed been held by some metaphysicians, but, as it seems to me on very insufficient reasons. It was not that they did not think some things were bad, but that they thought, in virtue of some theory, that nothing *could* be bad. But this view I need not much discuss. It is not important for my purpose. It is sufficient that those who hold it *do* admit that things are positively good, and that they *must* admit, if they deny the bad and the indifferent, that some of these good things are better than are others. The other view, the view that every thing, or element of things, is positively bad, has never, that I know of, consistently been held. And for that reason *it* does not need much discussion. I do not think that any one will hold it after careful introspection. If we are tempted to cry out that Every thing is bad, I think we shall find on examination that all we mean by this is that in every complex thing there is some element or part that is positively bad, or, at least, less good than other parts or elements. When, for instance, we say that we have nothing but a choice of evils before us, we may perhaps imply that the effects we contemplate as possible, are all *predominantly* bad; but we do not imply that there is absolutely no good in them. Moreover, we have not *always* nothing but a choice of evils; and even if we have, yet other people may not.

But even if we grant that there are things or elements of things that are bad in themselves, I think we still must hold, that those which are not bad but good may differ in degree of goodness. In judging of any complex thing, that it is better than another, we shall still be able to say of it that it is better, either because those parts which are good in it have in themselves a higher degree of goodness, or because it has less parts in it, that are positively bad.

Of any two perfectly simple elements we shall be able to say, that though both are positively good, and neither has anything what-ever that is bad within it, yet one is greatly better than the other. Thus, of two simple things, which both are ends, the one may be much more of an end than the other; and though it would be best to have them both at once, yet if we only can have one, there may be one which ought to be preferred. For instance, if it were a question of choosing between pleasure and consciousness, I should say certainly that it was better, as an end, to have them both together, but if that were impossible, then I should choose the consciousness much rather than the pleasure, because I think that it is better in itself, than is mere pleasure, of which we never can be conscious; even though such pleasure is itself a good.

So much, then, for ends in general. I do assume that some simple elements are good in themselves; and that the possibility of bringing any one of these into existence, if only one could so be brought, would be a sufficient reason for acting in one way rather than another. The possibility of realising any end whatever, at once gives us a duty; there is, if even one be possible, by means of any effort, something which we ought to do. But further of the many ends I think there are, I hold that some are better than others in themselves; and then if a better one be possible, and equally possible with the worse, it is our plain duty to aim at this one, which is better. Thus we have many different ends and many different degrees of goodness in them.

But yet there is one end which is The End, and one good thing which is The Good. It is only with reference to this, as the best of means for bringing this about, that any action can be completely rational. It is not, you see, sufficient that any action should result in some good, it must result in the most good that is possible; and in order that we may know what this good is, we must not only know what things are possible, but we must also first find out what, if it were possible, would be the greatest Good, the Summum Bonum, or the Ultimate End. This is what I have called The End, The Ideal, or The Good. It is *one*, not in the sense in which particular simple

181

ends are one, but in the sense in which a complex thing is one. It is the whole, composed of everything that is good, and of every good thing in infinite amounts.

This, then, is the Ideal—that which I have first to discuss to you to-day. The Ideal must contain everything that is good, and the very greatest amount of such things too. And it is this point of its amount that I want first to notice. From the quantitative point of view (if I may be allowed to treat under this head of quantity numerical considerations also) the Ideal may, so far as I see, be treated in three different ways. (1) There are the degrees of goodness of which I have been speaking, when I said that one simple element or quality might in itself be better than another. Now so long as each element in question is itself one and the same, the difference of goodness between them can never possibly be overcome. We shall have to have each good element in our ideal, and each of these, even in the Ideal, will still be better and worse than others. This is a conclusion which may seem strange to some: 'Your Ideal', they would say, 'is not the Best, if it includes some elements which are definitely worse than others'. I shall try to give one answer later on to this objection. But meanwhile there is some unreason in it, even from the point of view of quantity. Our adversary demands that it should be the best and nothing but the best; that is to say that it should be composed only of those good elements, which are all equally good and of the highest excellence. But, if this is so, will there not be less good in our Ideal, than might conceivably be there? We may, indeed, multiply the amount of these things of the highest excellence up to infinity; but we cannot make the excellence of each higher than it is, without changing that of which we predicate this excellence; we can only demand that each be present in infinite numbers. But, if this is all, could we not make our Ideal better, by demanding in infinite numbers each thing also, which in itself is worse than these, but still is positively good? We cannot have more than an infinity of what in itself is best, but by adding to this infinities of what in itself is worse, but still is positively good, we should seem to get a whole that is better still. I do not know what mathematical difficulties there may be, in thus comparing infinities with one another. If any one who knows them, can point them out to me, I shall be much obliged. But I trust the above argument may hold even in mathematics; and I may add that I am not always prepared to accept a mere mathematician's judgment, as to what infinity can mean. I conclude then, under this first quantitative head, that the degree of goodness of each good element, must in the Ideal remain the same; so that even there we still shall have some elements that are much better than others. And my second quantitative head is that to which I have just alluded, as liable to be confused with the degree of goodness of each simple element. (2) This second head concerns the number of specimens of each good element—the number of instances of each there are to be in the Ideal. I cannot myself avoid the conclusion, that the more of each good thing there is, the better. It is under this head I should treat all quantities, commonly so-called, both extensive and intensive. Suppose for instance it is good to be big; then certainly I should say, the bigger the better. But this I should interpret numerically. Bigness seems to be made up of so many units of extension: so too length of life, is made up of so many units of time. And what I should suppose to be meant, if it were said that bigness was good, is first of all that each unit of spatial or temporal extension was good in itself, and that, therefore, the greater number of such units there were, so much the better. And so, too, with intensive quantities. If it is good to be yellow, then it seems plausible to say: The more yellow you are, so much the better. And this I can only interpret as meaning that each existent unit of yellow is so much existent good, and that the greater the number of such existent units, so much the greater good exists. And this will apply to the instance that is most pertinent to Ethics. Pleasure, it will be admitted is an intensive quantity. Well, if we are to take Bentham's maxim, which, as I said, seems reasonable; if we are to say that, pleasure being good, the more pleasure there is, so much the better: here, too, I should say this meant that each unit of pleasure was good in itself, and that the greater *number* of such units that there was, the better it must be.—Of course, it seems also possible to take another view in all such instances—a view which appears to be contradictory to Bentham's and which may perhaps be hinted at by Aristotle, when he says that virtue is essentially a mean between two extremes. It may be held that only a certain fixed quantity of pleasure is good in itself, that more than this, occurring in one person, at one time, so far from being better, is positively bad; and that less than this is not only worse, though positively good, but actually, at once, is positively bad. But this view, I would submit, is based on a confusion—a criticism which will certainly apply to Aristotle's doctrine, whether that included this or not. For those who take it, would certainly admit, that for the same man to have this good fixed quantity of pleasure at other times, or for other men to have it at the same time, is better than if it were enjoyed but once. But to admit this is to admit my second quantitative principle—that the greater number of existent units that there are (units of any good thing) so much the better. And if this be admitted, then Bentham's rule will follow. For if it is really pleasure that we mean to praise as good, then the more pleasure, the better, at whatever time and in whatever mind. To limit our good to pleasure at this time, and in this place, is to make our good a complex good and not a simple one. We do not thereby contradict Bentham's maxim, although we may appear to. The plausibility of our view will either rest on a confusion between means and ends (and this, I think, is the case with Aristotle); we shall be thinking that for a man to have more pleasure at one time, would have the bad result of killing him, or at least of making him less fit for work: or else it rests on another principle with regard to complex ends, a principle which I shall discuss later, but which also can not contradict our present principle—the principle: That the greater the numbers of each good thing there are so much the better. Our Ideal, therefore, I would conclude under this head, must contain an infinite number of instances, of each distinguishable element that is positively good. (3) And my third head, for quantitative consideration of the Ideal, is much more simple. It is this, that the number of distinguishable elements that are good, may itself, for all we know, be infinite. There may be an infinite variety of good qualities, as distinct from an infinite number of instances of the same quality. It may be that both black and white and yellow, and so on with infinite others, may all be good in themselves, and all therefore demand a place in the ideal. Thus both pleasure and consciousness, and infinite other qualities of mind, may each be good; and this infinity is quite distinct from the consideration under our last head, that the number of minds which have each of them these very same qualities, which are for instance, each both pleased and conscious, should also be infinite.

Thus then we can say of our Ideal, in respect of its quantity (1) That the greatest quantity of goodness can only be secured to it, by addition to the number of good things that it contains. For, if we have really found out what the good thing in question is, then, though it may be better than another, yet, while it remains the same, its quantity of goodness can not be altered: we can make a better whole only by adding other things to it; and they will still be other things. (2) The Ideal must contain the greatest, i.e., an infinite number of instances of every element that is good in itself. So only can the Ideal be the Best or infinitely good. (3) It *may* contain, if there are such, an infinite number of different good elements, each of which, according to our last principle, is to be repeated in an infinite number of instances. We cannot tell that there is not an infinite number of such different elements.

These, then, we may call the formal quantitative or numerical determinations of the Ideal. And from them, alone I would have you note, it follows that we can never tell completely what the Ideal is. It involves, we have seen, an infinite number, certainly in one, and possibly also in a second, way. And an infinite number, as you probably know is inconceivable, if not absurd. For this reason some philosophers have called it a false infinite, and have raised objection to the application of any quantitative considerations in Ethics. If they could shew us, how we could say anything either of Ethics or any other matter without applying number: then, indeed, what they say might be well. But as it is, they are both inconsistent, since they must use quantitative determinations; and what they, at other times, propose to substitute for these, is at least equally absurd. I propose therefore to cling to an absurdity which I cannot avoid, rather than be both absurd and inconsistent. I dare not shrink from applying the notion of infinity to the Ideal, however false infinity may be. For if I say that it is one, then it may still contain infinite parts. And if I say it does not, then I must still say, that it contains two or three. And if I admit this, then I cannot refuse to add to those parts infinitely. I cannot see why one of what is good, should be better than two (except as a means), or two than three or any other number. On the contrary it seems to me that the larger number is always the better, other things being equal. So, at least, we seem commonly to judge. So Bentham judged of pleasure: and these philosophers themselves would, I think, shrink from maintaining that two good men were not better than one. And if two are better, then why not three? Is it 40 that are the elect, or 400, or 1066, or 4004, or 144,000? Why should any of these numbers be better than another? They may be so, indeed; but I cannot honestly say I think they are, on any other principle than that the largest is the best. I say, then, that the Ideal is one; *that*, in some sense, it must be, if it is *the* Ideal. But I cannot but say also that it contains infinite parts. That is unsatisfactory to be sure; but you will not mend matters, that I see, by saying it is finite. Wherever you may fix its limits, you will exclude some good thing that might have been within it; and that is surely worse than to include too much.

But let us turn from this discussion to something much more satisfactory. There is another formal determination of the Ideal, which has not these defects. This concerns the properties of any complex whole, which may be said to be good, as a whole. It is obvious that the Ideal, as I have just described it is such a whole. And, if I understand them rightly, some of those philosophers, who, as I said, object to the application of infinity, would seek to escape the difficulties, which are really involved in that notion, by the use of this notion of a whole instead. There has been in recent philosophical discussion, much talk of *organic* unities or wholes.

The notion of organism was much brought forward, as of philosophical importance, by Kant; the impulse to use it was encouraged by Hegel and by others; till now it has filtered through, I believe, even to the newspapers, where we find reference to the social organism and the demand that works of art should be organic wholes.

Now this notion of an organic, or even super-organic, whole rests in Kant, I do not hesitate to say, upon that confusion of 'end' as good and 'end' as effect, mediated by that third meaning of 'end' as purpose, against which I warned you in Lecture VI. And later writers have not, I think, done anything to clear up this confusion. Kant tried to make the matter clear, and in him therefore the confusion is most apparent: but later writers have withdrawn, like Vergil's goddesses, into the mist, where they refuse to answer further questions. They have enveloped themselves and their organic wholes in a luminous haze, which claims to be adored as something mystic and divine, and which at all events, if you will not adore it, makes it more easy for them to elude your grasp and serves to hide their spots and blemishes.

Well, what I have to say about organic wholes, is that in the first place they are no alternative to wholes which are mere sums: they are no higher synthesis of quantity or mechanism. And in the second place, that the notion will only apply, such as it is, to what is good—a work of art, for instance; it has no meaning at all in application to the human or the social organism. Let us consider what is said of these organic wholes. I imagine it is a fair statement, if we say that an organic whole is a whole of which all the parts are both ends in themselves and also means to one another; in which too all the parts are both ends-in-themselves and means to the whole. Whether it would be also said that the whole is not only an end in itself, but also a means to each of the parts, I do not know: but the rest is enough for my purpose. Now if in this definition of an organism, end means effect, and means means cause, then it is not wholly true of any organism in the scientific sense, and it is quite equally true of any inorganic whole: and if 'means' means mere necessary condition, then it is wholly true both of an organism like the body and of any other complex whole whatever. But if by 'end' be meant that which is good in itself, then we have first to decide whether every part of an organism is good in itself: the question becomes a merely ethical one and has no relevance either for scientific or for philosophical explanations, of what the whole in question is.

The ethical and only sense of an organic whole is this. Suppose we have a complex whole made up of various parts. That whole, as such, for scientific and philosophical purposes is a mere sum. But it may be that the parts of it are good in themselves and that the whole is also good in itself. In such a case, I think it cannot be denied that the degree of goodness of the whole is merely equal or fixed in proportion to the degrees of goodness of the various parts, if these degrees be added together. To take an instance: Pleasure may be admitted to be good in itself and so may consciousness: but the whole that is formed by both together, the whole of conscious pleasure, may, I think, be well maintained to have a higher degree of goodness, than could be obtained by merely adding the degree of goodness of pleasure by itself to the degree of goodness of consciousness by itself. And thus we have a want of equality between the goodness of the whole and the sum of the goodnesses of the parts. And that these two do not even always bear the same proportion may I think be seen in another instance. Suppose we take mere belief on the one side, and truth on the other, and combine them to form a true belief. Then I should say that the superiority of the true belief over the sum of the goodness of truth plus the goodness of belief, was greater than the superiority of conscious pleasure over the sum of the goodness of pleasure plus the goodness of consciousness. And similarly with a work of art. Suppose you take a great picture and cut it up into pieces one inch square. Now each of those pieces, or some of them at all events, would have some merit in them: you would say they were the work of a great artist. But nevertheless the sum of the merits of each piece taken separately, would not be equal to the merit of the whole picture. Nor would the proportion of its merit to the sum of merits of the parts be always the same. This proportion would, I think, differ with different pictures, which might, nevertheless, taken as wholes, be themselves of equal merit.

This, then, is my second formal determination of my Ideal. It must be good as a whole, nay the best as a whole; and the best whole may certainly be one in which there are parts of unequal goodness. We shall have to reckon in our Ideal both the sum of the goodnesses of all the parts, and the goodness of the whole as such: and each of these must be the very highest. And that is why I cannot see that this consideration, that the Ideal must be regarded as a whole, can do away with the need of admitting infinity within it. It is simply a different, not an alternative, consideration: we must consider both at once. Suppose for instance we have discovered what parts and what proportions of the quantities of each, are capable of combining to make the best whole: I cannot see but that by multiplying each to infinity while still retaining their relative proportions, the whole would be made better, not as a whole, but as containing more good parts. Here then is infinity brought in in one way. And supposing we have found such a best whole; then would not an infinite number of such best wholes, be better still? Would not that be our ideal? I cannot see that this suggestion is meaningless; and if it is not, then we have infinity brought in also in another way.

This consideration that the goodness of a whole need not be in proportion to the goodness of its parts is one which has been much used in Theodicies. It has been attempted to justify the ways of God, in that he allows vice and misery to exist in this world, by saying that if we saw the whole of things, as he does, we should see how these bad parts could fit into the general plan. But even if we did, then I think we must maintain those parts would still be bad in themselves: they cannot change their nature, by belonging to a whole; God would not be completely justified. But even granting this, it may be said, nevertheless the presence of those bad parts might add so much to the goodness of the whole, as would more than balance the badness that must belong to them. I do not think the possibility of this can be denied; but I see no reason for thinking that it is true; no one need admit it; for I know of no end in which it is obvious that the goodness of the whole is so much enhanced by the presence of a part which in itself is bad, as to overbalance the badness of that part. But what I think we must admit is this: that two bad parts together may form a whole that is distinctly better than either, whether it can be positively good or not. This seems to follow from our principle about good parts; and it will allow a justification of vindictive punishment. It seems to me certain that to punish an offender is a good thing in itself, quite apart from its effects on himself or others. And this is, on the present principle perfectly possible. The offence, we say, was bad in itself, and so is the punishment. But granted the offence has occurred, then we may make a better whole by adding the punishment, than, if the offence were left alone in its badness. This, you see, does not involve the admission of any bad part into our Ideal. It would have been better, we still can say, for no offence to be committed. The punishment is only added to make us a best possible. Even this it can only do if it be allowed that the addition of a bad part to a bad whole, may make that whole better than it was before. But it does not therefore follow that the addition of a bad part to a good whole, will make it better than it was before—that anything which may be added to the goodness of the whole will be greater in quantity than the badness added to the sum of goodnesses of parts.

This second formal determination of the Ideal makes it still more plain how hard it is to say what the Ideal is. Even if we could discover what are all its constituent parts, and could conceive the amounts of these to be infinitely multiplied, we should still have to balance the goodness of the whole against this sum of goodnesses, in order to determine by what proportions of the parts, the greatest sum of goodness might be come at. And this which is true of the Ideal, is also true of any complex thing. We cannot estimate its value, simply by summing the value of its various parts. We must also take into account its value as a whole, and see how we can get the greatest total, weighing this value of it as a whole, against the sum of the values of its parts. It is thus that in trying to judge of the value of a man or of a picture, considered in itself, we may say that it is perfect, meaning that the goodness of the whole bears the right proportion to the goodness of the parts—that the parts are all good, and that the whole is as good, as, with those parts, was possible. And this is one perfectly right way of judging. But also it may be that in another man or picture there may be a much larger sum of much more valuable parts, although the goodness of the whole is not in proportion to this sum of goodness. And in this way the man or work of art will be nearer the Ideal in another way. There will be more in such a man of that which must be in the Ideal. He will, considered in himself, perhaps be better than that other man, whom we called perfect. He will be a better part of the Ideal: he will contain more ends, and be more of the End, although he will be less of an end. There must be these two ways of judging any complex thing, considered in itself; and when we regard the fact that any such thing must also act in divers ways as means to other goods, it becomes plainer still how hard it is to judge. A man for instance may be a most valuable means, and yet of little value in himself; and it is very hard to say which of these he ought to be.

Well, after all this, I hope you will not expect me to tell you exhaustively what the Ideal is—what are all the elements that must make part of it, as being good in themselves and in what proportions they must be mingled to make the whole the best. What I have said should shew you how impossible this is. I will only say in general, how I try to conceive it.

In the first place it is obvious that there may be infinite good things of which we do know absolutely nothing. We must therefore, in imagining the Ideal, be limited to those good elements of which we have in some way had experience. The Ideal will therefore necessarily be very like this world in which we live, something not much less varied or less complex, and therefore far enough away from any such ideal as mere pleasure or pure will. It will be like this world, but with all the things in it which we think bad or mere means, left out; and all that we think good, indefinitely increased in amount.

And in the second place, you may fairly ask me what of the things that are in this world I think most definitely good and the best—which they are which we should most want to see increased in their amounts. Well, in this matter, I take the common view of

191

philosophers. I think that human minds are the best things that there are, and that these are best, when they know the truth, but also more especially when they strongly love the best—when they love other human minds, that are, in this way, like them. And of things that are not mental, I think that those which are most beautiful are the best. I have said in the Syllabus that the Aesthetic Ideal is subordinated to the Moral. I had an opportunity of explaining earlier what I meant by this. It is merely that everything that is beautiful must if it is to claim a value, claim it as being a part of the Moral Ideal. I think it can so claim it, and I think further that both Ideals are the *same thing*. But if you regard that one same thing, as good, then you can only say that it is also beautiful, because the beautiful is good. Or if you regard it as beautiful then you can only say that it is also good, because the good is beautiful. The good you can say is higher, because higher means better. But that is no disparagement of beauty; since beauty still remains the more beautiful. There is I think no difficulty here. But I do think that for a mind to contemplate external beauty is better than that such beauty simply should exist. And this can only be, according to what has last been said, if the mind itself is the most beautiful of objects. When one mind contemplates another, then there is most beauty; but this is by no means inconsistent with its also contemplating beauty in that which is not mind. In fine, I can find no better description for the Ideal than that which Aristotle and Plato found. It is θεωρία or a feeling of contemplation of all that is true and beautiful and good; the contemplating mind being also in these respects like that which it is contemplating. If you want to know more nearly what this is, you should read Plato's *Phaedrus* and the last book of Aristotle's *Ethics*.

Well, I have been led quite unintentionally into so long a discussion of the Ideal—a discussion which is more definitely than any other part of my lectures, of the nature which most people would call metaphysical—that I have but very little time left for the discussion of my other subject of to-day. This is the discussion of how we may best arrive at a decision on what we ought to do—

on what is the best possible, in any given case, both from the point of view of means and from the point of view of ends.

Well, I have tried to shew you how impossible it is that we should know the complete end. And it is obvious at once that the doctrine of means is also incomplete. No science can as yet predict with perfect certainty and accuracy, and some sciences and these the most important, have hardly yet begun. It is therefore obvious that the ideal of a rational belief as to what we ought to do, is infinitely far from being attainable for us. To attain it we should have to answer all the questions I have raised, and it is irrational to believe that we can answer them. What therefore is the best way to choose? And how can we say that it is best, without having first answered all these questions?

I think we can still say what is best *in general* and that for two main reasons:

(1) Most questions of practical conduct are for the most part questions of means and not of ends. The possible effects of choice are, in any case, very small; the amount of good attainable is whether by choice or not also very small in comparison of the ideal: we need therefore, in general ask no more than what is possible, and that we shall commonly arrive immediately at the best answer that can be given to this question, evolution guarantees us. It is only those who on the whole were best at foreseeing what will be the effect of what who could have come to survive as we have survived.

(2) And in the case of ends, we have a similar guarantee. We shall not in general, be able to think that anything is good beside what other people think so. For what we think has also been determined by the course of evolution.

Of course, cases will arise, where neither of these consolations can apply. It is a fact that, in some cases, one man will discover a better means than has been usual before him. But this I should say was chiefly in the region of the established sciences. Anything very markedly new and original in any other region of enquiry— in politics, for instance,—is likely to be wrong. In practical life therefore I think we should be on the whole conservative: only admitting a change in custom, where the change is slight and trivial.

In short we have a trained conscience for judging in the lump as to what we ought to do, including the question both of means and end. And if the individual finds his conscience markedly against that of common sense, there is good reason why he should hesitate to follow it. This conscience has indeed been trained to judge only of immediate effects. But here it may be trusted to tell us of any gross distinction between a good or bad effect and a right means or a wrong. It is for this reason that the hedonistic principle is so little likely to lead us wrong in general. Pleasure is very valuable as a means to keep us fit for doing other things; and we can [sic.], and we can generally judge pretty well what will lead to the most immediate pleasure. To aim at this will then have a good chance of being right. But Hedonism has not the slightest claim to be a scientific method. In order to be this, it would have to consider the far future—not only what will give immediate pleasure, but also how human capacities for pleasure must be modified. And when this is recognised, it becomes plain that its instructions have quite as little claim to be called scientific, as those of any other system.

I think reflection on particular moral questions cannot therefore be recommended. The more immediate the judgment is the better on the whole it will be. Reflection is, no doubt, good as an end-in-itself. To arrive at any truth whatever, even if it be only the truth that two things are in one point inconsistent, is good—good as an end. But reflection is not good as a means to the right action. Reflection is good, from the point of view of means, so long as it be scientific; for then it has but little bearing on the good. It is good, from the point of view of ends, always; such reflection we can sincerely recommend: but that is because the best ends are impracticable. To *act* on the results of reflection is hardly ever wise.

The result of the study of Ethics then should be, to convince us that any system which professes to give us precise and certain rules of conduct, any system from which there are obvious practical deductions, is certainly wrong. This is a most important result; though it has been anticipated by the common sense of most mankind. The pity is that some of the best minds are the most likely to be influenced by theories—to think a thing is right, because they can give reasons for it. It is something important to recognise that the best of reasons can be given for *anything* whatever, if only we are clever enough: sophistry is easy, wisdom is impossible; the best that we can do is to trust to

COMMON SENSE.

Index

Summum Bonum, 73, 90, 116, 117. *See also* The Ideal
Sylvester, Robert Peter, xxxii(n), xxxviii(n)

Ten Commandments, 120, 171
theology, 189
Trevelyan, G. M., xxi, xxii(n)
Tyndall, John, 30
Types of Ethical Theory, 139n

University of London, xv, xvi

Utilitarianism, 49, 65
utilitarianism, xl, xlii, 27, 64, 78–85, 94, 95, 96

Vergil, 187

Ward, James, xxiii(n), xxiv(n)
Ward, Mary (Mrs. Humphry), x, xviii, xix, xxxvi, xxxvii
Warnock, G. J., xxxii(n)
Woolf, Virginia, xxxvii
Working Men's College, xxii